Your First Step to
Celebrate
Recovery®

John Baker is the founder of Celebrate Recovery®, a ministry born out of the heart of Saddleback Church. Over the last twenty years, more than 11,500 individuals have gone through this Christ-centered recovery program at Saddleback. The Celebrate Recovery program is now being used in over 20,000 churches nationwide. In 1993, John and Pastor Rick Warren wrote the Celebrate Recovery curriculum which has been published and translated into twenty-three languages.

John began serving at Saddleback as a lay pastor in 1991. In 1992, he was asked to join the Saddleback Church staff as the Director of Small Groups and Recovery. In 1995, his responsibilities increased as he became the Pastor of Membership. In this position, John's responsibilities included pastoral counseling, pastoral care, Celebrate Recovery, support groups, small groups, family, singles, and recreation ministries. In 1996, he developed Saddleback's lay counseling ministry.

In June 1997, John became the Pastor of Ministries, responsible for the recruitment, training, and deployment of church members to serve in one of the more than 156 different ministries at Saddleback.

In 2001, Rick Warren asked John to become the Pastor of Celebrate Recovery. This is John's shape, his passion, and his calling. In addition, he serves as one of the five elders at Saddleback. John is a nationally known speaker and trainer in helping churches start Celebrate Recovery ministries. These ministries, in thousands of churches, reach out not only to their congregations but also to their communities in helping those dealing with a hurt, hang-up, or habit.

John and his wife Cheryl have been married over forty years and have served together in Celebrate Recovery since 1991. They have two adult children, Laura and Johnny. Laura and her husband, Brian, have twins. Johnny and his wife, Jeni, have three children.

INTRODUCTION BY
RICK WARREN

Your First Step to
Celebrate
Recovery®

How God Can Heal Your Life

JOHN BAKER

ZONDERVAN®

AUTHOR'S NOTE:

Because I have picked up a variety of quotes and slogans from numerous recovery meetings, tapes, and seminars, I have not been able to provide some sources for all of the material here. If you feel that I have quoted your material, please let me know and I will be pleased to give you the credit.

ZONDERVAN

Your First Step to Celebrate Recovery
Copyright © 2012 by John Baker

This title is also available as a Zondervan ebook.

Requests for information should be addressed to:

Zondervan, 3900 Sparks Dr., Grand Rapids, Michigan 49546

ISBN 978-0-310-53118-0

Published in association with the literary agency RKW Legacy Partners LP, 29881 Santa Margarita Parkway, Rancho Santa Margarita, CA 92688.

Cover design: Brand Navigation
Cover photography: David Robbins / Getty Images
Interior design: Michelle Espinosa

Printed in the United States of America

16 17 18 19 20 21 /QGM/ 20 19 18 17 16 15 14 13 12 11 10 9 8 7 6 5 4 3 2

CONTENTS

Introduction

WHAT IS
CELEBRATE RECOVERY?

BY RICK WARREN

The Bible clearly states "all have sinned." It is my nature to sin, and it is yours too. None of us is untainted. Because of sin, we've all hurt ourselves, we've all hurt other people, and others have hurt us. This means each of us needs recovery in order to live our lives the way God intended.

You've undoubtedly heard the expression "time heals all wounds." Unfortunately, it isn't true. As a pastor, I frequently talk with people who are still carrying hurts from thirty or forty years ago. The truth is, time often makes things worse. Wounds that are left untended fester and spread infection throughout your entire body. Time only extends the pain if the problem isn't dealt with.

Celebrate Recovery® is a biblical and balanced program that helps us overcome our hurts, hang-ups, and habits. It is based on the actual words of Jesus rather than psychological theory. Celebrate Recovery is more effective in helping us change than anything else I've seen or heard of. Over the years I've seen how God has used this program to transform literally thousands of lives at Saddleback Church and to help people grow toward full Christlike maturity.

Most people are familiar with the classic 12-Step program of AA and other groups. While undoubtedly many lives have been helped through the 12 Steps, I've always been uncomfortable with that program's vagueness about the nature of God, the saving power of Jesus Christ, and the ministry of the Holy Spirit. So I began an intense study of the Scriptures to discover what God had to say about "recovery." To my amazement, I found the principles of recovery — in their logical order — given by Christ in His most famous message, the Sermon on the Mount.

My study resulted in a ten-week series of messages called "The Road to Recovery." During that series, Pastor John Baker developed the participant's guides which became the heart of our Celebrate Recovery program. I believe that this program is unlike any recovery program you may have seen. There are six features that make it unique.

1. *Celebrate Recovery is based on God's Word, the Bible.* When Jesus taught the Sermon on the Mount, He began by stating eight ways to be happy. Today we call them the Beatitudes. From a conventional viewpoint, most of these statements don't make sense. They sound like contradictions. But when you fully understand what Jesus is saying, you'll realize that these eight principles are God's road to recovery, wholeness, growth, and spiritual maturity.

2. *Celebrate Recovery is forward-looking.* Rather than wallowing in the past or dredging up and rehearsing painful memories over and over, we confront our past and move on. Celebrate Recovery focuses on the future. Regardless of what has already happened, the solution is to start making wise choices now and depend on Christ's power to help us make those changes.

3. *Celebrate Recovery emphasizes personal responsibility.* Instead of playing the "accuse and excuse" game of victimization, this program helps us face up to our own poor choices and deal with what we can do something about. We cannot control all that happens to us, but we can control how we respond to everything. That is a secret of happiness. When we stop wasting time fixing the blame, we have more energy to fix the problem. When we stop hiding our own faults and stop hurling accusations at others,

then the healing power of Christ can begin working in our mind, will, and emotions.

4. *Celebrate Recovery emphasizes spiritual commitment to Jesus Christ.* The third principle calls for us to make a total surrender of our lives to Christ. Lasting recovery cannot happen without this principle. Everybody needs Jesus.

5. *Celebrate Recovery utilizes the biblical truth that we need each other in order to grow spiritually and emotionally.* It is built around small group interaction and the fellowship of a caring community. There are many therapies, growth programs, and counselors today that operate around one-to-one interaction. But Celebrate Recovery is built on the New Testament principle that we don't get well by ourselves. We need each other. Fellowship and accountability are two important components of spiritual growth.

6. *Celebrate Recovery addresses all types of hurts, hang-ups, and habits.* Some recovery programs deal only with alcohol or drugs or another single problem. But Celebrate Recovery is a "large umbrella" program under which a limitless number of issues can be dealt with. At Saddleback Church, only one out of three who attend Celebrate Recovery is dealing with alcohol or drugs. We have many other specialized groups.

I'm excited that you have decided to begin the Celebrate Recovery journey. You are going to see your life change in dramatic ways. You are going to experience freedom from your life's hurts, hang-ups, and habits as you allow Jesus to be Lord in every area of your life. To God be the glory! I'll be praying for you.

Chapter 1

WHY DID CELEBRATE RECOVERY GET STARTED?

You are not alone.

In the small city of West Monroe, Louisiana, men and women meet at Celebrate Recovery to share the hurts, hang-ups, and habits that have affected their lives. In greater Atlanta, Georgia, sixty-five churches are safe places where people come to Celebrate Recovery to find victory over their past. Elementary, junior high, and senior high school students are meeting in their own groups to talk about their hurts. In jails and prisons across the country, men and women are meeting in small groups to work through the participant's guides and the eight recovery principles based on the Beatitudes found in Matthew, chapter 5. Regularly, men and women from churches across the United States are making trips to countries such as Rwanda, Brazil, Great Britain, and Australia, to name a few, to share Jesus Christ as the one and only true Higher Power who can help them on their road to recovery.

You are not alone.

This book will help you understand how Celebrate Recovery got started, what the program is based on, and what to expect the first time you come to a Celebrate Recovery meeting. In addition, we will answer the questions that you may have as you begin this exciting, life-changing adventure.

I have asked my wife, Cheryl, to share with you our journey through recovery and how God's vision of Celebrate Recovery was born.

Cheryl and John's Story

I was born in St. Louis, Missouri. My dad was an Air Force sergeant and my mother loyally followed him throughout the United States as well as overseas. Alcohol was prevalent in my home, but my parents assured me that it was not a problem because they didn't drink at work, they just enjoyed the taste of beer, and they could quit whenever they wanted. I noticed that my parents were different after they drank, and I observed that my friends' parents drank very little, but I wanted very much to believe Mom and Dad's behavior was normal.

My mom had polio as a child and suffered a great deal of pain. She spent a lot of time in hospitals after surgeries and felt abandoned and alone. She said she could not believe in a God who would allow little children to feel such agony. Our family never went to church. When friends invited my brother and me, we were discouraged to attend.

By the time I was sixteen, we had lived in Missouri, Texas, Kentucky, New York, Portugal, Japan, and England. I learned early on how to use masks to hide my feelings of insecurity, to accept everyone, and to use a sense of humor when things got uncomfortable. These skills helped me to make friends by the end of the first day of every new school transfer.

My dad retired from the Air Force in the city where I was born, St. Louis, where I began to attend college. At a fraternity-sorority football game, I met John. At the party after the game, John told me that because he was president of his fraternity and I was president of my sorority, it was our "duty" to start off the dancing. Months later, I learned that John had arranged that entire evening so that he could meet me. (Years later, in Celebrate Recovery, I learned this was very manipulative and controlling!)

As John and I began dating, I learned that his childhood was very different from mine. He had been raised as an only child and had lived in a small town, Collinsville, Illinois, his entire life. Two years before John was born, his parents had given birth to a baby boy who died during his first few days of life. His mother never quite got over the pain of the baby's death, but her small Baptist church helped her deal with the loss. John grew up in that church and accepted Jesus into his heart at age thirteen.

It appeared that John had many successes while in high school: he was class president and lettered in baseball, basketball, and track. But John never felt that he was quite good enough. He was always certain that he was letting someone down — his parents, teammates, friends, and girlfriends. While searching for a college to attend, John had applied to several Christian universities to pursue a position in ministry. However, his feelings of low self-esteem caused him to feel unworthy to answer God's call, so he decided on the state university instead.

As soon as John arrived at college, he joined a fraternity and found the solution to all of his problems — alcohol. While he was the life of the party — it didn't start until he got there and wasn't over until he left — I approached the sorority life with caution. I had seen the effects of alcohol at home, and I was afraid that I might be someone who would not be able to handle it well. I didn't drink at all until I was twenty-one, and then I drank very little.

I was aware that John drank a lot in college, but I wanted to believe that it was normal behavior for someone just enjoying the college experience. I did not want to see it as a problem. Despite the warning signs, we got married in our senior year of school. We did not want to wait because we anticipated that John would be called to serve in the war in Vietnam.

John attended Officer Training School and pilot training, and he learned to act like an officer and drink like a gentleman. Again, it continued to cover his pain of low self-worth. He even discovered that the 100 percent oxygen in the plane could cure morning hangovers! When the war ended, he was assigned to a reserve unit and quickly began to pursue a business career. He joined a paper company and earned his masters' degree in business in night school.

After being married for four years, John and I had our first child, our daughter, Laura, and two years later, our son, Johnny, was born. John had been persistent in talking to me about accepting Christ. After our daughter was born, I did accept Him as my Lord and Savior. However, our church attendance was very irregular.

A few years later, when our son started attending a Christian preschool, Johnny explained to me that we could go back to his school on Sundays to hear more stories about Jesus. This tugged at my heart, and we finally committed to our first church home. Meanwhile, John continued to be promoted at work. He was achieving all of his life's goals before the age of thirty.

Each time John was promoted, our family moved. I was following in my parents' footsteps and going from city to city. I worried that my children would have feelings of insecurity from so many relocations. I also noticed that with each business success, John seemed unhappier. He certainly wasn't the life of the party anymore. He drank more and more and got quieter and quieter. I didn't know what to do or whom to turn to. I didn't want my children raised in an alcoholic home. By this time, church had become very important to me. I even taught preschool at our church, but I didn't feel like I could tell anyone there about our struggles. Everyone at church looked and acted as if their lives were perfect. The kids and I already felt different enough because John wasn't attending church with us anymore.

Gradually, things began to change between John and me. We didn't seem to understand one another, and we talked less and less. At first, I thought our relationship was shifting because of all of our relocations—we had moved seven times in the first eleven years of marriage. Or maybe we were losing touch because he traveled so much with his job. But I could see that his drinking was increasing and his relationship with our family was changing. He was emotionally distant and uninterested in our lives.

Each time I confronted John about his drinking, he assured me that it was not a problem, because he did not drink at work, he just enjoyed the taste of beer, and he could quit whenever he wanted. But even though I had grown up with those words, they had a different impact on me as a wife and mother. If he could "just quit whenever he wanted," then why didn't he quit? Maybe there was something about me that caused John to keep drinking. Maybe if I were prettier, or smarter, or funnier, or if I just worked harder, maybe then John would quit drinking. Since we didn't tell anyone about these struggles, to the outside world we looked like an average, normal family.

John began to be defensive about his drinking. He had grown up in the church and was starting to feel uncomfortable with some of his choices: his relationships with our family, his work practices, and the steady increase in the amount of alcohol. He knew that he had a choice—to continue to live by the world's standards or to repent and turn to God. Proverbs 14:12 (TLB) says, "Before every man there lies a wide and pleasant road that seems right but ends in death." But John turned his back on God, and the drinking escalated.

Our family continued to live as if the drinking was not affecting us. After all, John told me repeatedly, he had never lost a job due to alcohol. He had never even gotten pulled over by the police for drunk driving. He wanted so much to convince us that he was a normal, social drinker.

However, when John began drinking beer for breakfast, I knew that we had to face the family secret. John was an alcoholic. This time when I confronted him in anger, I gave him an ultimatum: quit drinking or leave our home. I was completely surprised when he packed his suitcase and announced that we were separating after twenty years of marriage.

Finally, the attempt to cover up John's hurts, hang-ups, and habits with alcohol was causing the breakup of our family. At first, alcohol seemed to be the solution to help him with his low self-esteem, but now it had become the problem in his life that was affecting him emotionally, mentally, physically, and most importantly, spiritually.

While on a business trip in Salt Lake City, John came to the realization that he could not take another drink, but he had no idea how he was going to live without one. Although he did not realize it, he had come to the first Christ-centered recovery step: *We admitted we were powerless over our addictions and compulsive behaviors, that our lives had become unmanageable.* "For I know that good itself does not dwell in me, that is, in my sinful nature. For I have the desire to do what is good, but I cannot carry it out" (Romans 7:18).

He had finally hit his bottom. He went back home and attended his first Alcoholics Anonymous meeting and attended over ninety meetings in ninety days. Then he became ready for Step 2: *We came to believe that a power greater than ourselves could restore us to sanity.* "For it is God who works in you to will and to act in order to fulfill his good purpose" (Philippians 2:13).

As it became clear to John that God loved him unconditionally, he began to find hope. It was time to make the decision to turn over his life and will to the care of God. This was a departure from the secular program he was attending where a "higher power" was very vague. As a child, he had learned who his Higher Power was: Jesus Christ!

John's stubborn willpower had left him empty and broken. The definition of willpower had to change. Willpower now became the willingness to accept God's power for his life. He began to accept, "I can't, God can, and I decide to let Him, one day at a time." He was ready for the third step: *We made a decision to turn our lives and our wills over to the care of God.* "Therefore, I urge you, brothers, in view of God's mercy, to offer your bodies as living sacrifices, holy and pleasing to God—this is your spiritual act of worship" (Romans 12:1).

God provided a sponsor to help navigate the road to recovery. The sponsor taught John that recovery is not meant to be a journey that is traveled alone—we need others to help us. He helped

John stay balanced and didn't judge him. He guided him through the fourth step: *We made a searching and fearless moral inventory of ourselves.* "Let us examine our ways and test them, and let us return to the LORD" (Lamentations 3:40).

Finally, John had to take a look at that young boy from Illinois and face the hurts, hang-ups, and habits that he had attempted to drown with alcohol for all those years. He discovered how the loss of his brother as an infant had impacted his family and affected his low self-esteem. This inventory made it clear that his alcoholism had destroyed all of his important relationships.

In Step 5 he learned: *We admitted to God, to ourselves, and to another human being the exact nature of our wrongs.* "Therefore confess your sins to each other and pray for each other so that you may be healed" (James 5:16). Finally, John was able to face the truth of his past and to accept the forgiveness of Jesus, which led him "out of darkness into his wonderful light."

I was completely unaware that John was beginning to deal with his alcoholism. I was busy putting all of my energies into using a mask, once again, to hide my pain. It was important to look as though nothing was wrong—I had to "hold it together." This is when my dysfunctions really began to surface. I had never told anyone about the breakup of our marriage. I didn't even tell my parents until they came to visit us seven months into the separation. I wanted so much to tell my close Christian friends at the church preschool where I worked, but I just didn't feel safe. I was afraid they might judge me. I didn't think they would understand. As I looked around my church, I wondered if there were others who were also struggling with pain that they were too afraid to share and feeling so different and alone.

Thinking that if we switched churches we would find a safe place to tell others about our pain, the kids and I began attending Saddleback Church. But we didn't want to feel different or alone, so we didn't tell anyone there about the separation either.

I was afraid that the church where I worked would judge me if they learned about the separation, so I accepted the position as the director of another preschool. This job paid more—and the pastor was understanding of my situation. The preschool had 400 families, 50 women on staff, and as I learned my first day on the job, was $40,000 in debt. The first thing I was expected to accomplish was for the school to pay back the money.

Up until this point, I had done a good job of pretending that I could manage all of the changes in my life. But after the first day of my new job, I fell apart. I couldn't stop crying as the pain of the drinking, the failed marriage, and now the impossible job came together. I couldn't believe it when John arrived at the house to visit the kids and to find out how my first day on the job had gone. I was embarrassed to have lost control, but I didn't seem to be able to do anything about it.

As I was crying about the job, I noticed that John had tears in his eyes as he tried to comfort me. He asked what he could do to help and offered suggestions. I realized that we were having a loving conversation—he seemed to be hurting right alongside me. This was confusing to me. John was showing signs of changing, and I had no idea how to cope.

Although I didn't know it at the time, I began working Steps 1 through 3. I knew I was completely powerless to get through the separation by myself. I began to trust Jesus and to lean on Him. Colossians 1:11 (NCV) tells us, "God will strengthen you with his own great power so that you will not give up when troubles come." I held onto that verse, but I didn't realize that Jesus was getting me ready for more changes.

John completed Step 6—*We were entirely ready to have God remove all these defects of character.* "Humble yourselves before the Lord, and he will lift you up" (James 4:10)—and Step 7—We *humbly asked Him to remove all our shortcomings.* "If we confess our sins, he is faithful and just and will forgive us our sins and purify us from all unrighteousness" (1 John 1:9). He allowed God to change everything in his life and rebuild his self-worth based on God's love for him alone, no longer trying to measure up to the world's standards.

Gradually, John began coming by the house more frequently. He said he was coming to visit the kids, but because they were teenagers, they were often not at home. I began to see a lot of changes in him. He would bring along a pizza or a movie, and we began spending some evenings together. John smiled more often, and sometimes he even laughed out loud. I hadn't seen him laugh like that in years. Although hesitant, Laura and Johnny asked him to join us at our new church. John loved Saddleback Church and said he felt like he was home. He began meeting us there every week on Sunday mornings.

Meanwhile, John began working on Step 8: *We made a list of all persons we had harmed and became willing to make amends to them all.* "Do to others as you would have them do to you" (Luke 6:31). After being separated for a year, John left a note on my table asking me to meet him for lunch.

I was surprised that John wanted to meet for lunch on February 14, 1991 — Valentine's Day! John explained that he was in recovery, and that he went to meetings every day. He was working on Step 9: *We made direct amends to such people whenever possible, except when to do so would injure them or others.* "Therefore, if you are offering your gift at the altar and there remember that your brother has something against you, leave your gift there in front of the altar. First go and be reconciled to your brother; then come and offer your gift" (Matthew 5:23–24).

John told me that he had a lot of names on his amends list, including former employers, employees, friends, and neighbors, but most importantly, he had very special amends to make to Johnny, Laura, and me. He said he was sorry for all of the pain he had caused by his drinking. He took full responsibility for his drinking and freed me from the doubts that I had been the cause of his alcoholism. He said he still loved me, and asked if I would be willing to work on the marriage.

God changed our lives with Step 9. John and I began to work on the issues that had torn apart our marriage. We made Step 10 a part of our daily lives: *We continued to take personal inventory and when we were wrong promptly admitted it.* "So, if you think you are standing firm, be careful that you don't fall!" (1 Corinthians 10:12).

Five months after John's ninth step to me, God opened our hearts and we renewed our wedding vows. As a family, we were baptized together, and we took all of the church's membership classes together. In the maturity class, John found one of his life's verses, 1 Peter 2:9 – 10 (TLB): "You have been chosen by God himself … you are the priest of the King … you are God's very own — all this so you can show to others how God called you out of the darkness into his wonderful light. Once you were less than nothing; now you are God's very own."

However, at John's secular meetings, some of the men made fun of him whenever he talked about his higher power, the one and only true Higher Power, Jesus. It seemed as though anything could be claimed as a higher power, just not Jesus. At church, we tried to find a small group where we could be open and honest about the issues that had torn our marriage apart. But we couldn't find that safe place — a group of other Christians who wanted to share openly about their struggles.

We began working Step 11: *We sought through prayer and meditation to improve our conscious contact with God, praying only for knowledge of His will for us and power to carry that out.* "Let the message of Christ dwell in you richly" (Colossians 3:16). Finally, John said, "We can't be this different from everyone at church. We can't be the only ones struggling with a hurt, hang-up, or habit." At the time, Saddleback Church had over 6,000 members.

John began writing down an outline for a program that would fit our needs. Realizing that "God never wastes a hurt," the pain and the heartache of his sin addiction to alcohol were finally beginning to have a purpose. In Joel 2:25, God promises to restore "the years the locusts have eaten." We discussed the ideas for the program for weeks while the vision from God continued to grow. We saw an opportunity to share our hurts with others as we began to work Step 12: *Having had a spiritual experience as a result of these steps, we try to carry this message to others and to practice these principles in all our affairs.* "Brothers, if someone is caught in a sin, you who are spiritual should restore him gently. But watch yourself, or you also may be tempted" (Galatians 6:1).

John finally finished a thirteen-page, single-spaced letter for a vision of a ministry called Celebrate Recovery—a Christ-centered recovery program. In summary, the letter said, "The vision for Celebrate Recovery is for the church to provide a safe place where families could find healing and restoration; where moms, dads, and their children of all ages could find freedom from their hurts, hang-ups, and habits."

John gave the letter to Rick Warren, the senior pastor of Saddleback Church. We were confident that Rick would find just the right godly man to head up this new ministry. Neither of us was prepared for Rick to call John into his office and say, "It's a great idea, John, I would like you to do it!"

The first meeting for Celebrate Recovery started on November 21, 1991. Saddleback Church did not have any property, so the only place we could find to hold our meeting was a psychiatric hospital! And, still, God used it—forty-three people attended! In order for the whole family to be able to come, we provided child care. Our son and daughter, Johnny and Laura, started the open share group for teens. A small group of volunteers led our worship, and the lessons were taught in a large group format. Since at that point we did not have any recovery stories from our program, we did not have testimonies. As time went on, testimonies were added to our large group as people began to want to share how Jesus Christ was changing their lives.

There were four groups: a woman's chemical addiction, a men's codependent, a men's chemical addiction (led by John), and a woman's codependent (led by me). I didn't even know what a codependent was! But I wanted to share with others who could identify with our struggles, so I was willing to learn.

After the meetings were over, we were all so excited to talk about our recoveries with other Christians that we went to a restaurant to keep sharing. Often we would close down the restaurant, and then go back to our house so that we could continue our conversations. It was such a relief to talk to others who understood our hurts, hang-ups, and habits. We had found a safe place; we were no longer different or alone.

This program was working for our family and that is all we hoped to accomplish. We just needed to keep the program going. But God had so many other plans! John was asked to join the Saddleback Church staff in 1992. He served at Celebrate Recovery as a volunteer while his job was to oversee the small ministries of the church.

In 1993, because lives were changing at Celebrate Recovery, Rick decided to take the entire church through "The Road to Recovery" sermon series of the eight principles based on the Beatitudes. This series helped us to experience another growing phase. But more importantly, Celebrate Recovery participants began to serve in other areas of the church. While finally experiencing freedom and forgiveness, and with many tears, Celebrate Recovery even served communion. Saddleback Church became a safe place for anyone with a hurt.

In order to better understand the choices that we had made in our lives, we began to feel that we needed something in addition to the open share groups. We decided to try some of the Christian 12-Step published materials. Often we would start off a group of twenty-five men or women, but only two or three would finish the study. The available, published resources did not work for us.

So the search began for a Christian study that was based on the Bible and would apply to anyone with a hurt, hang-up, or habit. We wanted the curriculum to be concise and easy to use while helping people deal with their past in a thorough manner. We studied many resources, but none of them seemed to be a good fit for Celebrate Recovery.

As the search continued for the right curriculum, our participants were having trouble getting through Step 4. John slowed down the lessons and took three months to teach on that principle. At the completion of those lessons, many had completed the step successfully and were ready to move on in their recovery. One of the leaders, Carl, was so impressed with John's teaching, that he suggested he put his teaching notes into a fourth step workbook.

Not having much confidence in his writing abilities, John quickly said he would consider the idea but within a few days had forgotten all about the request. However, as John would arrive at the next Celebrate Recovery meeting, Carl would greet him at the door and ask how the fourth step workbook was coming along. He repeated the same scenario at the Saturday night and Sunday church services. "How's that fourth step workbook coming?"

John finally decided that God was using Carl to encourage him to write the workbook, so he completed the participant's guide in 1994. The book was based on God's Word, so it was not addiction or compulsion based. We knew that it worked because the lessons had been so successful at Celebrate Recovery, and it applied to anyone with a hurt, hang-up, or habit.

Since Saddleback is a teaching church, it was not long before several churches in California were using the workbook. Then some churches in other states began incorporating the book into their programs. Much to our surprise, Canada and Australia contacted us about using this fourth step workbook. The workbook was helping people from all over the world get through their fourth step. Carl had been right.

And then it wasn't long before John began getting requests for the workbooks for steps one through three and steps five through twelve. All of a sudden, John had hundreds of "Carls" all over the country asking for step study workbooks. He went back to the computer and the late nights and completed all four workbooks—the participant's guides—in 1995. The workbooks included all twelve steps and the eight principles. Finally, the search for a Celebrate Recovery curriculum was over.

As we began to use the participant's guides, we had a huge

growth spurt. Leaders began to emerge from those step study groups and wanted to start new groups. Gradually, groups for newcomers, anger, eating disorders, food addiction, love and relationship addiction, sexual addiction, codependents in a relationship with a sexually addicted man, gambling, sexual/physical/emotional abuse, and adult children of the chemically addicted were added to the original four small groups.

The participant's guides began to be shipped all over the country, and people started calling the church office to find out how to start Celebrate Recovery at their churches. The questions were endless and complex. "How do you start the program? How do you find leaders? How can you prepare lessons with full-time jobs and family commitments?" In order to answer the flood of questions, a leader's guide was written in 1996.

For a couple of years, John and I printed those participant's guides and leader's guides and sold them from our garage. We had a post office box for the orders. It was a highlight of our week to pick up the orders and learn where Celebrate Recovery programs were being started. This Christ-centered recovery program was beginning to appear all over the United States, and other countries were starting the program as well!

In 1998, in order for the participant's guides and the leader's guide to receive wider distribution, Zondervan took over printing and distributing the materials. The participant's guides and leader's guide have now been published in twenty-three different languages and are in forty-five prison systems. Luke 4:18 (MSG) says, "God's spirit is on me; he's chosen me to preach the Message of good news to the poor, sent me to announce pardon to prisoners and recovery of sight to the blind, to set the burdened and the battered free …"

As the program continued, Celebrate Recovery leaders from across the country wanted to meet one another and to develop a network. In 1999, the first Celebrate Recovery Summit was held at Saddleback Church for that purpose and seventy-three people attended. Twelve years later, a sold-out crowd of 3,400 people met at Saddleback Church to learn how to meet the growing numbers of people with hurts, hang-ups, and habits. The network now includes regional and international directors, a prison director, and volunteer state representatives who help Celebrate Recovery programs get started and continue to grow. This was beyond our wildest dreams!

Celebrate Recovery began as a ministry at Saddleback Church so that our family could have a safe place to share the struggles that had torn us apart. We wanted to identify with others who would claim Jesus Christ as their Higher Power and were willing to turn their lives completely over to Him.

Now our "Forever Family" includes people from all over the world who want to break the cycle of dysfunction and live out 2 Corinthians 1:3–4 with us: "Praise be to the God and Father of our Lord Jesus Christ, the Father of compassion and the God of all comfort, who comforts us in all our troubles, so that we can comfort those in any trouble with the comfort we ourselves receive from God."

Victory Can Be Yours As Well

I hope you can see from Cheryl's testimony how God changed two broken lives and restored our marriage so that we could live out God's purpose in Celebrate Recovery. It is our prayer that you will read the rest of this book with an open heart, knowing everyone has hurts, hang-ups, or habits. One of the misconceptions about the word *recovery* is that it is only for those struggling with drugs and alcohol. Of over the million people who have gone through a Celebrate Recovery step study, only one out of three has been dealing with substance abuse.

The remainder of the book is designed to remove any fears, doubts, or questions you might have about attending a Celebrate Recovery meeting for the first time.

If you are going through any type of hurt, hang-up, or habit, Celebrate Recovery is for you.

God can give you the same victory He has given us!

Chapter 2

HOW DO I
KNOW CELEBRATE
RECOVERY WORKS?

Change Is Possible: The Eight Principles
of Celebrate Recovery

Since the beginning of time, men and women have searched for happiness—usually in all the wrong places, trying all the wrong things. But there's only one place where we can find tested-and-proven, absolutely-gonna-work principles that will lead to healing and happiness. These principles come in the form of eight statements from the truest of all books—the Bible—and from the most revered Teacher of all time—Jesus Christ. Jesus laid out these principles for happiness in the Sermon on the Mount in the gospel of Matthew, chapter 5. Today we call them "the Beatitudes."

Change, Jesus says, can be ours, but the pathway to change and happiness may not be exactly what we're expecting. From a conventional viewpoint, most of the following eight statements don't make sense. At first they even sound like contradictions. But when you fully understand what Jesus is saying, you'll realize these eight statements are God's pathway to wholeness, growth, and spiritual maturity.

"Happy are those who know they are spiritually poor."
"Happy are those who mourn, for they shall be comforted."
"Happy are the meek."
"Happy are the pure in heart."
"Happy are those whose greatest desire is to do what God requires."
"Happy are those who are merciful."
"Happy are those who work for peace."
*"Happy are those who are persecuted because they do what God requires."**

My Own Personal Journey

I know that the eight principles work. Why? Because they worked in my life. I have not always been a pastor. Prior to being called into the ministry, I was a successful businessman. I was also a "functional alcoholic." My wife Cheryl told my story in chapter one. I struggled with my sin addiction to alcohol for nineteen years. Eventually I came to a point where I was losing everything. I cried out to God for help, and He led me to Alcoholics Anonymous. Even then I knew that my Higher Power had a name—Jesus Christ! I started attending Saddleback Church in Lake Forest, California. After a year of sobriety, God gave me the vision for Celebrate Recovery, a Christ-centered recovery program. I answered God's call to start Celebrate Recovery. Since 1991, over a million courageous individuals have found the same freedom from their life's hurts, hang-ups, and habits that I did. If these eight principles worked for someone like me, I promise they can work for you too!

My Partnership with Pastor Rick

After Celebrate Recovery had been going for a year, Pastor Rick Warren, my senior pastor, saw how Celebrate Recovery was helping people in our church family find God's healing from their

---

* All quotations of the Beatitudes throughout this book are taken from the *Good News Translation (Today's English Version)*.

Principles That Will Change Your Life

The Road to Recovery
Based on the Beatitudes
Pastor Rick Warren

PRINCIPLE 1	Realize I'm not God. I admit that I am powerless to control my tendency to do the wrong thing and that my life is unmanageable (Step 1). *"Happy are those who know they are spiritually poor" (Matthew 5:3).*
PRINCIPLE 2	Earnestly believe that God exists, that I matter to Him, and that He has the power to help me recover (Step 2). *"Happy are those who mourn, for they shall be comforted" (Matthew 5:4).*
PRINCIPLE 3	Consciously choose to commit all my life and will to Christ's care and control (Step 3). *"Happy are the meek" (Matthew 5:5).*
PRINCIPLE 4	Openly examine and confess my faults to myself, to God, and to someone I trust (Steps 4 and 5). *"Happy are the pure in heart" (Matthew 5:8).*
PRINCIPLE 5	Voluntarily submit to every change God wants to make in my life and humbly ask Him to remove my character defects (Steps 6 and 7). *"Happy are those whose greatest desire is to do what God requires" (Matthew 5:6).*
PRINCIPLE 6	Evaluate all my relationships. Offer forgiveness to those who have hurt me and make amends for harm I've done to others, except when to do so would harm them or others (Steps 8 and 9). *"Happy are the merciful" (Matthew 5:7). "Happy are the peacemakers" (Matthew 5:9).*
PRINCIPLE 7	Reserve a daily time with God for self-examination, Bible reading, and prayer in order to know God and His will for my life and to gain the power to follow His will (Steps 10 and 11).
PRINCIPLE 8	Yield myself to God to be used to bring this Good News to others, both by my example and by my words (Step 12). *"Happy are those who are persecuted because they do what God requires" (Matthew 5:10).*

hurts, hang-ups, and habits. He decided to take the entire church family through a sermon series called "The Road to Recovery."

Pastor Rick's R-E-C-O-V-E-R-Y acrostic identifies eight principles. As you read the eight principles and the corresponding beatitudes (see box on page 29), you'll begin to understand the choices before you. (Throughout this chapter, you also will be introduced to the Christ-centered 12 Steps. These have been adapted from the 12 Suggested Steps of Alcoholics Anonymous, with the significant difference that we know our Higher Power to be Jesus Christ. To read these Steps and their biblical comparisons in one convenient spot, please see Appendix A on page 119.)

We will explore each of the eight Celebrate Recovery principles in the rest of this chapter. Let's begin with Principle 1. (NOTE: After four of the eight principles—4, 5, 7, and 8—you'll find a personal story, a testimony by a real person from the Celebrate Recovery family. You will see how with God's power, and working their program, they are overcoming their hurts, hang-ups, and habits. These courageous individuals come from very different backgrounds with a variety of problems and issues. As you read their stories, please keep your heart and mind open. You will see how their journeys relate to your own life or to someone's close to you.)

Principle 1

> **Principle 1:** Realize I'm not God. I admit that I am powerless to control my tendency to do the wrong thing and that my life is unmanageable.
>
> *"Happy are those who know they are spiritually poor."* (Matthew 5:3)

Your amazing recovery journey starts with Principle 1, where you admit that you are powerless to control your hurts, hang-ups, and habits and that your life has become unmanageable, out of control. But before you begin this exciting journey, you need to ask yourself the following two questions:

Am I wearing a mask of denial?
Over what do I really have control?

These questions are not just for you, but for everyone! Let's look at the first question: Are we wearing a mask of denial? Before we can make any progress in our recovery, we need to face our denial. As soon as we remove our mask, our recovery begins—or begins again! It doesn't matter whether someone is new in recovery or they have been in the process and working the principles and steps for years. Denial can rear its ugly head and return at any time. We may trade addictions or get into a new relationship that's unhealthy for us in a different way than a previous one. God says in Jeremiah 6:14 (TLB), "You can't heal a wound by saying it's not there."

Denial is serious. We can't heal our hurts, hang-ups, and habits by pretending they're not there. Denial will disable our feelings, isolating us from God and alienating us from others.

As soon as we start working on this principle and admit that we're powerless, we begin to change. We see that our old ways of trying to control our hurts, hang-ups, and habits didn't work. Our attempts were buried by our denial, and our problems were held close by our false sense of power.

This leads us to the second question we need to answer: Over what do we really have control? In Principle 1 we recognize our need to admit our powerlessness. Our lust for the power to control is rooted in our weaknesses, not in our strengths. We need to realize our human weaknesses and turn our lives over to God. Jesus knew this would be difficult. How difficult? He said this about a related issue, but it applies here as well: "With man this is impossible, but with God all things are possible" (Matthew 19:26).

Pride, worry, resentment, selfishness, and loneliness act like "serenity robbers" in our lives. We have to come to a place where we admit that we are powerless.

The power to change comes only from God's grace. In Principle 1 we start working and living this program in earnest. When we admit we're powerless, we go on to recognize that we need a power greater than ourselves to restore us. That power is the one and only true Higher Power, Jesus Christ.

Hebrews 12:1 invites us: "Therefore, since we are surrounded by such a great cloud of witnesses, let us throw off everything that hinders and the sin that so easily entangles. And let us run with perseverance the race marked out for us."

This verse spells out two important insights as we begin our recovery journey. First, God has a particular race, a unique plan, for each of us—a plan for good, not a life consumed with dependencies, addictions, and obsessions. The second thing is that we need to be willing to get rid of all the unnecessary baggage— hurts, hang-ups, and habits—in our lives that keep us stuck ("let us throw off everything that hinders and the sin that so easily entangles"). Working through the eight principles will allow us to discover God's plan and purpose for our lives. The journey begins by taking the first step.

The first step of the Christ-centered 12 Steps relates to Principle 1:

Step 1: We admitted we were powerless over our addictions and compulsive behaviors, that our lives had become unmanageable.

"I know that nothing good lives in me, that is, in my sinful nature. For I have the desire to do what is good, but I cannot carry it out."
(Romans 7:18)

Principle 1 Prayer

Dear God, Your Word tells me that I can't heal my hurts, hang-ups, and habits just by saying they're not there. Help me! Parts of my life—or all of my life—are out of control. I now know that I can't "fix" myself. It seems that the harder I try to do the right thing, the more I struggle. Lord, I want to step out of my denial into the truth. I pray for you to show me the way. In your Son's name, Amen.

Principle 2

> **Principle 2:** Earnestly believe that God exists, that I matter to Him, and that He has the power to help me recover.
>
> *"Happy are those who mourn, for they will be comforted."*
> *(Matthew 5:4)*

In Principle 2 you will find the power for your recovery as you earnestly believe that God exists, that you matter to Him, and that He has the power to help you recover.

Hebrews 11:6 tells us, "Without faith it is impossible to please God, because anyone who comes to him must believe that he exists and that he rewards those who earnestly seek him." And Psalm 62:5 invites, "Yes, my soul, find rest in God; my hope comes from him."

In the first principle, we admitted that we're powerless. It's through this admission that we're able to *believe* and *receive* God's power to help us recover. We do need to be careful, though, not to cover up the pit of our hurts, hang-ups, and habits with layers of denial or to try some quick "fix." Instead, we need to expose our hurts, hang-ups, and habits to the light so that through God's power we can truly find healing.

In the second principle, we come to believe that God exists, that we're important to Him, and that we're able to find the one true Higher Power, Jesus Christ. We come to understand that God wants to fill our lives with His love, joy, and presence.

In Luke 15:11 – 32 we find the parable of the lost son. This story about a father's love for his wayward son is really a picture of the love of God the Father for all of us. God's love is looking for us no matter how lost we may feel. God's searching love can find us no matter how many times we may have fallen into sin. God's hands of mercy are reaching out to pick us up, to love us, and to forgive us. He is the only place where we'll find hope.

The second step of the Christ-centered 12 Steps relates to Principle 2.

Step 2: We came to believe that a power greater than ourselves could restore us to sanity.

"For it is God who works in you to will and to act according to his good purpose." (Philippians 2:13)

In this principle we come to believe that a power greater than ourselves can help us recover — can restore us to sanity. This isn't to say we're crazy. The word *sanity* in this context means that as a result of admitting our powerlessness in Principle 1, we can move from chaos into hope in Principle 2. Hope comes when we believe that a power greater than ourselves, our Higher Power, Jesus Christ, can and will restore us. Jesus alone can provide that power, since on our own we are powerless over our hurts, hang-ups, and destructive habits. He alone can restore order and meaning to our lives. He alone can restore us to sanity.

A working definition of *insanity* in this context might be doing the same thing over and over again but expecting a different result each time.

Sanity, using this model, may, on the other hand, be defined as "wholeness of mind; making decisions based on the truth."

Jesus is the only Higher Power who offers the truth, as well as the power, the way, and the life.

We can't follow through with anything unless and until we get started. But just how much faith do we need to start working this principle? Jesus provides the answer in Matthew 17:20: "I tell you the truth, if you have faith as small as a mustard seed, you can say to this mountain, 'Move from here to there' and it will move. Nothing will be impossible for you."

It's reassuring to know that we don't need large doses of faith as we begin the recovery process. We need only a little faith, as small as the tiniest of seeds, to effect change, to begin to move away our mountains of hurts, hang-ups, and habits.

Eternal life doesn't begin with death; it begins with faith. Hebrews 11:1 explains what faith is: "Faith is being sure of what we hope for and certain of what we do not see." We can't find salvation through intellectual understanding, monetary gifts, good works, or church attendance. The way—the only way—to find salvation is described in Romans 10:9: "If you confess with your mouth, 'Jesus is Lord,' and believe in your heart that God raised him from the dead, you will be saved."

We'll find our true hope in the only Higher Power, Jesus Christ. As we take this step of hope, his Spirit will come with supernatural power to reside in our hearts. The Holy Spirit will give us the courage to reach out and take hold of Christ's hand, to face the present with confidence and the future with realistic expectancy.

Simply put, life without Christ is a hopeless end; with him life is an endless hope.

Principle 2 Prayer

Dear God, I've tried hard to fix and control my life's hurts, hang-ups, and habits. I admit that, by myself, I'm powerless to change. I need to begin to believe and receive Your power to help me recover. You loved me enough to send Your Son to the cross to die for my sins. Help me to open myself up to the hope I can find only in Jesus. Please help me to start living my life in reliance upon this hope, one day at a time. In Jesus' name I pray, Amen.

Principle 3

Principle 3: Consciously choose to commit all my life and will to Christ's care and control.

"Happy are the meek." (Matthew 5:5)

In Principle 3 you will make the one-time, permanent decision to turn over your life to the care of God—the most important decision you'll ever make. Your choice, not chance, determines your destiny. And that decision requires only putting your faith into action.

But what is faith? It isn't a sense, sight, or reason. Faith is simply taking God at His word. As we learned in Principle 2, God's Word tells us in Romans 10:9 that "if you declare with your mouth, 'Jesus is Lord,' and believe in your heart that God raised him from the dead, you will be saved." For some people that seems just too simple. But it isn't. Our salvation depends much more on God's love for us than on our love for him.

Many people don't understand that putting off the decision to accept Jesus Christ as their Higher Power, as their Lord and Savior, is really deciding not to accept him. Principle 3 is like opening the door: All you need is the willingness to make the decision. Christ will do the rest. He calls out to us, "Here I am! I stand at the door and knock. If anyone hears my voice and opens the door, I will come in and eat with that person, and they with me" (Revelation 3:20).

If we're going to successfully work Principle 3, we need to get past our old, familiar, negative barriers of pride, fear, guilt, worry, and doubt. But how do we break this cycle? The answer is that we need to be proactive, to take the initiative. In fact, Principle 3 is all about action.

Turning over our lives to Christ is a one-time, yet permanent, commitment. Once we accept Christ as Lord of our life, it's a done deal. We can't lose our salvation. It comes with a lifetime (in this case, eternal) guarantee from the Holy Spirit: "You also were included in Christ when you heard the message of truth, the gospel of your salvation. When you believed, you were marked in him with a seal, the promised Holy Spirit" (Ephesians 1:13).

The rest of the principle, though—the part about turning over our wills to Christ—requires a daily recommitment. We can begin by going to our Bible regularly, opening it prayerfully, reading it expectantly, and living it joyfully.

The third step of the Christ-centered 12 Steps relates to Principle 3.

Step 3: We made a decision to turn our lives and our wills over to the care of God.

"Therefore, I urge you, brothers, in view of God's mercy, to offer your bodies as living sacrifices, holy and pleasing to God—this is your spiritual act of worship." (Romans 12:1)

Principle 3 states that we choose to commit our lives and wills to Christ's care. In the secular 12 Steps, Step 3 gets the sequence confused, telling us to "turn our wills and our lives over ..." The fact is that we must first commit and surrender our lives to the one and only true Higher Power, Jesus Christ. Then and only then are we empowered to turn over our *wills* to Him.

Principle 3 constitutes the core difference between a secular 12-Step program and Celebrate Recovery. True and lasting recovery can be achieved only through a personal, committed relationship with Christ.

In the secular 12 Steps, Step 3 is: "We made a decision to turn our wills and our lives over to the care of God, as we understand him." But we need a God much, much greater than anything that stems from our own imagination or understanding. We need the one true God, the Almighty, the Creator of the universe. First Corinthians 13:12 tells us, "Now we see only a reflection as in a mirror; then we shall see face to face. Now I know in part; then I shall know fully, even as I am fully known." Someday we'll see Jesus face to face. The fog of interpretation will be lifted, and our understanding will be perfected.

Praise God that we don't need a complete understanding of Jesus in order to ask Him into our lives as Lord and Savior. Why? Because God does more than lead us day by day and year by year. He directs our way moment by moment, one step after another.

If you haven't asked Jesus Christ to be your Higher Power, the Lord and Savior of your life, what are you waiting for? All it takes is praying this prayer with a sincere heart:

Principle 3 Prayer

Dear God, I've tried—and failed—to do it all by myself in my own power. Today I want to turn my life over to You. I ask You to be my Lord and Savior. You're the one and only Higher Power. I ask You to help me think less about myself and my own will. I want to turn over my will, moment by moment, to You, to continuously seek Your direction and wisdom for my life. Please continue to help me overcome my hurts, hang-ups, and habits, so that victory over them may help others as they see Your power at work in my already changed, and still changing, life. Help me to do Your will always. In Jesus' name I pray, Amen.

Principle 4

Principle 4: Openly examine and confess my faults to myself, to God, and to someone I trust.

"Happy are the pure in heart." (Matthew 5:8)

Principle 4 begins the process of "coming clean." It's here that you openly examine and confess your faults to yourself, to God, and to another person you trust. You begin to chip away at the "truth decay" of your past. The negative effects of your hurts, hang-ups, and habits have built up, like a layer of tartar, over the years and have kept you from really seeing the truth about your past and present situations.

In the first part of this principle, we need to "openly examine" our faults. We need to list, or inventory, all of the significant events—both good and bad—in our lives. We need to be as honest as we can in order to allow God to show us our part in each event and how that has affected both ourselves and others. We need to do a searching and fearless inventory, to step out of our denial, because we can't put our faults behind us until we've faced them. We need to see through our denial of the past into the truth of the present—to identify our true feelings, motives, and thoughts.

Our inventory brings us to a black-and-white discovery of who we really are at our core. But if we look only at the bad parts of our past, we distort our inventory and open ourselves up to unnecessary pain. Lamentations 3:40 invites us, "Let us examine our ways and test them, and let us return to the LORD." Notice that the verse doesn't say, "Examine your bad, negative ways." We need to honestly focus on both the positives and the negatives of our past.

We accomplish that by taking a MORAL inventory. That word *moral* scares some people. But at its root, it simply means "honest."

In this principle, we list the people we resent or fear, the specific actions others have taken to hurt us, the ways in which those hurtful actions have affected our lives, and the wrongs or injuries we've inflicted on others.

This is done by taking a Spiritual Inventory. Through this process, we examine eight key areas of our lives:

Our relationships with others—Matthew 6:12–14
Our priorities in life—Matthew 6:33
Our attitude—Ephesians 4:31
Our integrity—Colossians 3:9
Our mind—Romans 12:2
Our body—1 Corinthians 6:19–20
Our family—Joshua 24:15
Our church—Hebrews 10:25

The fourth step of the Christ-centered 12 Steps relates to the first part of Principle 4.

Step 4: We made a searching and fearless moral inventory of ourselves.

> *"Let us examine our ways and test them, and let us return to the LORD." (Lamentations 3:40)*

As soon as we complete our inventories in the first part of Principle 4, we need to confess our faults to ourselves, to God, and to someone else we trust. After we share our inventories—the good and bad things of our past and present—we'll find the peace and freedom for which we may have been searching our entire lives. We need to confess our shortcomings, resentments, and sins. God wants us to come clean, to admit that wrong is wrong, that we're "guilty as charged."

In confession we agree with God regarding our sins, and our fellowship with Him is restored. Principle 4 sums up how we go about obeying God's direction in confessing our sins: First, we confessed our sins to God so we could be forgiven. Then we confessed them to another person we trust so we could start the healing process.

The fifth step of the Christ-centered 12 Steps relates to this part of Principle 4.

Step 5: We admitted to God, to ourselves, and to another human being the exact nature of our wrongs.

> *"Therefore confess your sins to each other and pray for each other so that you may be healed." (James 5:16)*

Some people feel that if they ADMIT their sins to another they have everything to lose and nothing to gain. The following is the truth about four things we have to lose and three things we have to gain by sharing our inventories with someone we trust:

We lose:

1. *Our sense of isolation.* Our feeling of aloneness will begin to vanish.
2. *Our unwillingness to forgive.* When people accept and forgive us, we start to see that we, in turn, can forgive others.
3. *Our inflated, false pride.* As we realistically see and accept ourselves, we begin to gain true humility, which involves seeing ourselves as we really are and God as He really is.
4. *Our sense of denial.* Being truthful with another person begins to tear away at our denial. We begin to feel clean and honest.

We gain:

1. *Healing that the Bible promises.* Look again at James 5:16. The key word here is *healed.* Notice that the verse doesn't say, "Confess your sins to one another and you will be forgiven," although we hope this will be so, at least in terms of the other person. God already forgave us when we confessed our sins to Him. Now He promises that we'll begin the healing process when we confess our sins to someone else.
2. *Freedom.* Our secrets have kept us in chains—bound, frozen, unable to move forward in any of our relationships, either with God or with others. Admitting our sins snaps the chains so God's healing power can be released.
3. *Support.* When we share our inventory with another person, we gain support. Our accountability partner can help us stay focused and provide valuable feedback.

An important part of Celebrate Recovery is for each of us to have accountability relationships. Don't attempt to work through this fourth principle alone. We need sponsors and/or accountability partners of the same gender for the following three reasons:

1. Having someone fill this role for us is a key part of our recovery program.

By walking alongside us on the road to recovery, a sponsor

and/or an accountability partner keeps us on track as we complete the eight principles.

Proverbs 20:5 says: "The purposes of a person's heart are deep waters, but one who has insight draws them out." We need a man or woman who understands us as an individual and who also understands what we're going through in order to help us in our recovery.

2. Having a sponsor and/or an accountability partner is biblical.

Ecclesiastes 4:9 – 10 tells us: "Two are better than one, because they have a good return for their labor: If either of them falls down, one can help the other up. But pity anyone who falls and has no one to help them up."

And Proverbs 27:17 points out: "As iron sharpens iron, so one person sharpens another." The phrase *one another* is used in the New Testament over fifty times.

3. Having a sponsor and/or an accountability partner is the best guard against relapse.

By providing feedback to keep us on track, a sponsor and/or an accountability partner can see our old dysfunctional, self-defeating patterns beginning to resurface and quickly point them out to us. This person can confront us in a spirit of truth and love without piling on shame or guilt.

Ecclesiastes 7:5 states: "It is better to heed the rebuke of a wise person than to listen to the song of fools." The trouble with most of us is that we'd rather be ruined by praise than saved by criticism.

As we complete Principle 4, we need to remember that no matter how bad our past actions may have been, we can hold on to the assurance offered by Romans 8:1: "Therefore, there is now no condemnation for those who are in Christ Jesus."

Principle 4 can be summed up in one verse, Isaiah 1:18: " 'Come now, let us settle the matter,' says the LORD. 'Though your sins are like scarlet, they shall be as white as snow; though they are red as crimson, they shall be like wool.' "

Principle 4 Prayer

Dear God, You know our past; You're familiar with all the good and bad things we've done. In this principle, we ask You to give us the strength and courage to list them so we can "come clean" and face both our past and the truth about our present and future. Please help us reach out to those special persons You've placed along our road to recovery. Thank You for providing them to help us maintain balance as we work on our inventories. In Christ's name I pray, Amen.

PRINCIPLE 4 TESTIMONY

My name is Marnie, and I am a grateful believer in Jesus Christ who struggles with sexual addiction and food issues.

I wish I could start this story "Once upon a time" or "There once was a little girl." But instead it starts like this: A broken home, tortuous abuse, fits of rage, and being stripped away from those I held dear to my heart. And this was just a fraction of my childhood that began my forbidden lifestyle filled with fantasy, sex, and lust.

My path to recovery started at Saddleback Church in November of 2000. I remember that night well. I crawled in broken and completely unaware of reality. My view on life had become so distorted and my actions had become so out of control, I don't think the enemy himself could've kept up.

That night I watched as people smiled, hugged, and celebrated, because it happened to be the ninth anniversary of Celebrate Recovery. I arrived an hour early, completely unaware that the worship service didn't start until seven o'clock. So, I sat and listened to the band rehearse.

I remember sitting there, *almost* all alone, with only a handful of people walking around setting things up. As I looked around, tears began to form in my eyes and it was all I could do to blink them back. I didn't know what I was doing there. My thoughts were wandering and had become so disjointed. Everything within me wanted to just get up and walk out. It was evident I was still in denial. I kept hearing the same thoughts repeating themselves in my head: *Whatever is wrong with these people is way worse than anything I could have done!* and *Whatever I've done, I'm sure I can fix it on my own!* But for some reason I just could not bring myself to get up out of that chair and leave.

I was startled as a man came up to me, put his hand on my shoulder, and said, "Excuse me, but this seat is taken." As I looked around the empty room, it took me a while to realize that he was kidding. But you know, just in those few words, I felt a sense of comfort and relief. I felt welcomed and a little less "out of place."

That night I attended Newcomers 101 where, for the first time, I confessed my secrets. I managed to utter the words that had gone unspoken for years — *"I cheated on my husband"* — and moments after that, I began to sob. That was it. That was all I said. The woman, who was leading 101 that night, leaned forward, cupped my hands in hers and told me for the first time "Everything's going to be okay. You've come to the right place." The sincerity in her voice warmed me.

Long before I was born, there was already turmoil brewing in my family. Before my first birthday, my parents had finalized their plan to divorce. My older sister and I were sent to live with my father and grandparents in Hawaii. Once we arrived, my dad conveniently left the scene. My grandparents were unofficially assigned to care for us as if we were their own. My fondest childhood memories are of the years I spent with my grandparents in Hawaii. They taught me about Jesus, and by their example, I learned Christian values. Thankfully, they showed me what it was like to live in a "normal" family. My parents, on the other hand, were diabolical opposites of my grandparents.

My father is a functioning alcoholic, who also has a wandering eye for women. I watched as my dad moved from relationship to relationship and as his addiction to pornography and alcohol grew. His complete disregard for his calling as a father allowed me plenty of time to explore as a young child. I can remember being crouched in a corner with my sister as we attempted to smoke cigarettes and drink some of my dad's beer. As a young girl, curiosity took me by surprise one day when I was snooping around the house and found my dad's *Playboy* collection hidden in his dresser drawers. I felt as though I had just stumbled upon a secret, and I ran out of the room. But at the same time, I was intrigued at the images I saw. Often, my dad would take my sister and me to his girlfriend's house where we were abandoned in the living room and told to watch television while Dad retreated into the bedroom with his girlfriend. Even at such a young age, I was well aware of what they were doing. I viewed this as a totally acceptable lifestyle. My last encounter with my father was when I was in my twenties. That day I wandered onto his patio to find an enraged, drunken man waving a butcher knife in my face.

At the age of five, I moved back to California to live with my mother. She has the personality of a raging alcoholic, minus the alcohol. The movie *Mommy Dearest* comes to mind. She was physically, verbally, and emotionally abusive. One unpleasant incident that sticks with me the most was when I was packing to go on a camping trip with family friends. I walked in on her in one of her fits of rage and she slapped me in the face so hard that my tooth punctured my lip. Needless to say, I had a huge fat lip and black eye the following day. I told everyone I had been eating and that my fork had slipped. She'd always apologize and say she hated what she had done, but in the next breath tell me I deserved it. I don't know how many times I ended up in the hospital as a young girl. I remember vividly my mother being sent out of the room and the doctors asking, "Did your mother hit you?" and with a stoic face, my response always being a simple shake of the head "no."

Throughout my childhood, I became my mother's human piñata—often a victim of choking and dodging mirrors she threw at me. I also was beaten with lamps, hangers, high-heeled shoes, and whatever else was within reach. To cope with my dysfunctional life, I escaped into a fantasy life, filled with lustful thoughts and pornographic images that were embedded in my mind. I would stay in bed for hours fanaticizing about sexual acts, replaying the same dreams over and over again in my head.

My upbringing was so filled with turmoil that I had no choice but to escape the insanity. Just before the start of my senior year of high school, I emancipated myself. At seventeen, legally, I was recognized as an adult. I moved out and was on my own. I was determined to break the cycle of dysfunction I had been living with all of my life. But I had become a product of my environment.

I married my high school sweetheart in June of '98. Marriage started off difficult for us. Although we had dated for eight years prior to getting married, it almost seemed that, in an instant we had grown miles apart, as if our years together had somehow been reversed. Our conversations were no longer familiar. Instead, we stuck to superficial topics. Hard times were beginning to materialize. We were struggling financially and we were living with his parents. The enemy sank his fangs into me as I viewed my marriage as a mistake; a "verbal blunder," so to speak; a prison. Bitterness, resentment, and hatred started to paint an ugly picture, as my visions of a "normal" lifestyle fell by the wayside. We went through months of arguing and a lot of broken promises. I felt like I was running in place. I felt taken advantage of, disrespected, and unappreciated. I felt like I had no voice and no control. I felt robbed of my dreams. Most of all, I felt emotionally bankrupt. It was then that my behavior exploded into an uncontrollable fury; my solution, adultery. Just ten short months into my marriage, I had cheated on my husband.

As my addictive lifestyle was starting to take shape, I took a new position at work, which would require me to fly to the Bay Area every Monday and fly home every Thursday. All of this free time away from my husband gave me the freedom to make my own choices, which only fueled my unhealthy behaviors. In my denial, life never felt so good. I was getting attention from men I hardly knew and who hardly knew me. Every day, I became more and more independent of my marriage. I felt in control. I was finally doing something I thought I wanted to do instead of having to live by someone else's rules. But in my heart, I knew something was desperately wrong. I struggled with confusion about the Christian values I had been taught as a child versus what the world deems as socially acceptable behavior. I suddenly felt as if I only knew these childhood beliefs intellectually. For the first time in my life, my faith in God had been tried and shaken, because at this point in my life, my relationship with the Lord was nonexistent. I ignored those feelings and instead replaced them with alcohol, anorexia, and adultery. I was now on a suicide mission *"devoted to a life of deception."* My life became intertwined with the very women I had been warned against in my childhood teachings of the Bible: Jezebel, Potiphar's wife, and Delilah. My life had now become a reflection of the woman whose *"greatest accomplishment in life was the destruction of the man who loved her most."* My forbidden lifestyle progressed into a double life. I continued keeping up the variety of appearances that had sustained me throughout the years. At work, I was balanced, poised, and professional. I would walk in with a smile on my face, go to my office, shut the door, and act out with Internet pornography and chat rooms. When I was with my college friends, I was the baby. I played the "innocent" codependent Marnie, the "good girl," the Marnie who never drank, but just took care of the rest of the bunch when they did. At church I was the devout Christian, pseudo listening from the concrete bench outside, but making sure my friends and family all knew I was present and accounted for. But the real Marnie, the uninhibited Marnie, surfaced after work hours where I would spend most of my free time at bars with the "good old boys club." I could tell a good dirty joke or two and just be one of the guys. The more I drank, the more I talked. The more I talked, the more I started blaming my circumstances for my behavior. My drinking buddies got the unvarnished story of how awful life was like for me at home. I became completely cavalier with a complete disregard and disrespect for myself and for those around me. My life was a riotous mess.

My insatiable appetite for more manifested itself as I attempted to fill the void within me, only to find out that this beast of ugliness would, in no way, be satisfied. My form of self-punishment and control was to starve my body, both spiritually and physically. Body image became more important to me than anything else in my life, including the people I loved the most. I was now on a quest for the perfect figure, no matter what the cost. Starving myself made me feel like I was making my own decisions. I put myself on a rigid diet which consisted of a handful of grapes each day and excessive amounts of Diet Coke. I decided what I put in my body. I decided what I would look like. I started working out obsessively, running between twelve and fifteen miles a day. This lifestyle, coupled with my sexual addiction, left my body weak and out of fuel. I weighed a mere ninety-two pounds, with a sunken face, and was rapidly self-destructing. My addiction was now in full throttle.

As I saw the scenes of my life unfolding, I became desperate to find freedom from my "web of deception." I picked up the phone and called Saddleback Church and they suggested I try Celebrate Recovery. During that time, I recalled the Christian values taught to me as a child by my grandparents, which I had buried due to my anger and resentment toward God. He had finally gotten my attention. It was then that I realized, *"I don't understand myself at all, for I really want to do what is right, but I can't. I do what I don't want to—what I hate. I know perfectly well that what I am doing is wrong, and my bad conscience proves that I agree with these laws I am breaking. But I can't help myself, because I'm no longer doing it. It is sin inside me that is stronger than I am that makes me do these evil things" (Romans 7:15–20).* At this point, I felt as if I had been hollowed out and the world, as I knew it, was slowly being erased. I didn't know how to reconcile these conflicting pieces of my past. The pain had finally become greater than the fear. I had reached my bottom.

Two months after that first fateful night at Celebrate Recovery, a women's step study group opened. So I picked up a Celebrate Recovery Bible and a set of Celebrate Recovery participant's guides and began a pilgrimage through the Christ-centered 12 Steps with women I could relate to and who could also relate to me ... and where secrets seemed all but impossible. At first I kept myself at a safe distance. I would guard my secrets so that no one could use what they knew to hurt me. I also felt hideously ugly, and thought the scars that had been left behind were visible to everyone. But, as I began to share, for the first time I saw women who just stayed silent throughout, listening without judgment. I began to grasp that this internal battle I was having was not uncommon. It was then that I started to understand how the pains of my past played a crucial part in my behavior. I started realizing that I was in a cycle of addiction. All my life I viewed men as objects, and I was imitating what I had learned in my childhood. I had kept *so* many secrets — childhood secrets, secrets in my adult life, and secrets in my marriage — but by saying them out loud, it brought some truth to my reality. I found comfort in the fact that I could not be perfect — there was no such thing as the perfect marriage or the perfect body. Most importantly, I saw just how far I had fallen away from my relationship with Christ. *"Problems far too big for me to solve are piled higher than my head. Meanwhile my sins too many to count; have all caught up with me and I am ashamed to look up" (Psalm 40:12).*

Principle 4 says, "Openly examine and confess my faults to myself, to God, and to someone I trust." "Happy are the pure in heart" (Matthew 5:8).

I began exploring this new, unchartered territory at Celebrate Recovery by working this principle, and the true healing began. It was then I heard God's promise of freedom and stopped acting out. *"It was then that I realized that whatever is covered up will be uncovered, and every secret will be made known. So then, whatever you have said in the dark will be heard in broad daylight" (Luke 12:2–3).*

As I laid my sins at the foot of the cross and turned from my addictions, God declared me not guilty. *He "blotted out the charges proved against you, the list of his commandments which you had not obeyed. He took this list of sins and destroyed it by nailing it to Christ's cross" (Colossians 2:13–15).*

I have reconciled my relationship with my husband and today my relationships are built on honesty and trust. My marriage has been restored. The challenges are still there. Marriage takes work. And my view on marriage is that every couple needs to argue every now and then, just to prove that the relationship is strong enough to survive it. We have been blessed with the most precious gifts of all, two beautiful baby girls. My new ministry in life is my family. Where they once played second fiddle to my work and my addictive behavior, they are now my priority. In fact, in this day and age, where people are so accessible with smart phones, iPads, iPods, etc., our family has a rule: "No electronics at the table." Most importantly, I am teaching my children that NOTHING is more important than my time with them. No email, text, tweet, phone call, whatever.

As for my mom and dad, I have found it in my heart to forgive them, although I still do not have a relationship with either of them. Though I have made attempts over the years, I remain steadfast in the fact that neither of them are safe people to have around me, my husband, or my girls. Neither of them has changed their behaviors, and unfortunately, they have been left to live in their own misery. I have learned how to embrace my pain and made the choice to abandon my life of deception and destruction.

As I reflect on my life now, I thank God for His never-failing truth and understanding. I look back at the journey I had to take through Celebrate Recovery to bring balance to the chaos of my life, and now the blessings that come with being able to help people use Celebrate Recovery as a tool to implement peace and joy in their own lives. I have used these same tools to continue my obedience and submission to Christ as a wife, mother, and employee. God has taken my tragedy and used it as a testament of my faith. Most of all, I thank God that, unlike Delilah, mine is not "a life wasted," and that He chose to spare me rather than erase me from history as He did Delilah. I'm no longer defined by my past mistakes and failures. It's only by God's grace that today, when I look at myself in the mirror, I no longer see myself as someone trying to be perfect, or an adulterer, or an alcoholic, or anorexic. I see myself as an incredibly blessed mother, wife, and forgiven child of God.

In corporate America I used to fly every week and find myself in compromising situations because of my husband's absence. Ironically, God is using the very same pattern of flying that was so instrumental in virtually destroying my life to restore me to wholeness. Today I get to serve on the Celebrate Recovery conference team, where it is my privilege to travel every other week to different cities nationally and internationally to help coordinate Celebrate Recovery one-day seminars. My accountability team now spans the nation, as I have filled my life with godly women and men from whom I seek guidance every day. With an accountability partner in almost every state, there's no hiding anymore.

This reminds me of God's promise that says, *"Even though you are at the ends of the earth, the LORD your God will go and find you and bring you back again" (Deuteronomy 30:4).*

You know, *"there was a time when I wouldn't admit what a sinner I was. But my dishonesty made me miserable and filled my days with frustration. All day and all night your hand was heavy on me. My strength evaporated like water on a sunny day until I finally admitted all my sins to you and stopped trying to hide them. I said to myself, 'I will confess them to the LORD.' And you forgave me! All my guilt is gone" (Psalm 32:3–5).*

Thank you for letting me share.

Principle 5

> **Principle 5:** Voluntarily submit to every change God wants to make in my life and humbly ask Him to remove my character defects.
>
> *"Happy are those whose greatest desire is to do what God requires."*
> *(Matthew 5:6)*

By the time you get to Principle 5, you will have already taken some major steps on the road to recovery. You admitted you had a problem that you were powerless within yourself to overcome. You came to believe that God could and would help you. You have sought Him and turned your life and will over to His care and direction. You've taken a spiritual inventory and shared it both with God and with another person. That was a lot of work—hard work, great work! Now you will be asking God to remove your character defects.

Principle 5 states that each of us is ready to voluntarily submit to every change God wants to make in our lives. The sixth and seventh steps of the Christ-centered 12 Steps relate to Principle 5.

> **Step 6:** We were entirely ready to have God remove all these defects of character.
>
> *"Humble yourselves before the Lord, and he will lift you up."*
> *(James 4:10)*

> **Step 7:** We humbly asked Him to remove all our shortcomings.
>
> *"If we confess our sins, he is faithful and just and will forgive us our sins and purify us from all unrighteousness."* (1 John 1:9)

Most, if not all, of us would be more than willing to have *certain* character defects go away. The sooner the better, we think. Good riddance! But the truth is that some defects are hard to give up. Like weeds in a garden, they've developed deep roots. We've developed our defects of character, our hang-ups, and our destructive habits over periods of five, ten, twenty or more years. In this principle you and God—together—are going after these defects. *All* of them.

To make these positive changes in our lives, we need to be entirely ready to let God be our life-changer. We're not the how-and-when committee. We're the preparation committee. All we have to be is ready.

Sometimes we discover in ourselves so many character defects that it's hard to know where to start. We need to go back to the wrongs, shortcomings, and sins we identified in our Principle 4 inventories. Remember, falling down doesn't make us a failure; staying down does. God doesn't just want us to admit our wrongs; He wants to make us right. He wants to give us "hope and a future" (Jeremiah 29:11). God doesn't just want to forgive us; He wants to change us. We need to ask Him first to remove those character defects that are causing us the most pain. Ask Him today, and be specific.

At first, our old self-doubts and low self-image may tell us we're not worthy of the growth and progress we're already making in the program. We need to turn off those old, negative tapes and yield to the growth. It's the Holy Spirit's work within us. Through His transforming power, we'll find the victory that keeps us from reverting back to our hang-ups and harmful habits.

Once we ask God to remove our character defects, we begin a journey that will lead us to new freedom from our past. We need to be careful not to look for perfection but instead to rejoice in steady progress. We need to seek, and be satisfied with, steady improvement.

The victory we receive in Principle 5 is summed up in Romans 12:2: "Do not conform to the pattern of this world, but be transformed by the renewing of your mind. Then you will be able to test and approve what God's will is—his good, pleasing and perfect will."

Principle 5 Prayer

Dear God, thank You for taking me this far on my recovery journey. Now I pray for Your help in making me entirely ready to change my destructive patterns. Give me the strength to deal with the character defects I've turned over to You. Allow me to accept all the changes You want to make in me. Help me to be the person You want me to be. In Your Son's name I pray, Amen.

PRINCIPLE 5 TESTIMONY

My name is John, and I am a grateful believer in Jesus Christ who struggles with codependency.

My earliest memories are probably kindergarten and the beginning of grade school. I was a pretty happy and extroverted little fella. I was very active, full of joy and energy, secure and comfortable in my own skin. We were Mom, Dad, my older brother (by three years), and then twin sisters a year younger—all together in Duluth, Minnesota. My parents were saved and belonged to an exciting new independent Pentecostal church. They were young and zealous, and had young and zealous friends, and a young and zealous pastor. My father worked at a men's clothing store and my mom stayed home with us kids. Some of the families from our young and zealous church got together and decided to buy some property just outside the city limits in a lovely, private wooded area. They all wanted to build some homes together, form a Christian neighborhood, with Christian kids riding their Christian bikes on a Christian road, with Christian dogs chasing Christian cats ...

Our family quickly signed on to that project and soon we were living in a freshly built log home on Morning Star Drive.

I guess I was in the second grade or so when, one by one, each of us four clueless siblings was called upstairs into our parents' bedroom for news of the divorce. This is how Mom wanted to break it to us. This is one of my few branded-in memories. I remember the unfinished texture of the wooden baluster on the balcony, my hand sort of trailing behind me on the railing trying to somehow slow my progress to my father and mother's room. My older brother came out sobbing, and I just kept walking toward their room, straining to look through their cracked door. There was something evil crouched beyond that door: depression, pain ... unwelcome, unasked-for change.

It was so quiet after the divorce announcement. My parents used to fight a lot before the announcement, but now my dad hadn't the spirit for fighting; he gave up. Again, the realization of past yelling matches came *after* the hush fell on that big log home. My father, one of the heroes, if there are any in this testimony, was so infinitely sad. My mom knew the pain she was causing—I do believe that—but at the same time, I have come to understand that she didn't. She was not making decisions based on the truth. She was lying to herself, and to us, about how much fun her new life, *our* new life, would be. It was a fresh start, a new and exciting adventure. Her world was a cleverly constructed fantasy of greener grass.

She packed us up and moved us away from my father, to a farm where a new family was waiting. I remember her turning her head to us in the passenger and back seats while driving and repeating over and over, "Isn't this exciting?"

At the first meeting of the soon-to-be-step-family, I remember lots of dogs and the smell of a dairy farm. I was game; it DID look exciting. My sisters took things in stride as well, but my older brother did not. I *adapted* to this new life. I did whatever I was told; I was compliant; I had fun; I rode motorcycles; I pitched in with the haying; I picked rocks in the fields; I camped out with my stepbrother; I shot a pistol, rode the three-wheeler, grabbed an electric fence on a dare to see who could hold on the longest. I did it. I conformed. My brother did not.

In the midst of my mother's chaotic relationship with this new husband, my brother went a little crazy. Our oldest stepbrother was a bullying beast of a teenager who had his father's temper. He was full of hate, full of rage, and I stayed out of his way, laughed at his dirty jokes, did what I was told. My brother did not laugh, did not do what he was told, did not stay out of anyone's way.

One night, out in the barn, my older brother had enough of our "bully stepbrother" and tried to crush his head with a lead pipe. He whiffed badly. I watched as my brother paid a terrible price for standing up to a bully. It was a terrifying experience, which led to me and my brother both moving back to our dad's. My brother and I carried on a new existence at my father's home in that huge, empty log tomb. Dad was not coping well, and we weren't enough to keep him going. He had seen his church collapse a few months earlier in a scandal. His church, his marriage, and his life had been taken from him; the rug had been pulled out; that was his new reality and ours.

Somewhere in the transition from grade school to middle school, depression took me like anesthesia. I remember it coming on, then I remember coming out of it. I ate a lot, I know that. I was like a Hoover vacuum on a very low setting. Whatever food was near me got sucked in, slowly but surely. I stared at whatever TV had to offer for hours after school, when other kids were outside playing. I began to skip school, constantly faking migraines. My mother was divorced again and off the farm. *I didn't care, I was depressed.* She had repented of her foolishness, and my brother and I were going to live with her and my sisters again in a nice little duplex. *I didn't care, I was depressed.* I was back with mom, my sisters, and my brother, and I was put in counseling. Now, I did care about that. I hated that. Maybe my hating counseling shocked me out of my depression. Counseling scared me straight.

When I did awaken from my depressed stupor, I found myself in the body of this scared, fat, introverted older kid. Mom was on welfare trying to get an education so I wore a lot of secondhand clothing. Bullies were a terror to me. I was much larger than most kids my age, but I was afraid of everyone. I was what others said I was. There was no doubt in my mind. I just wanted to disappear.

That's how I coped. I began to deal with problems through invisibility. A very big boy willing every part of his being to disappear into thin air best describes me at this time of my life. I was living a life of "quiet desperation." I was tortured and tormented by my classmates, physically and emotionally abused, and I felt like I deserved it.

I was helpless, powerless, and daily frozen with fear, being constantly silenced by crippling insecurity. This overwhelming insecurity at times reclaims its hold on me. A strange residual social fear lingers, but I have learned to trust that it remains for God's purposes. I choose to embrace this weakness and say with Paul: *"His power is perfected in my weakness. When I am weak, I am truly strong."*

One day it all began to change. It started when I stood up to a guy in my class who wanted to take my seat, and what do you know, he backed down. I started lifting weights, then I went by myself and tried out for the football team, and I made it. Then I went to the church youth group, started cracking jokes, starting talking to girls. By my junior year of high school, I was starting for the varsity football team and ENJOYING school for the first time in my life.

My grades stunk, but I was happy and independent. I had been getting more and more involved in the youth group, and I began developing a vibrant relationship with God. I had prayed for salvation at five years of age with my father, but now I was beginning to understand and answer a clear call to His service. At fifteen, I seriously committed myself to Jesus Christ. I made a vow to live for Him for the rest of my life.

I graduated from high school and eventually moved with my mom to the Twin Cities where I was back to being a "nobody." I had been lightly recruited by a couple local colleges for football and had received a small scholarship at a Christian university in Missouri, but that insecurity came back stronger than ever, convincing me all efforts to succeed were hopeless. I began a slow and steady roll back into depression. I was not in church, not in school. I was back to a day-to-day existence without meaning, without purpose, working the graveyard shift at a local gas station. My mom had many relationships over the years following the farm with one deadbeat after the other; but in St. Paul, Minnesota, she picked up their king in a bar one summer evening.

He told her that he was the son of a wealthy CEO, and that he would pay her back if she would spring for a weekend of partying in Duluth. He had no intention of paying for anything; he wasn't the son of a CEO; he was a con man running up her credit cards, depleting her savings, until finally he showed his true colors. One evening he took the rented Cadillac my mother had charged for their lavish weekend fantasy and disappeared. After my mom called the police a few days after his departure, I found him late one night passed out on the seat of the stolen Caddy.

I wanted to save my mom from these guys every time. She was always able to sell me on them, and then when she turned against them, I was right there with her, comforting her, consoling. I was blinded to her responsibility in these situations. I wanted to be somebody's favorite—to save someone—and she was beginning to rely on my shoulder to cry on. No matter what she had done to me, or to the family over the years, I loved her, I still believed in her, she relied on me, and that was what I desperately clung to. So, I called the police on the loser in the Caddy, and I was the hero, until my mom decided to bail the con man out of jail. When she walked through the door with him, I almost fell out of my chair. The king was back. I gave my mom an ultimatum. I was amazed and hysterical with anger when she gave me her answer. No. This man would stay, and I would go. Back to my dad's I went.

Soon after moving back to my father's, I had an opportunity to move north and play football at a community college. It was at this remote, "nowhere" school that I learned about the wonderful numbing effects of alcohol. It was easy to let it all go there in Virginia, Minnesota. I was alone, I was depressed, and I was a waste. My life consisted of football, a meager schedule of classes, alcohol whenever and however I could get it, and a girlfriend hand-picked to put up with my moodiness and drinking. I had plugged into a local church the moment I arrived, but it couldn't hold me; I was just too wrapped up in my pain, in coping. The discovery of alcohol was a revelation. It made me more depressed, but in a bittersweet, self-pitying, brooding sense.

I dropped out of college after my first year, and ended up rooming with my best friend from high school back in Duluth. I began working another graveyard shift cleaning the floors at a grocery store. I was sleeping through the days, stockpiling alcohol on the shelf, working a dead-end job that I could barely hold, picking fights. Now *I* was becoming the bully. I would drink at home, and then go out drinking, drive home drunk, and drink. There was nothing else in my future. This was my life, for the rest of my life.

One night I was alone, and I was sober, or I was drunk, or someplace in between. I do remember the shotgun in my hands. I had my grandfather's double barreled shotgun across my lap. I tried to put it to my head, but fear swept over me. Was I so pathetic that I couldn't even kill myself?

I began playing games with loading it and trying to peek down the barrel to see if I could get up the courage to take this seriously. I wept and screamed on the floor of my room for God to save me, but I was alone. He must have had enough and abandoned me; I couldn't blame Him. I wanted Him to leave me alone; I didn't deserve love. I was going to die, and I was going to be as insignificant in death as I was in life.

I was finally ready. Calm and determined, sniffing away the last of the tears, I said my last half-hearted prayer, "Lord, if You're there, it's time to let me know, or I'm finished." Another ridiculous ultimatum.

But, in that little upstairs apartment, God answered me. The room glossed over, and I was in a cave. Ribs became part of the infrastructure of the room, and I was inside something. It was a vision. The only one I have ever had. And it wasn't angels and harps. It was me clearly in the inner guts of a fish. I grabbed hold of that vision with two desperate hands, finding and opening my old Bible from youth group. I had no idea where the story of Jonah was. It was a book in itself. The story was familiar, but what did that have to do with me? Then I saw it, the prayer in the second chapter. Jonah's prayer is what was in me. My spirit had been speaking this in groans, in the throes of anguish. *"In my distress I called to the LORD, and he answered me. From the depths of the grave I called for help, and you listened to me cry ... I said, 'I have been banished from your sight' ... The engulfing waters threatened me, the deep surrounded me ... To the roots of the mountains I sank down; the earth beneath barred me in forever. But you brought my life up from the pit, O LORD my God. When my life was ebbing away, I remembered you, LORD, and my prayer rose to you ... What I have vowed I will make good. I will say, 'Salvation comes from the LORD'"* (Jonah 2:1–9).

I dedicated myself to the Lord that moment, telling Him that what I had vowed as a committed Christian in my youth, I would make good.

I signed up for the fall to go to the Christian university in Missouri where I had initially, upon graduation, received a seed scholarship for football. I had no idea where the funds would come from, but it was clear that was the place God wanted me. It was where He had wanted me all along. I had been running from a call. Like Jonah.

I was accepted to the school and the money somehow was there for me to attend. Life was so sweet these three years of school. I was away at school, playing football. I had Christ-centered classes and Christian friends, so why was I still struggling to maintain my sobriety? There were rules against drinking. I had even signed a covenant that I would abstain from alcohol. But that didn't mean opportunities didn't present themselves; it didn't mean opportunities weren't created. My last binge ended late one night after staring into the disappointed eyes of the most beautiful woman God has ever breathed life into. My girlfriend had been able to melt away some of the walls that were again forming around me—we even began talking about marriage, about kids, about everything—but we hadn't talked about this drinking stuff before.

Another stamped-in, burned-in memory is when I stopped by her off-campus apartment after having a few drinks, and then a few more drinks with some friends who lived in the same apartment complex. My girlfriend didn't say so, but it was all over her face when she saw me. She was disappointed. I don't think she ever really thought twice about us—we were in love and flying recklessly and blissfully toward our future—but in that instant, I saw a loss of respect ... even some doubt. She loved me for the right reasons—for the Christian man I wanted to be—and this wasn't it. It was in this moment, confronted with this past-and-once-again-present coping strategy, that the double-standard I was keeping between my Christian ascent and my worldly descent came to a head. I was either going to become the man God had created and called *or* go back to despair, loneliness, death, and hell. I chose life, and have never, in over a decade of sobriety, ever regretted my decision.

My girlfriend and I got married, and I received a degree in criminal justice, but ended up enjoying a counseling group I was placed in during my practicum so much that I began to explore counseling and social work as a career. Together we moved to my wife's home state of Delaware where I began working for the state's Division of Family Services as a family crisis therapist.

During my five years in that office, I toiled through a master's program in social work, and began group and individual work at a private counseling agency on the side to earn hours for my clinical licensing. I loved the work, I loved counseling, and I loved group process.

What I didn't realize is that in working two to three jobs ministering to others, I was neglecting my ministry at home to my family. Three jobs at times kept me away constantly, and I was even volunteering any leftover hours at the church. It was exhausting—and a trying time for my marriage.

I tried to convince my wife, unsuccessfully, that this work was my mission field. I was giving my all in answer to "the call." But my absence was wearing on her, on us. We had two girls, and I didn't see much of them. My explanation to them, to myself, and to God was that I was needed out there; people needed me; they needed saving! She had her parents to lean on, my kids had their grandparents. Those I helped didn't have anyone but me. Isn't being a Christian about helping the helpless AT ANY COST?

What I didn't fully realize is that through college, working toward a degree, playing football, and now with my career goals, my master's degree, my striving for success in counseling others, I was succumbing to the pressure of trying to earn back my value. The value I had lost by being a fat, spineless nobody without any answers. My professional life was a tenuous balance of keeping everyone happy with me, spinning anything negative, running from conflict, blaming others, justifying my very existence, running, running to keep that distance ... keeping the helpless loser I once was far behind me.

One day, God called me to a fast. A one-week fast. I managed to doubt it and fight it for a good month, but I finally relented. When the fast was over, I was incredibly disappointed. No lightning bolts, no giant handwriting on the wall.

What a rip-off! Oh well. It was done and I had been obedient. A few weeks later, my brother-in-law, a youth pastor working in a little church in West Virginia, called and asked if I would travel to West Virginia to talk to his church's men's ministry about outreach.

His pastor had felt God leading the church to do more for those outside their four walls. I said I would be glad to do it, and soon found myself talking to a small group of men in Clarksburg, West Virginia about Celebrate Recovery, and some other outreach programs I was heading up in our church in Delaware.

A week later, I was being asked to consider interviewing in this same church to do outreach ministry full-time. God was orchestrating a miraculous life-change, and soon I was chugging through the mountains in a U-Haul contemplating this new direction in my life and ministry.

Now the recovery program I had started in Delaware was very loosely based on the Celebrate Recovery curriculum, and I had plans in West Virginia to veer even further off the Celebrate Recovery course. I have since discovered why I was reluctant to conform to the program. Running my own program, my way, was all about pride. Tailor-making my own recovery program elevated me to the keeper of all the keys, giving me the illusion of being in complete control and helping me stay aloof in a "therapist" role. It kept people looking to me for the answers. I wanted to be their savior. *"I, even I, am the LORD, and apart from me there is no savior" (Isaiah 43:11).*

After several months of running the "John" recovery program in my new ministerial role in West Virginia, with frustratingly minimal success, my wonderful little church sent me to my first Celebrate Recovery Summit. It was during those three days in August 2006 where I felt challenged to make a commitment to run this ministry by the letter. I had been fighting it, as I was to learn later, mainly because I would rather help "those people," than be *one* of "those people."

However, as I listened to the testimonies given at the Summit, as I worshiped with the thousands of lives being transformed by the power of God through the truths of this program, I felt the gentle conviction of the Holy Spirit calling me to submit and SURRENDER. I had been asking everyone to share their lives with me, to open up, be completely transparent so they could find healing and hope for their lives. However, I had never really done that myself. What hypocrisy! During a question-and-answer time at one of the Summit workshops, I made a public confession that I had been using the Celebrate Recovery name, but had not been following the model. It was at that vulnerable place, the giving up of my power, where my own healing began. You could say that my journey of discovery into my own emotional and spiritual DNA finally began when I submitted to the Celebrate Recovery DNA.

While I had been trying to construct a new me through meeting the needs of others, God had wanted nothing more than to deconstruct me by exposing my own many hurts, hang-ups, and habits. Through the work of this ministry, especially going through the step study, I finally dared to get honest about my past.

Principle 5 says, "Voluntarily submit to every change God wants to make in my life and humbly ask Him to remove my character defects." "Happy are those whose greatest desire is to do what God requires" (Matthew 5:6).

Finally, I would have to take a real look at myself and either change or continue in my own pride and ego. Then, as I wrote my inventory, I realized something that broke me to a point where I hadn't been broken before. I started to see and feel how much my efforts to replace God with self-sufficiency and self-righteousness had grieved my God and Savior Jesus Christ. After sharing my inventory, with the help of another minister, I made my first heart-wrenching amends. My first amends were offered to God, and through that process I felt His forgiveness, mercy, and love for me like never before.

In that place of grace, He gave me a new awareness of a value I could never earn, and a value I will never lose.

"How deep the Father's love for us, how vast beyond all measure that He would send His only Son, to make a wretch His treasure."

Today I have come to a new realization and reliance on His economy. It is not by my strength, not by man's might, but truly by His Spirit that I (and others) find true recovery. My wife and I celebrated our twelfth anniversary in June. I have four beautiful daughters. (Yes, I am powerless and my life is truly unmanageable.) My family has now become my most important and cherished ministry.

I want to encourage anyone who is feeling the overwhelming weight of insecurity to let go, get vulnerable, and trust in the Lord. In Principle 7 we are taught: *"Reserve a daily time with God for self-examination, Bible reading, and prayer in order to know God and His will for my life and to gain the power to follow His will."* Celebrate Recovery rightly emphasizes this complete dependency on Christ as the only opportunity we have for true peace, security, and salvation.

I thank God for His love, and I thank God for my family; I thank God for this program and for my incredible Celebrate Recovery family; and I thank God for the opportunity to share my testimony with you.

Thank you for letting me share.

Principle 6

> **Principle 6:** Evaluate all my relationships. Offer forgiveness to those who have hurt me and make amends for harm I've done to others, except when to do so would harm them or others.
>
> *"Happy are the merciful." (Matthew 5:7)*
>
> *"Happy are the peacemakers." (Matthew 5:9)*

Principle 6 is all about making amends and offering forgiveness. "Forgive me as I learn to forgive" sums up Principle 6. This is right in line with Jesus' words in the prayer He taught his disciples: "Forgive us our debts, as we also have forgiven our debtors" (Matthew 6:12). But some of us balk at making amends. If God has forgiven me, we think, isn't that enough? Why should I dredge up the past? After all, making amends doesn't sound natural. The answer to that objection is simple: Making amends isn't about our past so much as it is about our future. Before we can enjoy the healthy relationships we desire, we need to clean out the guilt, shame, and pain that have caused many of our past relationships to fail.

Luke 6:31 instructs each of us to "do to others as you would have them do to you." This verse reminds us to treat others the way we want to be treated. For some of us, that may be difficult. We've been badly hurt and/or abused. Many of us had nothing to do with the wrongs committed against us.

The first part of Principle 6, "Evaluate all my relationships," deals with our willingness to consider making amends and offering our forgiveness. The second part, "Offer forgiveness to those who have hurt me and make amends for harm I've done to others," calls us to action. We need to pull out the dead weeds in our past broken relationships so that we can clear a place where new relationships can be successfully planted or old ones nurtured. That's why this principle is so important.

It's so important to make amends because we can become addicted to our bitterness, hatred, and revenge, just as we may have become addicted to alcohol, drugs, or unhealthy relationships. A life characterized by bitterness, resentment, and anger will kill us emotionally and shrivel our souls. Such a life will produce the three Ds:

Depression
Despair
Discouragement

An unforgiving heart will cause us more pain and destruction than it will ever cause the person who has hurt us.

The inability to accept and offer forgiveness can stall, block, or even destroy our recovery. Forgiveness breaks that negative cycle. It doesn't settle all the questions of blame, justice, or fairness, but it does allow relationships to heal.

Principle 6 addresses three types of forgiveness. The first and most important kind of forgiveness is extended by God to us. Have we accepted God's forgiveness? Have we accepted Jesus' work on the cross? By His willingness to take our punishment, all our sins were canceled. Our debt was paid in full—a free gift for those who are willing to put their faith in Him as the true and only Higher Power, Savior, and Lord. Jesus Himself exclaimed from the cross, "It is finished" (John 19:30)—possibly the most significant three words ever uttered. No matter how grievously we may have injured others or ourselves, the grace of God is always sufficient. His forgiveness is always complete, with no strings attached.

The second kind of forgiveness is the kind we extend from ourselves to others. This type of forgiveness is a process. We first need to be willing to forgive. But in order to become truly free, we have to let go of the pain of the past harm and abuse caused by others.

The third kind of forgiveness may well be the most difficult for us to extend: We need to forgive ourselves. We may find the grace within ourselves to forgive others, and we may accept God's forgiveness, but we may feel as though the guilt and shame of our own past are just too horrendous to forgive. But this is what God wants to do with the darkness of our past: "'Come now, let us settle the matter,' says the LORD. 'Though your sins are like scarlet, they shall be as white as snow; though they are red as crimson, they shall be like wool'" (Isaiah 1:18). No matter how unloved or worthless we may feel, God loves us and values us highly. Our feelings about ourselves don't change God's assessment of us and our potential one bit.

As we grow as Christians and move through our recovery process, we want to follow the guidance and direction of Jesus Christ. As we get to know Him better, we want to model His teachings and His ways. We want to become more like Him. If we're going to implement Principle 6 to the best of our ability, we need to learn to model God's grace.

As we learn to model God's grace, we'll be able to complete Principle 6 and discover healing in our lost and broken relationships—at least as far as that healing depends upon our action. As Romans 12:18 directs us: "If it is possible, as far as it depends on you, live at peace with everyone."

The eighth and ninth steps of the Christ-centered 12 Steps relate to Principle 6.

Step 8: We made a list of all persons we had harmed and became willing to make amends to them all.

"Do to others as you would have them do to you." (Luke 6:31)

Step 9: We made direct amends to such people whenever possible, except when to do so would injure them or others.

"Therefore, if you are offering your gift at the altar and there remember that your brother or sister has something against you, leave your gift there in front of the altar. First go and be reconciled to them; then come and offer your gift." (Matthew 5:23–24)

Forgiveness is all about letting go. Remember playing tug-of-war as a child? As long as the people on each end of the rope are tugging, you have a war. You let go of your end of the rope when you forgive others. No matter how hard they may tug on their end, if you've released yours, the war is over. But until you release that rope, you're a prisoner of war.

Principle 6 Prayer

Dear God, thank You for Your love, for the grace You freely offer. Help me model Your ways when I make my amends to those I've hurt and offer my forgiveness to those who've injured me. Help me set aside my selfishness and speak the truth in love. Help me focus on my own responsibility in the issue, so my actions won't be conditional. I know I can forgive others because You first forgave me. Thank You for loving me. In Jesus' name I pray, Amen.

Principle 7

Principle 7: Reserve a daily time with God for self-examination, Bible reading, and prayer in order to know God and His will for my life and to gain the power to follow His will.

"Happy are the pure in heart." (Matthew 5:8)

When you get to Principle 7, you will have arrived at an important junction. You will have come to understand that you could never have made it this far on your own power. In fact, the only reason you were able to have reached this point is the decision you made way back in Principle 3 to turn over your life and will to God's care.

Jesus explains it this way in John 8:31–32: "If you hold to my teaching, you are really my disciples. Then you will know the truth, and the truth will set you free." Then in John 14:6 He defines truth by identifying it with Himself: "I am the way and the truth and the life. No one comes to the Father except through me." We've been set free from our habits because of the Truth (Jesus Christ) we've invited into our hearts.

Step 10: We continued to take personal inventory and, when we were wrong, promptly admitted it.

> *"So, if you think you are standing firm, be careful that you don't fall!" (1 Corinthians 10:12)*

We've arrived at the crossroads of our recoveries. This isn't a place to stop and rest on our past accomplishments. We need to thank God for getting us this far on our road to recovery; to praise Him for the many victories over our hurts, hang-ups, and habits that we've already seen in working the first six principles; and to continue working the last two principles with the same devotion and enthusiasm that got us to this point in our recoveries. First Corinthians 10:12 puts it this way: "If you think you are standing firm, be careful that you don't fall!"

Most recovery material refers to Steps 10 through 12 (Principles 7 and 8) as the maintenance steps. It's certainly true that in these principles we'll live out our recoveries for the remainder of our time here on earth—one day at a time! But we need to do much more than just maintain our recoveries; we need to continue to *grow* them.

In Principle 7 we desire to grow daily in our new relationships with Jesus Christ and others. Instead of attempting to be in control of every situation and every person with whom we come into contact, or instead of spinning out of control ourselves, we're starting to exhibit self-control, living the way God wants us to. Remember that "self under control" is what we're initially seeking but that self under *God's* control is what we're ultimately striving for.

As we begin to work Principle 7 and Step 10, we'll see that this step involves three key actions:

1. Taking time to do a daily inventory.
2. Evaluating both the good and the bad.
3. Admitting our wrongs promptly.

One way to keep daily track of our good and bad behaviors is to keep a journal. Our journal isn't a place to jot down the calories we ingested for lunch today or our carpool schedule for school. It's a tool for us to review and record the good and bad things we did today. We can look for negative patterns, issues that we're repeatedly writing down and having to make amends for. We can share these pitfalls with our sponsors or accountability partners and set up an action plan to overcome them with God's help.

Journaling will help us live in daily humility — in reality, not in denial. Through God's guidance we can make choices about the emotions that affect our thinking and actions. When we take this step seriously, we can begin to take positive action — instead of getting caught up in a continuous spiral of *reaction*.

In Principle 7, we actually do three different inventories:

1. *An ongoing inventory.* We can maintain an ongoing inventory throughout the day. The best time to admit we're wrong is at the exact time we're made aware of it. Why wait?

2. *A daily inventory.* At the end of each day we can look back over our daily activities, both the good and the bad, paying special attention to points at which we might have harmed someone else or reacted out of anger or fear. But once again, we need to remember to keep our daily inventory balanced. We should be sure to include the things we did right throughout the day, no matter how easy they may be to overlook or discount.

3. *A periodic inventory.* We should take a periodic inventory every ninety days or so. We may want to get away on a mini retreat. We should bring our daily journal with us, and pray as we read through the entries for the last ninety days. We should ask God to show us areas in our life in which we can improve during the next ninety days. But we should also remember to identify and celebrate the victories we've already experienced.

Principle 7 is so important. It also includes Step 11 of the Christ-centered 12 Steps.

Step 11: We sought through prayer and meditation to improve our conscious contact with God, praying only for knowledge of His will for us and power to carry that out.

"Let the word of Christ dwell in you richly." (Colossians 3:16)

By this point in our recoveries we've learned that when we start our day working Principle 7 and having a quiet time with God, and when we end it by doing our daily inventory, we have a pretty good day — a reasonably happy day. Not only will this help to prevent relapse, but it will cultivate in us an attitude of gratitude.

To help maintain this grateful attitude, we can focus our thankfulness on at least four areas of our lives: God, others, our recovery, and our church.

Principle 7 Prayer

Dear God, help me to set aside the hassles and racket of the world, so I can focus my mind and listen just to You for the next few minutes. Help me to get to know You better. Help me to better understand Your plan and purpose for my life. Father, help me to live this day within the boundaries of today, seeking Your will and living this one day as You would have me live it.

I pray that others may view me as Yours, not just in my words but, more importantly, in my actions. Thank You for Your love, Your grace, Your perfect forgiveness. Thank You for all those important individuals You've placed in my life—in my program, in my recovery, and within my church family. Your will be done, not mine. In Your Son's name I pray, Amen.

PRINCIPLE 7 TESTIMONY

My name is Monty, I am a grateful believer in Jesus Christ who struggles with gambling.

I was born in a little town called Okemah, Oklahoma. My dad met my mom after he returned from World War II; he was in the Army, where he drove tanks. My mom, on the other hand, was one of seven siblings raised on a farm not far from Okemah. I came into this world at about one o'clock in the morning January 2, 1951, and just nine months later we were living in Richmond, California, across the bay from San Francisco.

I entered into the first grade in Richmond, but my dad had so many different jobs, we moved so many times, and I attended so many schools that I didn't stay long enough to pass the first grade. That's right, I flunked the first grade. I remember feeling very stupid and not like other kids who had no problem passing the easiest grade in school. This affected my educational outlook for most of my first twelve school years. My grades were barely passing all the way until I graduated from high school. But I got my diploma!

At my graduation, when they were calling out each of the names of my classmates to receive their rolled-up reward for twelve long years of both good teachers and bad, it was my turn to be handed my diploma. Over the loud speaker came someone else's name, not mine.

I know my face must have shown an expression of failure because at that moment I went back in time to being a five-year old again. I was being told by a loudspeaker — to all my friends, family, and everyone in the bleachers — "YOU FLUNKED."

I was dumbfounded and embarrassed, but the wise teacher who was giving out the diplomas held my right hand in a very tight adult handshake, looked at me and my horrified expression, and then whispered in a calm voice, "Just wait!"

The next name, read loud and clear, was mine. Wow, close call! But I made it, and now it was time for the next step in my education: "finally" off to college in the fall.

In college, I had professors and instructors teaching everything from math, science, and logic to history, English, and world religions including Christianity, Hinduism, Islam, Buddhism, and Atheism. I met students who claimed to be witches and followers of Scientology, Mormonism, Jehovah's Witness, and other cults. Of course, I had my own brand of homemade religion that I believed which I called Monty-theism.

This religion was made up in my own mind, not from any Bible or any formal religion, just my own way of believing. But it was this very belief system that formed my understanding about God and just who He was. *Proverbs 14:12 says, "There is a way that seems right to man."*

It was while I was attending Cerritos College in 1976, studying to become an accountant, that Jesus changed my life and this wrong way of thinking. I was going to school during the day and working part-time in a small machine shop in Paramount, California. I was going to parties and lots of dance clubs all over Southern California almost every night, drinking cheap wine and smoking marijuana. My friends and I were completely caught up in the culture of the '70s. One of the standard sayings of that day was, "Keep on truckin'." That is exactly what we were doing: living and loving this carefree lifestyle.

The Vietnam War was the only threat to my college commitment. I was ready any day to be drafted and sent off to fight for our country. I was living at home with my parents rent-free. My parents paid my auto insurance, most of my school expenses, food, and even the gas for my car, a 1962 Ford van that they had also purchased. I had it all.

I never gave much thought to things like religion, church, growing up, and being an adult. Pretty much all I cared about was myself and a few close friends.

My first girlfriend in school was my first love and brought me to my life's big crossroad—I emphasize the "CROSS" in the road. She and I were together through most of junior high and some of senior high school, but broke up just before my junior year. My friends used to tease me because I talked about her all the time.

Do you remember your first love? They say "Your first car is like your first love, you will never forget them!" We experimented with pot together while we were going steady. Except for a couple of tries of a very strong drug called angel dust, which I was told afterward is some kind of animal tranquilizer that stays in your brain for years, I never went on to use any other drugs. However, my girlfriend did go on to stronger and more dangerous drugs.

One morning in January, I got up to go to work and my mother told me that my former girlfriend was very sick and in the hospital. I decided to go after work and pay her a visit, not aware of how sick she really was. When I got there she was tied to the bed, tubes in every part of her body, hooked up to all kinds of machines with lights, bells and beeping sounds. She was in the final stages of Hepatitis C. Her eyes and skin were yellow and she could barely speak. I could not believe what I was seeing. My very first love was dying right in front of me. There was nothing I could do; I was totally helpless to help her.

I did not know how to pray, and I didn't know God in any way, shape, or form. She was barely able to communicate, but through her slurred words she asked me to read to her. I was fresh out of reading material, so I grabbed the book that is in most hospital rooms: a Gideon Bible. So with all the expertise of a "not-so-great first-year Bible student," I opened to a book called John. I can't remember much of what I read, but it seemed to give her some comfort.

After I left the room, I completely came apart. Totally uncontrolled tears ran down my face and a feeling of being more lost than I have ever felt in my life overcame me.

The next day when I went to see her, I stopped first at a flower shop across the street from the hospital. I was weeping so much that the lady couldn't understand what I was asking for. She guessed my emotion and cried herself at my grief. I come by these tears naturally and I am in good company as Jeremiah was known as the "Weeping Prophet," and John tells of Jesus weeping for Lazarus at his death.

As I walked into the room with flowers in hand, I was surprised to see that my ex-girlfriend was sitting up in a chair, not as yellow or as sick. She seemed to be getting better. Our communication was clearer, and we visited a couple of hours. She wanted me to read to her again. Again, I got the Bible and read some more, not understanding it one bit better. Two unbelievers reaching out to God for help, and we wouldn't have known what to do with that divine help if we got it. God would save both of us, although not in a way either of us could or would understand for some time. Jesus, in His infinite wisdom, knew perfectly what each of us needed.

Her salvation came the next day, by way of her death, mine after her funeral. A young man shared the gospel with me after her funeral. He said he had remembered seeing my girlfriend at several services before she got sick. He thought she had told him that she had asked Jesus into her life and that may be why she wanted me to read from the Bible. Only God knows. This young man took the time to explain to me that God sent His Son into the world in human form to save mankind—and me. He patiently answered my questions about the Bible, God, death, and most importantly, my grief.

That night when I was alone with all the thoughts of that dark and terrible day, I prayed "Jesus, I don't know if I can live this new life with You, but if You will forgive me, I promise to trust You with all my heart." At that very moment on my bed in the middle of the night, I felt the weight of that dreadful day and my whole life lift up from my soul. It felt like I rose up from my bed and floated when Jesus came into my life. I've never been the same and never wanted to return to the past life. I started reading the Bible the next day in the weirdest place for a new Christian to start reading.

God's plan was for me to read a very special verse, *Revelation 2:4: "Nevertheless I have this against you, that you have left your first love."* God came into my life because I thought I had lost my very first love. God in His Bible was telling me two things: my first love is really Jesus Christ and He loves me much more than I could ever love anyone else in my life.

The next step in my life was entering into the family of God by way of the church. About six months later, I was asked by my brother to go on a blind date. My date's family went to a church in Bell Gardens.

The next day was Sunday, and I asked her if I could meet her at her church, and she said yes; so I went to my first Sunday school class and a worship service. This became my home church and is to this day.

We dated for two years and during that dating time, we got engaged. I would come to find that my new wife was the perfect example of a Proverbs 31 woman. We got married September 16, 1978, in our home church and have been married for over thirty-four years! I can't believe that she has been able to put up with me for all these years. God did not bless us with children of our own, but He provided many opportunities for us to work with the youth groups from the church and community.

In fact, I became a junior high Sunday school teacher and then started working as a youth pastor with the junior high kids. I eventually became the senior high youth pastor and an associate pastor.

Wow, what a great story of salvation—so far.

But like the famous Paul Harvey would say: And now, the rest of the story ...

My addiction to gambling started very slowly. One night after our Wednesday youth meeting, I asked my new assistant youth leader to go to dinner with me at a restaurant in Downey, California. While we were seated at a table waiting for our waitress to take our order, I noticed a numbered game panel on one of the TV screens near our table. As we watched the graphics, little white balls would float across the multicolored game board and light on one number at a time, a lot like BINGO. I asked my friend what it was and he said it was called Keno, a legal gambling game new to California. I had been to Las Vegas a few times in my life, and even played Keno there along with many other games of chance. I always lost my money pretty easily, but had a lot of fun.

I never realized how much my need to gamble was addicting, because it was always so far to go to Vegas to play. I was never comfortable in the local poker casinos, so I didn't consider them to be a temptation for me. But these local restaurants and 7–11's were right up my alley, so to speak. They were simple and easy gambling establishments, fun places to get involved in a very wrong way of spending my hard-earned money. Slowly but surely, I spent more and more money for my addiction. Some of that money was supposed to be for bills and everyday expenses. I started getting money out of our checking and saving accounts. I actually depleted our savings account two times. I was caught by my wife many times and, of course, I promised I would stop. My "stopping" was really my sick way of thinking "getting money without being caught" by my wife.

I was a textbook example of a full-blown addict; I needed my "gambling fix" just like a person hooked on any other kind of habit. And I exhibited all the behaviors that go along with addictions: stealing, lying, denial, and just plain being too proud to admit I had an out-of-control habit.

My life was in a downward spiral. While at work, church, or home, I made out that I was living up to the principles taught from the Bible. But in my alone times, with no accountability, I was in the uncontrolled addiction of my struggle. I was spending money and using funds that were meant to buy food, gas, and pay bills. I was in love with trying to be the next winner, no matter how much it cost.

In 2008, my wife called me at work and asked the deadly question, "Have you been gambling again? There is a lot of money missing from our accounts." I admitted how out-of-control I was, and how sorry I was, and that it would never happen again. Translated: "I'll try to control my gambling and hide it better to not get caught." In *1 John 1:8–10* the Bible reminds me that *"If we say we have no sin, we are only fooling ourselves, and refusing to accept the truth. But if we confess our sins to him, he can be depended on to forgive us and cleanse us from every wrong. If we claim we have not sinned, we are lying and calling God a liar, for he says we all have sinned."* Although I admitted to my wife that I had messed up, I was not willing to admit it to God or to confess my sins to Him.

As you can imagine, my wife saw right through this lame excuse because she had a very close friend who was in 12 Step meetings and could tell when an addict was lying. My wife informed me she had found a Gamblers Anonymous meeting on Saturday nights in Downey, and I needed to attend or else. I went and was involved with that organization for about a year. My accountability to the meeting was enough to make me stop for over a year, but it was just another "white-knuckle experience." I truly spoke every Saturday night about my struggle by saying "Hi, my name is Monty and I haven't placed a bet in over a year." Accountability really works, but after a year, I felt like I was cured. So, I stopped going to the meetings and within a few weeks, I would spend two or three dollars on scratchers or a couple of games of Keno. In just a short time, I was back in as deep as before. Still being a practicing Christian and a practicing gambler every chance I would get.

On April 9, 2010, I got that bitter call from my wife. Again! I knew this time it was the "or else." But after many strong warnings and a time of clarity, we decided it was time to look for a Christian recovery program.

This time, she located a Christ-centered recovery program called Celebrate Recovery. I was informed that my choice was: to go on Friday, or I could go on Friday. She left it up to me.

I went to Celebrate Recovery that Friday. I started going to the groups, and the change came almost from the first night when I told my wife this is truly a Christ-involved program. I was welcomed, loved on, and felt the presence of the Holy Spirit when I entered those rooms the first time!

Since coming to Celebrate Recovery, my life has been changed in more ways than I could have ever dreamed of or hoped for. The program was filled with many helpful tools to guide me into a wonderful transition from guilt, lying, and bad behaviors to forgiveness, honesty, good habits, new friendships, and a brand-new relationship with our God, His church, and the Bible.

After attending a few meetings, my new friends told me about another great tool in Celebrate Recovery called a step study group and how it had changed their lives both physically and more importantly, spiritually. I decided to take the leap of faith and began attending a step study group at Emmanuel Church. The real teacher is God's Holy Spirit. Through the Word of God and the step study participant's guides, which are based upon the eight principles, I've learned more about God's great love and care for my hurts, hang-ups, and habits.

Principle 7 says, "Reserve a daily time with God for self-examination,

Bible reading, and prayer in order to know God and His will for my life and gain the power to follow His will."

I've learned to trust the wisdom of my heavenly Father to make me into a new creature filled with truth, love, and grace, and to walk in the newness of life promised by our wonderful Redeemer.

Second Corinthians 5:17 states, "Therefore, if anyone is in Christ, he is a new creation; the old has gone, the new has come!"

As the weeks and months passed, the step study became more and more a part of my everyday life. My friends, family, and coworkers have noticed the changes in me, and I didn't have to tell them. By the grace of God and applying the eight principles based on the Beatitudes, I have not gambled since April 9, 2010. This is a miracle and now I know what people mean when they say, "Don't leave before the miracle happens." God has replaced my need to gamble with a need to know Him and His Word. The Holy Spirit is leading me "one day at a time," and I am definitely "enjoying every moment at a time."

I would like to share a Scripture that has helped me on this road to recovery: *"For as many as are led by the Spirit of God, these are sons of God. For you did not receive the spirit of bondage again to fear, but you received the Spirit of adoption by whom we cry out, 'Abba, Father.' The Spirit himself bears witness with our spirit that we are children of God, and if children, then heirs—heirs of God and joint heirs with Christ, if indeed we suffer with him, that we may also be glorified together" (Romans 8:14–17).*

I know that God is on this road to recovery with me, and He is helping me every day to stay out of my mess. My work in the church is one area that has benefited because of my attendance at Celebrate Recovery. I'm much more effective as an assistant pastor, teacher, and shepherd. Even in my home I am becoming the kind of man my wife deserves by being the husband God wanted me to be all along.

God bless you and God bless Celebrate Recovery!

Thank you for letting me share.

Principle 8

> **Principle 8:** Yield myself to God to be used to bring this Good News to others, both by my example and by my words.
>
> *"Happy are those who are persecuted because they do what God requires." (Matthew 5:10)*

Major, miraculous progress and growth will have occurred in your life since you started your recovery program, since you began working Principle 1. You will have stepped out of your denial into God's grace. You will have taken an honest spiritual inventory. Worked on getting right with God, yourself, and others. And most of all, you will have grown in your relationship with Christ. Discovered a new way to live life, and you will be finding the serenity you have always sought. But the most exciting part is yet to come—in Principle 8.

Principle 8 is the "giving back" principle. It's about giving back because we *want* to, not because we *have* to. We want to share the freedom and victory God has given us with others who are still trapped in their hurts, hang-ups, and habits.

What is giving back all about? What does it truly mean to give? First of all, Principle 8 doesn't ask us to give in unhealthy ways, ways that might hurt us or cause us to relapse into our old, codependent behaviors. No, Principle 8 is all about healthy, non-codependent giving of ourselves—giving freely, without the slightest expectation that we will receive anything in return. No one has ever been honored, after all, for what they've received. Honor has always been a reward to those who gave.

Matthew 10:8 sums up the heart of Principle 8: "Freely you have received; freely give."

Once we understand how to freely give of ourselves in healthy ways, we can start living the eighth principle, and in particular Step 12 of the Christ-centered 12 Steps.

Step 12: Having had a spiritual experience as the result of these steps, we tried to carry this message to others and to practice these principles in all our affairs.

"Brothers, if someone is caught in a sin, you who are spiritual should restore him gently. But watch yourself, or you also may be tempted."
(Galatians 6:1)

Sometimes we get to Principle 8 and feel as though we really don't have anything to offer someone else. We feel as though we're not worthy of helping another person, that we're not eligible to be used by God in this way. Nothing could be further from the truth.

As an example, take an old, beat-up soft drink can—dirty, dented, even squashed. A few years ago, it would have been thrown into the garbage and deemed useless, of no continuing value. Modern technology has changed that. Today it can be recycled, melted down, purified, and made into a new can—shiny and clean—that can be used again.

That's what Principle 8 does. It recycles our pain by allowing God's fire and light to shine on it—to melt down our old hurts, hang-ups, and habits so we can be used again in a positive way. Our lives can be recycled to show others how we've worked the principles and steps, with Jesus' healing, and how we've come through the darkness of our pain into Christ's glorious freedom and light.

Society tells us that pain is useless. In fact, some people believe that *people* in pain are useless. At Celebrate Recovery, we know that pain has value, as do the people who experience it. So while the world says no, Principle 8 shouts a resounding YES:

Yield myself to God.
Example is important.
Serve others as Jesus Christ did.

The road to recovery leads to service. Some will choose to serve at Celebrate Recovery. Others will prefer to devote their skills to other areas in the church.

We need to share our experiences, victories, and hopes with newcomers. We do that as leaders, sponsors, and accountability partners. But the church also needs our service. As we lend a hand outside Celebrate Recovery, we can share with others and motivate them to get into recovery when they're ready to face their own hurts, hang-ups, and habits.

The world is populated by two kinds of people—givers and takers. The takers eat well, but the givers sleep well. Be a giver. There are many, many areas in which to serve. Make suggestions. Get involved.

Principle 8 comes down to this: Do what you can with what you have from where you are. Make your life a mission, not an intermission.

Live out Principles 7 and 8 on a daily basis for the remainder of your time on this earth, and your life will be full and rewarding as you follow God's purpose for you.

Every morning, before you get out of bed, pray this prayer:

Principle 8 Prayer

Dear Jesus, as it would please You, bring me someone today whom I can serve. Amen.

PRINCIPLE 8 TESTIMONY

My name is Mac, and I am a grateful believer in Jesus Christ who struggles with drug and alcohol addiction. I have lived to see a milestone in my recovery. After twenty-four years in recovery, I've finally been sober longer than I was using.

My childhood was pretty uneventful in terms of abuse. My parents loved me and set good standards to live by. So I can't look back to blame others for my actions, actions that brought great shame. Today because of Jesus Christ, I don't have to live in the past anymore. I am free!

Ironically though, I spent a lifetime searching for freedom in all the wrong things. My dad was in the military, so by the time I was fifteen, I had moved eight times. I learned to blend in and make friends quickly.

My dad preached wherever he was stationed. So I knew about God, heaven, and hell. I was taught that unless you were a Christian you would go to hell. I remember fear being the motivating factor for being baptized when I was twelve. I appeared to enter a relationship with God, but for all the wrong reasons. Two weeks later at summer camp, I was introduced to marijuana by one of the counselors. I found a group of people who looked like they were having a lot of fun, so I decided, "Who needs to live in fear? These people aren't worrying about anything!" I became fearless and believed I was invincible, not realizing I had set the pace for eventual destruction.

My dad retired from the military and went to seminary to become a full-time pastor, so we moved to Louisiana when I was fifteen. I hated the fact that we were moving and I wondered how I would ever find friends who liked doing what I liked to do now. Amazingly within the first week, I found the same people there. I never ran out of drugs, and acceptance was immediate.

Once we arrived, my parents sent me to church summer camp to straighten me out and that's where I met Mary.

Mary: My name is Mary. I am a grateful believer in Jesus Christ who struggles with codependency.

I grew up an elder's kid. My parents lived out the Deuteronomy verse: "to tie God's word as symbols around your hands and teach them to your children as you walk by them day after day." There were always guests at the dinner table in our home. Missionaries from foreign countries stayed with us for recharging, while others flocked to our home seeking wise counsel, Bible study, and to repair wrecked marriages.

During my childhood, my mother would write Bible verses on three-by-five cards and tape them up all over our bathroom walls. As I would get dressed in the morning, there staring me in the face would be several verses I would read over and over. It just became a habit without me even realizing it. My sister and I would throw our heads under the covers at night and giggle, thinking how silly it was having our mama reciting those verses to us, never realizing the impact they would have on me in years to come.

I confessed Jesus as Lord of my life when I was twelve years old and was baptized telling myself, "I would *never* sin again!" I wanted to please God with all my heart.

Mac: A new school year began; Mary was a senior and I was a junior. Life was great! After a few months of dating, I talked her into having sex, the first time for both of us, by using the manipulative "if you love me" line. Two weeks later, she didn't start her period, but we thought, *No way; surely one time can't get you pregnant.*

Mary: Four months later I finally consulted a doctor and, yes, I was pregnant. No one had been pregnant outside of marriage in our church, so we had a secret. I felt alone and was convinced Mac couldn't support us. He was only sixteen at the time.

By the time I was five months pregnant, I decided it was confession time to my dad. During my childhood, my mother had a mental illness. Doctors put her through experimental procedures such as electric shock treatments. She suffered in mental hospitals and was a test subject for drugs that often kept her debilitated. So needless to say, my sweet mother who loved me the best she knew how didn't notice I had a growing belly.

I had always been able to talk to my dad, and I knew I couldn't keep it from him any longer. I walked into the den where my dad was taking a nap. I had snuggled up next to him many times throughout the years on that big old flowered sofa, while he read Bible stories to me and we talked about God's love. I knelt down next to him, eye to eye, and said softly, "We need to talk, Daddy."

I was prepared for him to point his finger and say all kinds of harsh words.

But tears began streaming down his cheeks as he said he

would support and love me always. I told him my plans for moving out of town and giving my baby up for adoption.

I left home for my secret summer trip. Three months later it was August 17, 1975. That date is significant later in our story. The doctor left me in a tiny room all alone. Labor lasted for twelve hours with no anesthesia and no family. As they rushed me into the delivery room, a nurse shoved a gas mask over my face. I thought they were suffocating me to punish me for what I had done.

I awoke later in bed sheets soaking wet from perspiration and tears. I experienced emotions that were alien to me. A time that was supposed to be the happiest time of my life was my saddest. I moved to a Christian college out of state. My dad was hoping to get me away from Mac.

Mac: But I followed her there. My parents thought by sending me to a Christian college, they would fix me. Guess what? I found the people who loved to party my first day on campus. In fact, I found the guy who first introduced me to pot six years earlier at church camp. Halfway through the semester, I was kicked out of college after sneaking out of the dorm past curfew to smoke a joint with a friend. Mary and I both went home and married three weeks later.

Married life was great. We partied all the time. Later we would come to understand it helped us to mask the guilt of giving up our baby. When we had been married three years, we started trying to have another baby. Mary told me she was quitting the partying. I said, "Go ahead, but I'm not." Even in the midst of my addiction, I set a boundary and decided to quit everything except smoking pot. I convinced myself that marijuana wasn't so bad.

As I continued down the road of drug addiction, the conflict began between us. Our two daughters were born during this time. However, we lived separate lives under the same roof while growing further apart. I stayed away from the house as much as possible, working overtime to pay for my drug habit. By this time, meth had become my drug of choice.

Mary: In time, I came to the realization that our marriage was totally unmanageable, and I couldn't survive without turning my life and hurts over to God. I had to quit trying to be Mac's Holy Spirit and fix him and instead work on my own shortcomings. I started seeking the pathway to peace while Mac continued to run down the path to destruction. This pattern continued for seven years.

I held on to the verses I remembered reading as a child on my bathroom wall. *In Isaiah 55:11, it says when God's word is spoken; it does not come back empty but will accomplish what He desires and achieve the purpose for which He sent it.*

I would also repeat *Isaiah 41:10* to myself the way I remembered my mother quoted it, slowly and distinctly. I felt God was speaking to me.

"Do not fear for I am with you. Do not be afraid for I am your God. I will strengthen you and help you. I will uphold you with my righteous right hand."

All those Scriptures I heard as a child were coming back to me, comforting me during the dark and lonely nights. Now I had two secrets I carried. We had a son we would never know and I had an insane husband! I say insane because I didn't know all the drugs he was doing and their effects.

So I walked on eggshells to keep peace. I wore my mask to church every Sunday. I just wanted my insides to feel like everyone else looked on the outside: perfect, I thought.

Mac: Amazingly enough, even as a drug addict, there was a line I said I would never cross. The last two years of my addiction I was shooting up ten to twelve times a day. I wore long-sleeve shirts all the time so no one would notice the marks on my arms. I slept only about sixteen hours a week. One Sunday morning, God gave me a great gift at the time and I didn't even realize it. It was a moment of clarity.

I was crashed out in the bed, and our four-year-old daughter stood beside the bed and said to her mother, "Why doesn't Daddy go to church with us anymore?" Mary said, "He's been working hard. He needs sleep." Our daughter replied, "If he doesn't go to church, then I'm not either!" I pretended to be asleep and not hear what she said.

They left for church and then all of a sudden I felt like I ran into a brick wall. God used a little girl to break my heart. I realized I was killing everybody I claimed to love. It was as if my eyes were opened for the first time seeing the insanity of it all. So I collected all my drugs and paraphernalia and burned them.

Mary: I was crushed realizing our children were being affected. That Sunday the sermon was on confession and how good it is for the soul. I remember the song "It Is Well with My Soul." The words hung in my throat. I couldn't breathe. I wanted to just run out of the building. Arriving home, I found Mac sitting in his recliner with tears in his eyes.

Mac: I was raised to believe that men shouldn't cry or show any weakness. But what I found in those tears that morning was relief like I'd never known. I told Mary all that I had done and that I wanted to start a new life. For the first time, Mary stepped out of her codependency and said,

Mary: "Who are you going to call? I'm tired of keeping secrets."

Mac: "I told you I'm through with that life. What more do you want?"

Mary: "We need someone to help us. Would you talk to our pastor?"

Mac: Our pastor had been coming to my cabinet shop for years, getting me to build things for him, only to find out later they were things he really didn't need. He saw something in me that nobody else did. So he came over to pray with us. He said I didn't have to confess before the church, but I might help someone else if I did. I knew I needed to be held accountable.

Mary and I responded to an altar call that Sunday night, expecting to be shunned by people. The whole church came down afterward and cried with us. They didn't know what to do with me—I was their first drug addict—but they loved me and said to keep coming back.

There was one lady who said I needed to go to AA. I thought she was talking about some kind of car club. She said, "Not triple A, but double A—Alcoholics Anonymous."

Mary wanted me to talk to someone at a rehab center the next day. I told her I wasn't crazy and didn't need that. I finally agreed to talk but nothing more. After much discussion with the head guy, he asked if I would stay. I said, "Okay, I guess I'll stay. But I've got to go home and get my stuff."

Mary: "That's okay; your stuff is in the trunk!"

Mac: Our life became a whirlwind with rehab, ninety meetings in ninety days, Bible studies, and making new friends. A whole new life had begun for us. We started Overcomers two years later, which we led for fourteen years. We had approximately twenty to thirty people who came on a regular basis.

Mary: The only other people who knew about our son were my dad, my brother, and his wife. Fast-forward to spring 1988, one month after Mac yielded to God, when God gave us a surprise gift. Our church youth group was going to a rally five hours away and my sister-in-law was one of the chaperones.

They were assigning groups to stay in homes and by the time they got to my sister-in-law's group, they had run out of homes. So they were asked if they would mind staying in a town close by. As the suitcases were being loaded into the car of a friendly couple, my sister-in-law asked if they had any children. When the woman said they had a son named Heath, a funny feeling came over my sister-in-law. So she asked his age. Heath's mother said he was twelve. So my sister-in-law went one step further and asked, "When is his birthday?" Heath's mother said August 17—the date our firstborn, Heath, arrived on August 17, 1975!

At 2:00 a.m. our phone rang. My sister-in-law whispered, "You'll never imagine where I am." I said sleepily, "Where?" She replied, "Heath's bed!" A family at our church has the last name, Heath, so I questioned her, "What are you doing in Mr. Heath's bed?" She exclaimed, "No, no—Heath, *your son*!" Mac and I feel

God gave us that gift at that time in our lives to reassure us our son was loved and cared for in a Christian home.

After waiting seven more years, in August 1994 we got the call we always hoped we would get. When Heath was about to turn nineteen, his parents contacted us and said that he would like to meet us on his birthday. My dad was in charge of videoing the momentous occasion, but as we sat down later to view it, the whole first part of the reunion video was showing the ground. My dad was so excited he forgot he was holding the camera!

It's been seventeen years now since we first met Heath. We didn't get to see Heath's natural birth, but we were blessed with witnessing his spiritual birth as Mac baptized him! In 2005, Heath's parents moved to our city and Heath's mother and my mom became best friends as she took care of my mom after my dad died. We also attend the same church and celebrate holidays together. Our family continues to grow as God has blessed us now with eight grandchildren!

Mac: After leading Overcomers Outreach for thirteen years, Mary's brother "happened" to be at Saddleback Church and told me about a ministry called Celebrate Recovery and said I ought to check it out. So in 2004, we attended the Summit. During the second day I told Mary, "We're stopping what we're doing and starting this! Look how many more people we can help—more than just drug addicts and alcoholics, anyone with a hurt, habit, or hang-up!" After 120 days of prayer and preparation, we started Celebrate Recovery at our church on New Year's Eve 2004! During this preparation time, I learned about Principle 8 and realized that this is exactly what God had in mind for us.

Principle 8 states: "Yield myself to God to be used to bring this good news to others, both by my example and by my words." "Happy are those who are persecuted because they do what God requires" (Matthew 5:10).

This is why we went through all of these trials and then we found out there was more!

I love watching God's plan for our life unfold. A few years

ago, a pastor of forty years tried to commit suicide. The "Pharisees" in the church finally got to him. And the only way he could get through his week was by doing something he said he would never do—take a drink. That one drink turned into every Monday. He had been drinking the last ten years and nobody knew except his wife. Finally he couldn't take the hypocrisy of his own life anymore and that's when he attempted suicide. Along with the bottle, he took a handful of pills. He was moved from pastor to one of "those" people. So I got the call to go visit him.

I visited him in the ICU and even though he was unconscious, I prayed over him and said, "Don't give up. God still has a plan for you." Over the next few weeks, I was able to share with him about the hope that God still had for him. He later became a part of our Celebrate Recovery ministry. While at one of our small groups, he shared with me that he had just met our son's parents at church on Sunday. I said, "Everybody has; they go to church here now!" And he said, "No, no, you don't understand. Forty years ago when I first became a pastor I performed their marriage ceremony!" Before our son was conceived, God had a plan to use this man to marry the couple that would adopt our son! And then later, allow me to be instrumental in giving him the hope that his relationship could not only be restored, but also that God would continue to use him! God always sees the big picture, and He is always right on time!

Mary: We went from the twenty to thirty people attending our Overcomers' group, a ministry that was already working, to an average attendance of over 250 every Friday night at Celebrate Recovery. Our children are a part of Celebrate Recovery. They serve in roles of state rep, ministry leader, training coach, open share group leaders, nursery worker, videographer, and youth minister.

Twenty-four years ago, I prayed God would just keep Mac awake in church. God has truly taken the ashes of our lives and turned them into something beautiful. I believe when God said in *Joel 2:25, "I will repay you for the years the locusts have eaten."*

We can't keep quiet about what the Lord has done in our lives and in the lives of our Celebrate Recovery Forever Family! If there is restoration for us, there is hope for you too! Don't give up; put your faith in action by making life's healing choices.

Mac: Being on the front line of what I believe is THE outreach ministry of the church, we are able to bind up the brokenhearted, to proclaim freedom for the captives of sin in Jesus' name, and release from darkness the prisoners of hurts, hang-ups, and habits.

Celebrate Recovery has helped us reach more hurting people to find healing than we could've ever imagined. How can we repay the Lord for His goodness! We share the hope we've found in Jesus! Today we are making life's healing choices and that's Celebrate Recovery!

Thank you for letting us share.

Chapter 3

WHAT CAN I EXPECT TO HAPPEN AT MY FIRST CELEBRATE RECOVERY MEETING?

A simple reply to that question is a lot! But before we answer in detail, it might be helpful to give you an overview of a typical Celebrate Recovery meeting.

A typical Celebrate Recovery meeting includes:

- A pre-meeting dinner
- A large group meeting
- An open share small group
- Newcomers 101 (for your first week only)

Participants are encouraged to invite their families and friends to the pre-meeting dinner if they so choose; the dinner is designed for a time of great fellowship and great food at affordable prices with other Celebrate Recovery participants.

The large group meeting is designed for the participant to set aside the busyness and stress of the outside world by entering into a time of prayer, praise and worship, and teaching as a way of getting in touch with the one and only Higher Power, Jesus Christ.

The open share small group meets immediately after the large group meeting and provides a place for the participant to connect with other Celebrate Recovery attendees. This is a safe place where participants can be in gender-specific groups and issue-specific groups.

Newcomers 101 is for first-time attendees and will help you better understand what Celebrate Recovery is all about as well as provide you the opportunity to ask questions or process your feelings in a safe environment before you make a commitment to a small group.

After you've attended Celebrate Recovery for a while, you will join a step study. The step study small group is for those who are ready to delve deeper into their past and the choices they have made. This is where participants will see real, lasting changes start to happen. Step studies take place another night of the week.

Now let's take a closer look at the components of each meeting on any given night at Celebrate Recovery.

The Pre-Meeting Dinner

At Saddleback, the evening usually starts off with a dinner around 6:00 p.m. Times and menus might vary for different Celebrate Recovery locations. We serve a Bar-B-Que at our program that runs from 6:00 to 7:00 p.m. You can choose from the following menu items:

Recovery Dog Dinner
12-Step Chicken
Serenity Sausage
Or a Denial Burger
With 60-Day Chips and
Keep Coming Back Onions

This event provides great fellowship and great food at very affordable prices. For the recovery dog dinner, which includes a hot dog, soda, chips, and salad, we only charge $2.50. Watch out, McDonald's!

For four months of the year (due to the severe winters we have in Southern California!), we shut down the Bar-B-Que and have an inside pizza dinner. We encourage you to invite your friends and family.

Large Group Meeting Format: Worship and Teaching Time

At 7:00 p.m. we begin our "large group" worship and teaching time.

During the large group time, everyone meets together — all the men and women combined. This time is designed to help everyone to focus by participating in a twenty-minute time of prayer, praise, and worship.

> "Praise the LORD. Praise God in his sanctuary; praise him in his mighty heavens. Praise him for his acts of power; praise him for his surpassing greatness. Praise him with the sounding of the trumpet, praise him with the harp and lyre, praise him with timbrel and dancing, praise him with the strings and pipe, praise him with the clash of cymbals, praise him with resounding cymbals. Let everything that has breath praise the LORD. Praise the LORD." (Psalm 150:1–6)

It also includes a time for teaching a lesson from the *Celebrate Recovery Leader's Guide* or a testimony of a "changed life." This time begins to unfold the **safe** environment that is essential to any recovery program. It allows all of us to get in touch with the one and only Higher Power, Jesus Christ.

The evening typically follows this agenda:

6:30 p.m.: Doors open

As you come into the meeting, the greeters will hand you the Celebrate Recovery bulletin for the evening (see box on page 96).

The Celebrate Recovery Bulletin

The bulletin contains the following information:

- Song sheet of words (unless they are projected on screen)
- Solid Rock Cafe/Bar-B-Que information sheets
- Small group meeting guidelines
- Eight recovery principles and the Christ-centered 12 Steps
- Twelve Steps and their biblical comparisons
- List of all the open share groups that are meeting that night and room assignments
- List of the open step study small groups that meet during the week
- Announcements of upcoming special events
- Prayer request sheets
- Serenity Prayer

7:00 p.m.: Opening song, welcome, and opening prayer

We attempt to begin our large group meeting promptly at 7:00 p.m. and end by 8:00 p.m. This will ensure that you have a full hour for your small group meetings that meet from 8:00 to 9:00 p.m. After the first song, someone on the leadership team welcomes everyone and prays the opening prayer.

7:05 p.m.: Praise and worship

The music continues with songs chosen to go along with the particular principle we will be working on that evening. This praise and worship time is extremely important! We encourage everyone to participate. But if you are not comfortable doing so, you can remain seated. We completely understand.

7:20 p.m.: Reading of the Eight Recovery Principles or the Christ-centered 12 Steps

Two individuals are selected to read the eight principles or the 12 Steps. The purpose is twofold: (1) to reinforce the biblical foundation of the program, and (2) to allow increased participation for Celebrate Recovery leaders. The opportunity to read is used to recognize leaders and encourage prospective new coleaders.

One person is asked to read the principle/step and another reads the Bible verse for that principle/step until all eight principles/12 Steps are completed.

Example:

First reader: "Principle 1: Realize I'm not God. I admit that I am powerless to control my tendency to do the wrong thing and that my life is unmanageable."

Second reader: "Happy are those who know they are spiritually poor." (Matthew 5:3 GNT)

7:25 p.m.: Celebrate Recovery news

The purpose of the Celebrate Recovery news is to help you feel welcome and informed. You will hear about the special group for newcomers where you can get your questions answered—Celebrate Recovery Newcomers 101.

While the Celebrate Recovery news is an important part of the program, announcements can be rather "dry," so we attempt to make them light and fun. The remainder of the time is used to announce upcoming events at church and Celebrate Recovery and to introduce the "special music" for the evening.

7:30 p.m.: Special music

Special music supports the teaching or the testimony for the evening. It is usually a solo performed by one of the Celebrate Recovery singers. Also, during the special music selection, a collection, or "love offering," may be taken. The money collected could be used to support child-care, to pay for special speakers, and to offset regular expenses. *We make it clear that no one is obligated to give to this offering!*

7:35 p.m.: Teaching or testimony

The speaker will teach one of the twenty-five lessons from the

Celebrate Recovery Leader's Guide. Typically, the next week follows with a testimony which supports the teaching of the previous week's lesson.

7:55 p.m.: Serenity Prayer and dismissal to open share groups
The large group meeting ends with one of the leaders leading the group in the reading of the complete version of Reinhold Niebuhr's Serenity Prayer. The prayer is printed on the inside cover of the bulletin jacket. Then we sing the closing song and everyone is encouraged to quickly go to their small group meetings located throughout the church campus. Meeting locations are also noted in the bulletin. If you have questions, you can stop by the Celebrate Recovery information table or ask one of the Celebrate Recovery leaders. The leaders are easy for you to spot because they wear a Celebrate Recovery leader's shirt or lanyard.

Celebrate Recovery's Small Group Formats
Open Share Small Group
These small groups meet immediately after the large group concludes. There are separate groups for men and women. The format is as follows:

8:00 p.m.: Opening prayer, welcome, introductions, and guidelines
When you enter the room you will find the seats arranged in a circle. Feel free to sit in any of the open seats.

The leader will welcome everyone and then say, *"Good evening. My name is _____; I am a believer who struggles with _____."*

The reason we introduce ourselves this way ("I'm a believer …") is that our identity is in Jesus Christ—the One and only Higher Power. Then we go on to say, "who struggles with _____." Our struggles are not our identity! Our struggles are our hurts, hang-ups, habits, and sins. But you and I are children of God!

You may be wondering, "Do I have to believe in God and Jesus to participate in Celebrate Recovery?" The answer is "absolutely not." All that we ask is that you keep your heart and mind open. Outside of the group, if you ask, your leader will be happy to talk to you about what it means to make the decision to ask Christ into your life!

The leader then says, *"Let's take a minute now to introduce ourselves. I'll begin, and we'll go around the room. Again my name is _____; I'm a believer who struggles with _____."*

You can do the same, or if you are not ready to make that statement you can simply say, *"I'm _____."*

Don't be surprised that after each person introduces himself or herself, the group will respond by saying, *"Hi _____"* back to you.

The leader then says, *"Before we open the meeting for sharing, we have the reading of the small group guidelines.* (Note: The five small group guidelines can be found on page 104.) *These guidelines are designed to provide a safe and productive meeting for everyone. Please listen carefully and honor these guidelines throughout the meeting."*

8:05 p.m.: Leader's focus on the principle

The leader starts the group's sharing by reading the focus question from the large group lesson. If there was a testimony that evening, the leader could ask the group to focus on what part of the testimony touched them the most.

8:10 p.m.: Group open sharing

This is the heart of the small group time. Everyone can choose to share on the focus question or just feel free to share whatever is on their hearts. Remember, you have the guidelines to keep your sharing safe! If you do not feel ready to share, that is not a problem. All you have to do is say, "Pass." You will find that as the weeks go by, you will be sharing! Just keep coming back!

8:50 p.m.: Wrap-up and closing prayer

Wrapping up the session is the leader's responsibility. It is up to the leader to see that the group has enough time for closure—that the meeting does not just come to an abrupt halt or go on and on and on.

9:00 p.m.: Invitation to the Solid Rock Cafe

The meeting can now continue "unofficially" at the Solid Rock Cafe, a place designed specifically for fellowship. At the cafe, you have an opportunity to continue to share with those with whom you feel safe. This, like the dinner before the meeting, is a time for you to continue developing accountability partners and sponsorship relationships.

Step Study Small Groups

The step study groups are the second type of Celebrate Recovery small groups. This is where you delve deeper into your past and the choices you have made. This is where you will see real, lasting changes start to happen in your life! Quite honestly, at first you may not be able to see the changes God is making in your life. But others will start seeing the changes in you. This is the beginning of restoring relationships!

Don't worry: you do not need to join a step study group in your first week. In fact, I suggest you keep attending the large group and your open share small group for at least three to six months before you consider joining a step study.

By then, you will have formed your accountability team. They can help you decide when you are ready!

Step study groups meet on a different night of the week from the large group and open share group meetings. The step study groups go though the four Celebrate Recovery participant's guides together. It usually takes the group about a year to complete them. You will answer and discuss the questions at the end of each lesson together. The group will close (i.e., no new participants) after they have completed the lessons on the third principle. There are separate groups for men and women.

The typical step study group agenda is as follows:

7:00 p.m.	Opening prayer and welcome
	Introductions
	Serenity Prayer
	Reading of the eight principles and/or the 12 Steps and their biblical comparisons
	Reading of Celebrate Recovery's small group meeting guidelines
	Leader's focus on the principle or topic
7:15 p.m.	Group discussion of that night's lesson from the participant's guide. (The leader will go around the group and let everyone have a chance to share their answer to *each question*. Depending on the size of your step study, it may take two weeks to cover one lesson.
8:50 p.m.	Wrap-up, prayer requests, closing prayer
9:00 p.m.	Closing

A Comparison of the Three Celebrate Recovery Groups

The following illustration will help you see the components of each of the three types of Celebrate Recovery groups: large group, open share small group, and the step study small group.

Large Group
- Worship
- Read the steps or principles
- Announcements (Celebrate Recovery news)
- Teach lesson from the *Celebrate Recovery Leader's Guide* or have a testimony
- Serenity Prayer
- No opportunity to share
- Mixed group
- Dismiss to open share groups or Newcomers 101
- Information table

cont.

Open Share Group

- Recovery issue specific
- Immediately follows large group meeting
- Gender specific
- One-hour meeting
- Share struggles and victories
- Acknowledge sobriety (chips)
- Open to newcomers
- Find a sponsor and/or an accountability partner
- Follow the five small group guidelines

Step Study Group

- Use *Celebrate Recovery* participant's guides
- Answer and discuss questions at the end of each lesson of the guides
- Follow the five small group guidelines
- Two-hour meeting
- Mixed recovery OR recovery issue specific
- High level of accountability
- Weekly attendance expected
- Gender specific

Newcomers 101

"Praise be to the God and Father of our Lord Jesus Christ, the Father of compassion and the God of all comfort, who comforts us in all our troubles, so that we can comfort those in any trouble with the comfort we ourselves receive from God." (2 Corinthians 1:3–4)

After the large group (8:00 to 9:00 p.m.) I suggest that you attend Newcomers 101. It is a group designed just for you. You only need to go to this group your first week. Why is it important? Because we have found that when someone comes to Celebrate Recovery for the first time he or she may be overwhelmed with feelings of fear, pain, humiliation, sadness, or hopelessness. The whole concept of recovery may be unfamiliar and a little frightening.

Selecting and identifying with an open share group may seem an impossible task.

Newcomers 101 will help you better understand what Celebrate Recovery at your local church is all about and you will be able to ask questions. The group will be divided into two parts: an informational large group meeting and an open share group. The following is a typical schedule:

1. Welcome and handing out of Solid Rock Coupons
The leaders of the group will welcome you and pass out Solid Rock Coupons, the coffee time hosted at the end of the meeting (or coupons for the meal the program provides before next week's meeting).

2. Opening prayer
After everyone is seated, a leader will open in prayer.

3. Showing the newcomers' video
The video will introduce you to leaders from different areas of recovery talking about the changes God and the program have made in their lives. Usually the senior pastor will share a few words about Celebrate Recovery and how it has changed their church.

4. The leaders will introduce themselves and briefly state the goal of the Newcomers 101
The goal of Newcomers 101 is to explain how Celebrate Recovery works and to help you find a group to attend next week. The newcomers group is a one-time attendance group only.

You will learn that the Newcomers' large group will be divided into a men's group and a women's group during the second half of the evening—just like the open share groups that are meeting throughout church.

Questions will be welcomed after the Newcomers' open share group sharing. However, questions are not a part of the regular open share groups.

5. Announcing time and place for Celebration Station and The Landing

These are programs for elementary school, junior high, and high school students. Celebrate Recovery is a place that the entire family can find healing in one program. (These programs may not yet be available at every Celebrate Recovery.)

6. Explaining the different components of the program

Very briefly the leaders will mention the tools of Celebrate Recovery: the *Celebrate Recovery Bible*, the four participant's guides, and the *Celebrate Recovery Journal. Life's Healing Choices* is the recommended book to better understand the eight recovery principles and to be encouraged by an additional sixteen great testimonies.

7. Reading the five small group guidelines

1. Keep your sharing focused on your own thoughts and feelings. Limit your sharing to three to five minutes.
2. There is no cross talk. Cross talk is when two individuals engage in conversation excluding all others. Each person is free to express their feelings without interruptions. (For the Newcomers 101 event, we break the cross talking guideline when we accept questions at the end of the sharing. At future meetings, this guideline will be obeyed. Otherwise, we will abide by the rest of the guidelines.)
3. We are here to support one another. We are not here to "fix one another."
4. Anonymity and confidentiality are basic requirements. What is shared in the group stays in the group. The only exception is when someone threatens to injure themselves or others.
5. Offensive language and graphic descriptions have no place in a Christ-centered recovery group.

8. Dividing into men's and women's small groups

You will be encouraged to give your first name, to state the group you can identify with, or just to say what brought you to Celebrate Recovery for the first time. Of course, you will have the opportunity to pass if you are not ready to share. If you decide to pass, you can meet with a leader one-on-one at the end of the meeting, while the rest of the group talks informally. Leaders will let everyone know that they are always available to answer any future questions.

9. Closing in prayer
The group will stand and a leader will pray the closing prayer.

Summary
Here's a quick review of the evening: The dinner or Bar-B-Que meets at 6:00 p.m., at 7:00 we meet for our large group time, and at 8:00 we break up into our smaller open share groups. After our groups, at 9:00, we go to Solid Rock Cafe for coffee and dessert. Remember, at the dinner and coffee, you can make new friends and start to form accountability partners and sponsors. You will learn more about building your accountability team in our large group meetings.

I know you will enjoy Celebrate Recovery! Just keep coming back! As I travel around the country, I hope to see you at a meeting.

Chapter 4

HOW CAN I GET MORE QUESTIONS ANSWERED ABOUT CELEBRATE RECOVERY?

The purpose of this chapter is to answer as many of your questions as possible. I want you to attend your first Celebrate Recovery meeting free of any doubts or fears and fully able to focus on God's power to help you remove your mask and start the recovery process.

So I asked Celebrate Recovery's leadership team to help me develop a list of Frequently Asked Questions to help you with any concerns.

Frequently Asked Questions (FAQs)

Q: What is Celebrate Recovery?
A: *The following is a list of things we ARE:*

- A safe place to share
- A refuge
- A place of belonging
- A place to care for others and be cared for
- Where respect is given to each member

- Where confidentiality is nonnegotiable
- A place to learn
- A place to grow and become strong again
- Where you can take off your mask
- A place for healthy challenges and healthy risks
- A possible turning point in your life

The following are the things we are NOT:

- A place for selfish control
- Therapy
- A place for secrets
- A place to look for dating relationships
- A place to rescue or be rescued by others
- A place for perfection
- A long-term commitment
- A place to judge others
- A quick fix

Q: How can I find a Celebrate Recovery near me?

A: Celebrate Recovery has a national website telling where groups meet all over the United States: *www.celebraterecovery.com*.

Q: Do I have to belong to the same denomination to go to Celebrate Recovery at the church where it is held?

A: No, everyone is welcome at Celebrate Recovery, no matter your denomination. You do not have to belong to a church to come to Celebrate Recovery.

Q: Do I have to be a Christian to attend?

A: No, all you have to do to qualify is to have a hurt, hang-up, or habit and a desire to get well.

Q: Is it okay for me to be in the same small group as a family member?

A: No, we feel that it is easier to be in a separate group so that you can feel safe to share more deeply. Sometimes we hold back when our family members are with us.

Q: Is it okay for me to take notes?

A: It is okay to take notes during the large group portion. We do, however, ask that during open share group you refrain from bringing out any note-taking materials, because it is distracting to others.

Q: Do I have to sign up to come to Celebrate Recovery?

A: No, just show up. You are welcome to arrive early if you would like to ask some questions before the group time starts. If not, we have a group that is offered for all first-time attendees. It tells a little about who we are and gives the participants a chance to ask questions.

Q: Are your leaders trained counselors or psychiatrists?

A: No. The group leaders are those who know what it is like to be lost, broken, or hurting. Your leaders have overcome the same issues that you are going through. They now are committed to helping you and others find hope and healing as well.

Q: How long will I need to attend Celebrate Recovery to find healing?

A: Healing from our hurts, hang-ups, and habits is a journey. If we surrender our lives to Christ, He saves us (Principle 3). The twelve steps and the eight principles help us work through the issues we face. For some, the journey lasts a year. For others, the journey can last a lifetime. The length of time depends on the depth of your hurts, hang-ups, and habits. Remember, that your hurts, hang-ups, and habits occurred over a long period of time. They will not go away overnight!

Q: I've heard people introduce themselves in a very different way at Celebrate Recovery than at most secular programs. Why is that?

A: In Celebrate Recovery, you will hear folks introduce themselves like this: *"My name is _____ and I am a grateful believer in Jesus Christ and I struggle with _____."* We do this in order to emphasize that though we do still struggle with hurts, hang-ups, and habits, our identity is in our relationship with Jesus Christ. He is the one and only true Higher Power.

Q: How do I know which group to go to?

A: Upon your first visit to Celebrate Recovery, it is highly recommended that you attend the ministry's Newcomer 101 group in order to get an overview of the program and an orientation to what groups are available.

Q: Do I have to buy the *Celebrate Recovery Bible* for the step study?

A: Although it is not required, it is highly recommended. The *Celebrate Recovery Bible* is a seamless tool for navigating the timeless recovery principles found in your step study and in Scripture. You will need a Bible.

Q: Why do I have to go to the large group? Can't we just go to an open share meeting and eliminate all of the singing and lessons and testimonies? What's the point of all that stuff?

A: The Celebrate Recovery large group time is structured to provide a starting place for the night. This time allows us to start the process of clearing our minds and preparing our hearts for the message or testimony that will be delivered that evening. It also gives us a time to connect with others before going into the small groups.

Q: What is the purpose for separate men's and women's groups? Why can't we have co-ed groups?

A: The purpose for Celebrate Recovery having gender-specific groups is that it provides another opportunity to have a safe place to share. Separate groups allow men to be open in their groups and speak freely about their issues, and the same for women. It also protects the groups from being a place for people who are looking to impress the opposite gender during their sharing by embellishing their story. And there are some people who are not comfortable talking in front of the opposite gender and will shut down and not share at all. It also eliminates a "dating" scene from developing within the groups.

Q: What is the difference between a sponsor and an account-ability partner?

A: First of all, an accountability partner and sponsor should be the same gender as you. A sponsor is like a coach and an accountability partner is like a teammate. When you are out on the field and do something that goes the wrong way, your teammates are there to encourage you. When you return to the bench where your coach awaits, he/she is there to correct your methods and suggest a better way to try to prevent errors.

Q: How soon do I need to get a sponsor/accountability partner?

A: The sooner the better! The benefit of walking with a sponsor and/or accountability partner is that you will have support for every step along the road to recovery. The Bible tells us that we cannot do life alone, and therefore, we cannot do recovery alone. There will be times when temptation is overwhelming and you will need to contact someone to discuss the temptation and work out a solution to prevent a possible relapse.

Q: What do I do if my spouse or someone close to me relapses?

A: The great thing about Celebrate Recovery is that we are taught that we must first work on our own recovery. The hard thing to realize is that we are no good to anyone who is struggling if our recovery is not solid. We need to be supportive of our spouses and encourage them through their recovery, but we cannot fix them. Only as their relationship with God gets stronger will they be able to avoid relapse. When you come and learn all of the necessary tools of Celebrate Recovery, then you can be an example to your spouse that the program works. It can work for them too.

Q: Is Celebrate Recovery court-mandated approved?

A: We have found nationwide that many local courts recognize Celebrate Recovery as a proven and effective 12 Step program for alcohol- and drug-related mandates. However, we strongly suggest that you confirm with your local court to ensure that they approve Celebrate Recovery.

Q: Do you have any groups to help my teenage son or daughter?

A: Yes, we have a group called "The Landing." It is based on the same principles as Celebrate Recovery, but it presents them in a way that students will connect with. The lessons deliver hope-filled truths and real-life strategies for giving young people the tools for making wise choices and developing healthy patterns for living. The curriculum is experiential and includes small groups.

Q: Do you have groups for grade-school children?

A: Yes, we have a group called "Celebration Station." It is a pre-recovery program based on the same principles as Celebrate Recovery, but it presents them in a way that grade-school-aged children will understand. The age-appropriate lessons deliver hope-filled truths and real-life strategies for giving young children the tools on how to start making wise choices and developing healthy patterns for living. The curriculum is experiential and includes small groups.

Q: Are there Celebrate Recovery groups available in other countries? Is the curriculum available in other languages besides English?

A: Yes, there are groups in several countries around the world and they are making a big difference in people's lives. The curriculum is currently available in over twenty-four languages. For more information on either of these questions, you can check out *www.celebraterecoveryglobal.com*.

Q: I have a family member in another country—how can I get information on the groups available in each country?

A: You can find out more information about where groups are around the world by checking out *www.celebraterecovery global.com* or by emailing *bobwood@celebraterecoveryglobal.com*.

Q: Why are the Celebrate Recovery step studies so important and why do they take about a year to complete?

A: We learn about recovery and celebrate our victories in the large group. Then we share our struggles and victories in the open share groups. However, the "meat and potatoes" of recovery happens when we join a step study and answer the questions found in the four Celebrate Recovery participant's guides. Given the number of participants in a step study group, the process of moving through the guides can take from nine to twelve months of meeting weekly. The process of asking ourselves deep questions and finding healing does not happen overnight—but it does happen if we are willing to take this Christ-centered journey.

Q: What exactly does "codependency" mean?

A: Generally speaking, being "codependent" means that I value someone else's happiness and situation over my own. If I constantly make excuses for a loved one's behavior and not allow them to experience the consequences of their actions, I am operating in a state of "codependency." This term can sometimes be confused with "acting Christian," but in Celebrate Recovery we learn how to love others as Christ loves us and allow others to live their lives with their own choices. We learn what it means to have boundary lines that foster healthy relationships.

Q: Can I still go to my other secular recovery meeting if I attend Celebrate Recovery?

A: This is completely up to you. Attendance at Celebrate Recovery is a personal choice, just like attendance at any other program.

Q: Can I have a sponsor from a secular program?

A: Celebrate Recovery encourages participants to find their own sponsors, but we do have suggestions for things to consider before asking someone to fill this role. A sponsor should be the same gender, have at least one year of sobriety (preferably more), in the same area of recovery as you. A sponsor should also demonstrate a mature and growing relationship with Jesus Christ. With these characteristics, a good sponsor from a secular program will also honor the Celebrate Recovery process. Hopefully, they will attend Celebrate Recovery meetings with you as well.

Q: Why don't you have a group for _____?

A: Celebrate Recovery takes the role of leadership very seriously. Newcomers to recovery can be very vulnerable, and it is important that those leading the groups have walked through the process and found healing for themselves first. Therefore, the open share groups that are offered at an individual church will reflect the recovery journeys of the local leadership. All programs will offer a men's and women's group. The principles of recovery are the same for all issues, and participants can find support and help for their issue in any group. As the leadership of the program grows, more groups covering more specific recovery issues can be offered.

Q: I am not an addict. Why should I attend Celebrate Recovery?

A: Celebrate Recovery is for any kind of struggle in our lives. Less than a third of the people who attend Celebrate Recovery struggle with substance abuse—the rest may come for anger, marriage struggles, adult children on drugs, overeating, you name it! Many of us come because someone in our family is struggling. If a family member is struggling, it is affecting the whole family—and we need support too! Everybody needs recovery!

Q: What if I want to leave after the large group?

A: You are certainly welcome to do so—we will not hold you captive! However, it is important for you to know that this recovery process is much like baking a cake. If you leave one of the ingredients out of the recipe, it just won't taste the same. In the same way, in recovery there is a reason we have the three ongoing groups to the Celebrate Recovery process. We encourage everyone to jump in with both feet. Many people will say that they just don't have time to do all three components—the large group, the open share group, and the step study group. As a wise accountability partner once told me, "We need to spend as much time on our recovery as we have on our junk." Those who work the process by doing the proven three groups really see much more significant and longstanding growth. It truly does work if you work it and won't if you don't.

Q: I'm not a believer, but I have some issues I need to deal with. Can I still go to Celebrate Recovery?

A: Absolutely! We are a Christ-centered recovery ministry and are going to acknowledge God and His role in our recovery, but we do not require you to become a believer in order to attend and participate.

Q: How do I keep my attendance a secret from the rest of my family? I don't want them to know I have a problem.

A: Celebrate Recovery is a safe place to share your hurts, hang-ups, and habits because we follow five simple small group guidelines. They make the ministry safe. We honor confidentiality and anonymity. We don't tell others who attends Celebrate Recovery or who is in our groups. Everything that is shared in the groups stays there. Celebrate Recovery is a safe place to share our struggles.

CLOSING
THOUGHTS

As we come to the end of *Your First Step to Celebrate Recovery*, I want to congratulate you for preparing to begin this healing journey. As you choose what Celebrate Recovery group you will attend, and as you walk through the doors for the first time, I want you to know my prayers are with you! You will find others there who will walk alongside you on your road to recovery! This is only the beginning of what God has planned for you.

I would like to share one of my favorite prayers with you. It is called the Prayer for Serenity:

> *God, grant me the serenity*
> *to accept the things I cannot change,*
> *the courage to change the things I can,*
> *and the wisdom to know the difference.*
> *Living one day at a time,*
> *enjoying one moment at a time,*
> *accepting hardship as a pathway to peace,*
> *taking, as Jesus did, this sinful world as it is,*
> *not as I would have it;*
> *trusting that You will make all things right*
> *if I surrender to Your will;*
> *so that I may be reasonably happy in this life*
> *and supremely happy with You forever in the next. Amen.*
>
> Reinhold Niebuhr

In this prayer, we are asking God that we *be reasonably happy in this life*. That's what we have been really striving for as we work through the eight principles—a reasonable, healthy way to live life in the reality of today.

We are no longer expecting perfection in ourselves or others. As you work through Celebrate Recovery, it is my prayer that your definition of happiness will change. I hope you find that true happiness is in having a personal relationship with Jesus Christ. Happiness is being free from your hurts, hang-ups, and habits. Happiness is having honest and open relationships with others.

Just reading this book is not enough for your recovery. It's only the beginning. It takes commitment, and it takes relationships. That begins when you attend Celebrate Recovery for the first time and find people there to love and support you. If you already have a church family, start attending their Celebrate Recovery. If they do not have Celebrate Recovery yet, make an appointment with your pastor, share this book, and help start one!

I really want to know how you are doing. You can follow me on *www.Facebook.com/celebraterecovery*. I post almost daily. I'm also *@CRFounder* on Twitter. And please continue checking *www.celebraterecovery.com* for updates!

To God be the glory!
John Baker

Twelve Steps and Their Biblical Comparisons

1. We admitted we were powerless over our addictions and compulsive behaviors, that our lives had become unmanageable.

   "I know that nothing good lives in me, that is, in my sinful nature. For I have the desire to do what is good, but I cannot carry it out." (Romans 7:18)

2. We came to believe that a power greater than ourselves could restore us to sanity.

   "For it is God who works in you to will and to act according to his good purpose." (Philippians 2:13)

3. We made a decision to turn our lives and our wills over to the care of God.

   "Therefore, I urge you, brothers, in view of God's mercy, to offer your bodies as living sacrifices, holy and pleasing to God—this is your spiritual act of worship." (Romans 12:1)

4. We made a searching and fearless moral inventory of ourselves.

   "Let us examine our ways and test them, and let us return to the LORD." (Lamentations 3:40)

5. We admitted to God, to ourselves, and to another human being the exact nature of our wrongs.

   "Therefore confess your sins to each other and pray for each other so that you may be healed." (James 5:16)

6. We were entirely ready to have God remove all these defects of character.

   "Humble yourselves before the Lord, and he will lift you up." (James 4:10)

7. We humbly asked Him to remove all our shortcomings.

   "If we confess our sins, he is faithful and will forgive us our sins and purify us from all unrighteousness." (1 John 1:9)

8. We made a list of all persons we had harmed and became willing to make amends to them all.

   "Do to others as you would have them do to you." (Luke 6:31)

9. We made direct amends to such people whenever possible, except when to do so would injure them or others.

   "Therefore, if you are offering your gift at the altar and there remember that your brother has something against you, leave your gift there in front of the altar. First go and be reconciled to your brother; then come and offer your gift." (Matthew 5:23–24)

10. We continued to take personal inventory and when we were wrong, promptly admitted it.

    "So, if you think you are standing firm, be careful that you don't fall!" (1 Corinthians 10:12)

11. We sought through prayer and meditation to improve our conscious contact with God, praying only for knowledge of His will for us and power to carry that out.

    "Let the word of Christ dwell in you richly." (Colossians 3:16)

12. Having had a spiritual experience as the result of these steps, we try to carry this message to others and to practice these principles in all our affairs.

"Brothers, if someone is caught in a sin, you who are spiritual should restore him gently. But watch yourself, or you also may be tempted." (Galatians 6:1)

HOW GOD HAS CHANGED MY LIFE THROUGH CELEBRATE RECOVERY

Allen R. — Celebrate Recovery is a mirror that allows me to see the things in my life that God wants to change.

Mary L. — Celebrate Recovery has taught me compassion, and with compassion came my healing.

Cory R. — Celebrate Recovery allowed me to finally see the woman of God I was designed to be!

Mark Z. — Before I was eating out of dumpsters. Now, with Celebrate Recovery, I'm living on God's Word.

Jeanne P. — Four years ago, I walked into my first Celebrate Recovery fellowship with fears and doubt. Through this blessed program, I have gained a stronger grasp on God's plan for my life.

Cheyenne S. — I started going to support my son but quickly found that God had much more planned! I've been in Celebrate

Recovery almost a year and have been healed with many, many blessings.

Wynette C. — I came to Celebrate Recovery a day after attempting suicide. I remember going up to get a blue chip, ready to surrender a life of drug abuse, depression, and suicide attempts. I stood before people whose eyes were focused on me, not with that usual judgmental stare but with a look of love and compassion. When I took that chip and sat down, it felt as though the weight of the world had been lifted off of my shoulders. At Celebrate Recovery I found love, acceptance, and sincere concern not only for my mental and physical well-being, but also for my spiritual well-being.

Yvette M. — Celebrate Recovery helps me with every aspect of my life!

Sherrie B. — Celebrate Recovery has helped me heal a lot of wounds that years of counseling could not heal. Because of Celebrate Recovery I have become a better mother and wife!

Sarah B. — I grew up in church and I've always known that God was the answer to my problems, but I was so bound by my hang-ups and struggles that I couldn't find peace. Celebrate Recovery is completely changing my life! For the first time I have hope and peace, while God is gradually shaping me into the woman He has called me to be.

Julie A. — I never felt "good enough for church," yet I wasn't "bad enough" for AA anymore. After twenty-five years in recovery, Celebrate Recovery brought what I was missing all along — the power of God to heal me.

Terie P. — Celebrate Recovery showed me that no matter how bad or how worthless I thought I was, God still loves me. I also learned that what people did to me was not my fault, but what I did to people I had to assume responsibility for. No matter how low on the ladder of life I feel, Jesus put me right up on the top rung by His sacrifice for me.

Michael B. — Five years ago I walked into a Celebrate Recovery program hating myself, hating others, and hating God. Today, through the healing and restoring grace of Jesus who I met at Celebrate Recovery, I'm in love with God, in love with the person who He has made me to be, and I'm the ministry leader of a beautiful Forever Family at the very same Celebrate Recovery program I walked into five years ago.

Janet R. — Celebrate Recovery helps me find a way out of the forest life gives me each day and gives me a special way to help hurting people heal!

Mary Beth F. — I worked my Celebrate Recovery steps in prison and when I was released I became a leader and a Sunday school teacher.

Jennifer E. — I first attended Celebrate Recovery to find out how to get and keep my husband sober. After working through a full step study, I realized I had just as much of a need to change. Six years later, he's sober (all through his journey in Celebrate Recovery) and I've worked more and more on own my issues. Today I am able to boast of my weakness and to help lead other women to find truth.

Andrew H. — When I first attended Celebrate Recovery, I didn't believe anything was wrong with me. After all, I had never messed with drugs or alcohol ... what good was a 12-Step program for me? How wrong I was! Anger, lust, codependency ... Celebrate Recovery is helping me allow God to put my life back in order. Thank you, John Baker, for allowing God to do His work through you!

Teresa L. — I had been a Christian for over thirty years, even in positions of leadership but never really experienced true freedom in Christ. After attending Celebrate Recovery and a step study, I was finally able to gain accountability, confess my sins to other godly women, and begin to see healing from codependency, divorce, abuse, and so much more, as things that had been hidden for so many years were finally brought into the light! It's more than a program; it's a way of life, and it works!

Mandi L. — I found Celebrate Recovery before I even knew who God was. Not only was Celebrate Recovery a turning point for my life, it was also a starting point for me to develop my relationship with God and to become a Christian.

Loretta D. — I came from secular recovery looking for a Christ-centered recovery program that could help me grow in my relationship with Christ, find support in maintaining my sobriety, and work on my very present issues of codependency. Celebrate Recovery was home for me!

Julie T. — My life has turned around because of Celebrate Recovery. I have made so many true friends who have encouraged me to do the hard things I had to do, with love and acceptance all the way.

James M. — Celebrate Recovery helps you learn to apply God's Word to the struggles in your own life, just as Jesus did in His temptation. There is power in the Word and Celebrate Recovery teaches you how to apply it.

Malinda C. — Celebrate Recovery helped me see that it doesn't matter where we came from. What matters is where we are going.

Melodie W. — God changed my life through Celebrate Recovery by giving me sisters who understand because they have been where I have been. Trust and safety, there's no feeling like it in the world. When we're together at meetings, I feel Jesus' arms around us!

Marvin M. — Through Celebrate Recovery, God took a messed-up pastor and gave him a second chance.

Darlene M. — Celebrate Recovery was the open hand I needed to lift me out of the hell of my addiction and into true relationship with God.

Elmer D. — Celebrate Recovery is God with "skin on" for the things we all face today.

Wendy F. — I came to Celebrate Recovery broken and needing healing from abuse in my childhood. Years of counseling touched the surface, but didn't do the deep work that is happening now through a step study. I stay with Celebrate Recovery because it helps me find hope for each day.

Marty K. — I finally realized I mattered to God!

John M. — Thanks to some great people at Celebrate Recovery, I am finally at peace with God and myself. It is an awesome feeling. Today, I have a smile that nothing can take away and I mean — nothing!

Fran H. — Celebrate Recovery works if you work it — and you are worth it!

Diane C. — For eighteen years I kept God in my bookcase on a shelf. I never allowed Him to heal what He so desperately wanted to until I walked through the doors of Celebrate Recovery! Since that day, over five years ago, I have grown in Christ and am loving life as never before! Thank you, God and Pastor John.

Debbie H. — Celebrate Recovery took a very depressed, lonely woman and made her whole again! Me! It was nice to know there were several depressed ladies in my group and by working through the eight principles, we all found victory in Christ. You can find it as well! Praise God!

Jonathan S. — In Celebrate Recovery, I found the power in Jesus Christ to stop doing the things that caused me and my family so much pain.

Marianne S. — Codependency was my life. I hit rock bottom when I found out my husband was having an affair and addicted to porn. Shortly after, we started attending a Celebrate Recovery at our church and my life began to change. Celebrate Recovery gave me tools, strength, family, comfort, and a place where I could feel safe to be myself. I asked that my husband attend with me if he wanted our marriage to work. Celebrate Recovery saved our marriage! We are now ministry leaders and my husband is now a state rep for Celebrate Recovery! This program works and saves lives through God's amazing grace!

Karen R. — Through Celebrate Recovery I found help, healing, and a deeper, restored relationship with God. I've learned boundaries, communication skills, and how to have healthy relationships. I've learned how to trust God and others again. I've learned how to focus on the truth and not the trials. Thank You, God, for Celebrate Recovery.

Sue V. — Before Celebrate Recovery, I was a miserable mess. I was alone and I was an out-of-control glutton. But when I turned my mess completely over to God, He took it, made me new, and turned my mess into a message. Today, I have a life in Christ and a testimony that glorifies God. And rather than an abundance of food, I'm now enjoying an abundant life filled with the fruit of the Spirit. And this fruit — love, joy, peace, and self-control — is far better than any food I ever binged on!

Harry H. — I lived fifty-five years believing that God existed, but was unable to feel a true relationship with Jesus Christ. Through Celebrate Recovery and witnessing the never-ending victories in others' lives, I learned that I AM a son of the King — that He had always been with me and always will be. All I had to do was surrender, and His light warmed my soul and showed me the way to live in Him!

Janet C. — I came to Celebrate Recovery wearing a mask that said, "I'm fine; how can I help you?" Now, four and a half years later, the mask is gone, and I've been healed from past events I thought I'd gotten over. I know I have worth because God loves me just the way I am.

Tim M. — After being stuck in an addiction to pornography for twenty-five years, Celebrate Recovery offered me something that nothing else had … HOPE!

Micah H. — Through Celebrate Recovery I have found Christ-centered accountability — men of God who support me, confront me, cry with me, and celebrate with me. It is truly "iron sharpening iron" so that we can bring glory to God.

Brenda Y. — God has brought me to my knees through the struggles of my marriage, my codependency, and my husband's sexual addictions. I was ready to run away from the problem and let the wind carry me away. Celebrate Recovery provided a solid foundation to hold on to through my time of need. Praise God for bringing me to my knees; my pride was strong and I was not easily bent. God knows what is best even when I can't see it.

Lynne F. — The hardest part about coming to Celebrate Recovery the first time was getting across the parking lot from my car to the door. But I was welcomed with genuine smiles and love, not pity. The easiest part of coming to Celebrate Recovery is making the decision to keep coming back!

Amber A. — Because of past hurts, I took a detour off the path that God had intended for me. I got lost, hit a few bumps, and got a few cuts and scrapes. Because of God and through Celebrate Recovery, I am no longer lost. My feet are firmly planted back on His path and this time the bumps aren't so bad and the cuts and scrapes don't hurt as much. Thank you, Jesus, and thank you, Celebrate Recovery!

Jeff P. — I found my sobriety in secular recovery, but I kept my sobriety by starting a Celebrate Recovery at my church. Celebrate Recovery showed me what the Bible had to say about recovery and allowed my church to see the healing benefits of a support group ministry.

Ingrid B. — Celebrate Recovery has taught me what true mercy and grace is all about. Though I have been and worked in church most of my life, Celebrate Recovery has shown me what God's true love looks like. It is now my first ministry.

Mary S. — Even though I was full of anxiety walking into Celebrate Recovery that very first time, I was even more anxious that the rest of my life would be the continuing cycle of disappointments, failures, and pain I had experienced so far. Celebrate Recovery has changed my life into one full of joy, hope, peace, and just sheer happiness. To get something I never had, I had to do something I never did — go to Celebrate Recovery!

Celebrate Recovery Kit

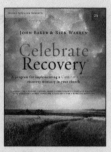

For over 25 years, *Celebrate Recovery* has helped the church fulfill its role as Christ's healing agent. Since 1991, over 1.5 million people have participated in the Celebrate Recovery programs offered at more than 29,000 churches, prisons, and rescue missions in 21 different languages. Developed by John Baker and Rick Warren of Saddleback Church, *Celebrate Recovery* draws from the Beatitudes to help people overcome their hurts, hang-ups, and habits. Rather than setting up an isolated recovery community, this powerful program helps participants and their churches come together and discover new levels of care, acceptance, trust, and grace.

Included in the 25th anniversary kit is the brand new, revolutionary step study of *The Journey Continues* which are four participant's guides that take your recovery journey deeper. The kit also includes:

- 1 leader's guide
- 1 each of *The Journey Begins* participant's guides #1-4
- 1 each of *The Journey Continues* participant's guides #5-8 (ALL NEW)
- 1 Pastor's Resource DVD with sermon transcripts, MP3 sermons, and three videos featuring John Baker, Johnny Baker, and Rick Warren
- 1 Leader's Resource DVD with 25 customizable lessons from *The Journey Begins* curriculum and three videos featuring John Baker, Johnny Baker, and Rick Warren
- 1 personal size *Celebrate Recovery Study Bible*
- 1 copy of *Your First Step to Celebrate Recovery*
- 1 copy of *Celebrate Recovery Booklet: 28 Devotions*

Available in stores and online!

Celebrate Recovery The Journey Begins Participant's Guides

John Baker

Recovery is not an overnight phenomenon, but more like a journey. The purpose of Celebrate Recovery is to allow us to become free from life's hurts, hang-ups, and habits. By working through the eight principles of recovery based on the Beatitudes, we will begin to see the true peace and serenity that we have been seeking.

The four participant's guides in the Celebrate Recovery program are:

- Guide 1: Stepping Out of Denial into God's Grace
- Guide 2: Taking an Honest and Spiritual Inventory
- Guide 3: Getting Right with God, Yourself, and Others
- Guide 4: Growing in Christ While Helping Others

The participant guides are essential to the person in recovery to take part in because it makes everything personal.

Available in stores and online!

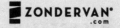

ZONDERVAN·
.com

Celebrate Recovery
The Journey Continues
Participant's Guides

John Baker and Johnny Baker

Celebrate Recovery introduces *The Journey Continues* — four new participant's guides designed as a revolutionary new second step study curriculum. This step study is taken after completing The Journey Begins (Participant Guides 1–4).

The final four participant's guides in the Celebrate Recovery program are:

- Guide 5: Moving Forward in God's Grace
- Guide 6: Asking God to Grow My Character
- Guide 7: Honoring God by Making Repairs
- Guide 8: Living Out the Message of Christ

By working through the lessons and exercises found in each of the four Participant's Guides of *The Journey Continues* you will find a deeper sense of true peace and serenity, continue to restore and develop stronger relationships with others and with God, and find deeper freedom from life's hurts, hang-ups, and habits.

NIV Celebrate Recovery Study Bible

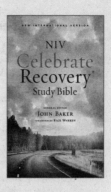

The *NIV Celebrate Recovery Study Bible* offers everyone hope, encouragement, and the empowerment to rise above their hurts, hang-ups, and habits. This life-changing Bible is based on the proven and successful Celebrate Recovery program developed by John Baker and Rick Warren.

With features based on eight principles Jesus voiced in his Sermon on the Mount, this insightful Bible is for anyone struggling with the circumstances of their lives and the habits they are trying to control.

- Articles explain eight recovery principles and the accompanying Christ-centered twelve steps
- 112 lessons unpack eight recovery principles in practical terms
- Recovery stories offer encouragement and hope
- Over 50 full-page biblical character studies illustrate recovery principles
- 30 days of devotional readings
- Side-column reference system keyed to the eight recovery principles and topical index
- Complete text of the New International Version

Available in stores and online!

Daily Devotions to Encourage & Inspire

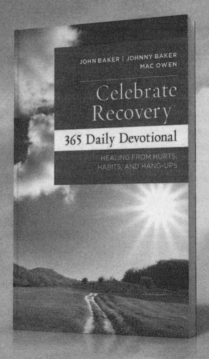

The *Celebrate Recovery Daily Devotional* is designed to inspire readers during weak moments and encourage them in strong moments. These daily devotions bring just the right strength for each day and provide words of hope, courage, and triumph!

Celebrate Recovery Journal

This journal is specially designed to complement the Celebrate Recovery program. The content guides you through the recovery process in a step-by-step fashion. Includes tips on how to benefit from journaling, specific Scriptures pulled from the Celebrate Recovery program, a section to help facilitate a 90-day review of your journaling progress, and a prayer request area to document God's answer to prayer.

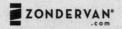

"You want something. So do I. Let me help you."

Meghan looked at him as if he'd lost his mind. Maybe he had. He'd never been considered one of those white knights charging to rescue ladies in distress. He found jackets and ties confining enough; armor would be murder.

"I'll take another look into your sister's accident for you. In return, you'll cooperate by allowing your nephew to assist us in any way we need him. You get what you want, I get what I want. It'll be strictly business."

Sensing the protest she was about to utter, he went on. "Of course, maybe you'd rather work with Officer Wadrell instead...."

"Believe me, I find cops eminently resistible. For that matter, how can I be sure that I wouldn't have to fight off *your* advances, Detective?"

"'Cause I make it a point to steer wide of your type."

* * *

Don't miss *Born in Secret* (IM 1112)
Kylie Brant's emotional, sensual contribution
to the FIRSTBORN SONS series.
Coming next month!

Dear Reader,

Once again, Silhouette Intimate Moments brings you six exciting romances, a perfect excuse to take a break and read to your heart's content. Start off with *Heart of a Hero,* the latest in award-winning Marie Ferrarella's CHILDFINDERS, INC. miniseries. You'll be on the edge of your seat as you root for the heroine to find her missing son—and discover true love along the way. Then check out the newest of our FIRSTBORN SONS, *Born Brave,* by Ruth Wind, another of the award winners who make Intimate Moments so great every month. In Officer Hawk Stone you'll discover a hero any woman—and that includes our heroine!—would fall in love with.

Cassidy and the Princess, the latest from Patricia Potter, is a gripping story of a true princess of the ice and the hero who lures her in from the cold. With *Hard To Handle,* mistress of sensuality Kylie Brant begins CHARMED AND DANGEROUS, a trilogy about three irresistible heroes and the heroines lucky enough to land them. Be sure to look for her again next month, when she takes a different tack and contributes our FIRSTBORN SONS title. Round out the month with new titles from up-and-comers Shelley Cooper, whose *Promises, Promises* offers a new twist on the pregnant-heroine plot, and Wendy Rosnau, who tells a terrific amnesia story in *The Right Side of the Law.*

And, of course, come back again next month, when the romantic roller-coaster ride continues with six more of the most exciting romances around.

Enjoy!

Leslie J. Wainger
Executive Senior Editor

Please address questions and book requests to:
Silhouette Reader Service
U.S.: 3010 Walden Ave., P.O. Box 1325, Buffalo, NY 14269
Canadian: P.O. Box 609, Fort Erie, Ont. L2A 5X3

Hard To Handle
KYLIE BRANT

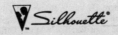

Silhouette®

INTIMATE MOMENTS™

Published by Silhouette Books

America's Publisher of Contemporary Romance

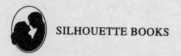 SILHOUETTE BOOKS

ISBN 0-373-27178-6

HARD TO HANDLE

Copyright © 2001 by Kimberly Bahnsen

Visit Silhouette at www.eHarlequin.com

Printed in U.S.A.

Books by Kylie Brant

Silhouette Intimate Moments

McLain's Law #528
Rancher's Choice #552
An Irresistible Man #622
Guarding Raine #693
Bringing Benjy Home #735
Friday's Child #862
Undercover Lover #882
Heartbreak Ranch #910
Falling Hard and Fast #959
Undercover Bride #1022
†*Hard To Handle* #1108

*The Sullivan Brothers
†Charmed and Dangerous

KYLIE BRANT

lives with her husband and five children in Iowa. She works full-time as a teacher of learning-disabled students. Much of her free time is spent in her role as professional spectator at her kids' sporting events.

An avid reader, Kylie enjoys stories of love, mystery and suspense—and she insists on happy endings! When her youngest children, a set of twins, turned four, she decided to try her hand at writing. Now most weekends and all summer she can be found at the computer, spinning her own tales of romance and happily-ever-afters.

Kylie invites readers to write to her at P.O. Box 231, Charles City, IA 50616.

To Aunt Red, with love and fond memories.

Acknowledgments:

Special thanks to Sergeant Charles Holz
of the Chicago Police Department, 8th District,
for answering endless questions about CPD procedures.
Your infinite patience and generosity of time were
greatly appreciated! Any mistakes that occur in accuracy
are the responsibility of the author.

Prologue

His mom was dead.

Danny huddled in the corner of the blue-patterned couch clutching his Pokémon backpack to his chest. The lady, his aunt Meghan, he reminded himself, had gone to get him a glass of milk. He hadn't really wanted one, but she'd had to leave the room to get it. That was good 'cuz he didn't want to hear her say the words out loud. He already knew what she was thinking. It made his stomach hurt and he felt like he might throw up.

His mom had been killed in a car accident and she wasn't coming back for him this time. Not ever.

He reached up a hand to swipe at his eyes furtively. Only babies cried. That's what his mom always said, but she wouldn't be saying that again. No, not anymore. He knew then, deep down in his stomach where he felt sickest, that not saying the words out loud didn't make them not true. He was all alone.

His aunt came back into the room and handed him the glass. He took it, but didn't drink. He couldn't. There was a hard ball in his throat and he didn't think he could swallow anything. He wrapped his fingers tightly around the glass and scooched down farther in the couch. He wanted to run away before his aunt could tell him, but he couldn't do that, either. There was nowhere to run. No one to run to.

"You know, don't you?"

He didn't look up at the words, just nodded. He'd had a real bad feeling when his mom didn't come home last night. She'd left him alone before, and so that hadn't scared him. Not really. He was almost six. He'd stayed home at night lots of times. Once his mom hadn't come home for two days, and maybe *that* had scared him, just a little. But last night had been different. The bad thoughts, the *knowing*, wouldn't go away. And so he'd waited for someone to come, wanting it to be his mom, already sure that it wouldn't be.

"What's gonna happen to me?" His aunt didn't answer right away, so he did look up then and stared hard at her, concentrating on her thoughts. That's where the truth was, his mom said. People would lie and lie out loud, but they kept the truth in their heads, where people couldn't see. At least, most people couldn't.

Danny didn't really understand words like *telepathic* and *clairvoyant,* but he understood that he was different, just like his mom had been. Sometimes she would tell him that they had this superspecial gift, one that made everyone else jealous. He liked that. He liked to pretend that they were a team, like Superwoman and Spiderkid, with cool powers no one else had. But deep in his heart he'd known the real truth was what his mom had said all those other times; after two empty bottles, when her words would start running together. They were freaks, him and her.

He knew what freaks were. They were bad and ugly and made people afraid. Meghan had been afraid the only other time he'd met her, and that had made him feel bad. He'd never had an aunt before, and Meghan was pretty, with long, curly blond hair and big blue eyes. He looked into her eyes now and beyond, searching for a comfort he wouldn't find.

"I don't want you to worry." Meghan sank down onto the couch beside him. She pushed her hair back from her face and tried to smile. "I know that sounds pretty dumb. Of course you're worried. And sad. Me, too. But I'm not about to let anything happen to my only nephew."

With a child's single-minded logic, he asked, "Where will I live?"

Meghan didn't answer, and for just an instant he could see a flash of white, as if her mind had been wiped clear. Then it was like she drew a big curtain over her thoughts. He couldn't see them anymore, no matter how hard he tried to peek.

"Well...you'll stay here, of course. At least for now."

He thought about that, and he wondered what thoughts she was hiding behind that curtain. She put her hand on his shoulder then, and the hated tears filled his eyes again.

"How about if you stay with me until we sort this out? Then later...you and I will talk about our options. Is it a deal?"

Her hand left his shoulder, and she held it in front of him. He looked at it, then at her. He tried poking under that curtain one more time, but it was closed tight. He couldn't tell what the truth was. And although he didn't have the words for it, he knew he was out of choices.

Slowly, tentatively, he loosened his grasp on the glass and placed his hand in hers.

Chapter 1

Three Months Later

Gabe Connally had been alive and he'd been dead. It'd taken a few years, but he'd developed a preference for being alive.

His gaze met his partner's in a silent exchange before he lifted his fist to pound on the door. "Police, D'Brusco. We have a few questions for you."

There was a tiny noise in the apartment, and the detectives had an instant to act before bullets splintered the wood in a miserable parody of a greeting.

With his cheek resting against the smooth, cool tile of the hallway floor, Gabe recalled being told that it had taken a miracle to return him from the ninety seconds he'd spent suspended above his bullet-ridden body in St. Lucien's emergency room. In the tension-filled moments that followed the barrage of gunfire, he fleetingly wondered how many miracles a man was allowed in one lifetime.

Scrambling into position, he glanced at Cal Madison as the other man mouthed the signal. On "three" he kicked the shredded door in and entered the room low. He heard Cal mutter a curse behind him. Weapons drawn, they stalked through the well-furnished apartment.

"Empty," Cal pronounced disgustedly a few moments later.

"Only one other way out." Without wasting a motion Gabe went through the open terrace door, following D'Brusco's escape route.

"When are you going to learn that we move *after* three. How many times do I have to tell you that?" Madison craned his neck, scanned the wide cobblestone alley. In a neighborhood as trendy as this one, even the alleys had ambiance.

Gabe ran across the terrace to the fire escape. "After? Since when? We've always moved *on* three." Deftly he swung over the wall of the terrace and began his descent.

"We've never gone on three. It's always been after." Even with the exertion of following him, Madison's voice wasn't winded. The man could nag without taking a breath.

"The problem is, you're always changing the rules." Gabe kept his weapon steady as he observed the alley for signs of life. "On three, after three, who could keep it straight? Leave things uncomplicated. They go smoother that way."

"Only you could complicate a simple count to three," Madison muttered. He dropped lightly down beside his partner, and without a word they fanned out, covering the alley.

Minutes later, they rejoined, holstering their weapons. "Damn. If he was on foot he's either a champion sprinter or else he ducked into one of the shops' back doors." Gabe hunched his leather-clad shoulders against the biting wind. Chicago in the spring was a malicious tease, coupling promising bouts of bright sunshine with frigid blasts of air. The sunlight had already begun to fade over the fashionable skyline, but the winds blowing off the lake showed no sign of abating.

Cal didn't react to the weather since he was sensibly outfitted in his winter parka and muffler and would be until the flowers started blooming. He believed going out in varying temperatures was a leading cause of pneumonia. "Think he had a car stashed back here?"

"It's a tow area. But he could have had one waiting."

"Meaning he was expecting company," concluded Cal.

"Judging from his greeting, he wasn't expecting friends."

"Not exactly the reaction I'd expect from a penny-ante ex-con like Lenny D'Brusco."

Gabe grunted his agreement, already tallying the doors lining the alley. "Front or back?"

An eternal optimist, Cal replied, "Back. We'll work our way to the front, maybe catch a lead, grab a sandwich and be home in time for tip-off."

Gabe was more realistic. With a wave of resignation, he mentally kissed off his plan for a quiet evening in the recliner with pizza, beer and a lively Bulls game on television. He hadn't set the VCR. Something told him the only parts of the game he'd see tonight were the highlights reshown on ESPN.

"I don't know," Meghan told her nephew with mock seriousness. "I'm still considering buying something educational for your birthday present. Maybe a set of encyclopedias."

Danny clutched his throat and made gagging noises. His antics forced a smile from his aunt. They'd come to the quaint toy store in search of ideas for Danny's upcoming birthday. After spending almost an hour there, it appeared that the boy wouldn't be dissuaded from the items that had seized his attention almost immediately.

"But, Aunt Meggie, I can't even read that good yet. And

I could learn from these electronic dinosaurs, too. My teacher says we should study animals that are extincted."

"Extinct."

"Yeah. And if I got two of them, Alex could play with one with me, and he'd be learning, too."

"You've got it all figured out, huh?"

Danny's eyes were alight with an excitement she'd rarely seen there, and the sight sent an odd pang to Meghan's chest. "I could take them outside again and you could watch what they can do. They can have fights and make noises and everything."

She glanced at her watch. She'd arranged for the cab driver to return for them, and the allotted time was almost up. "Tell you what. You put the dinosaurs back in the display case, and I'll keep them in mind. Your birthday isn't for three more weeks."

"Nineteen and a half days," he corrected. On this subject he was very exact.

"Nineteen and a half days," Meghan repeated. "So we still have plenty of time." She followed Danny as he went over to replace the toys, taking his time positioning them. The toy store was as unique as her friend Callie had promised, with inviting displays of unpackaged items that allowed children to manipulate the toys. As a marketing ploy it was amazingly effective, Meghan thought, as her gaze wandered to the front of the store, watching for the taxi through the plateglass window. Fifteen minutes spent playing with the dinosaurs on the patio in the alley had certainly hooked Danny.

The door opened then and a tall dark-haired man entered. His gaze swept the interior of the store. When it landed on her for a moment, she felt it like a physical touch. An inexplicable shiver skated down her spine, and she turned to hurry her nephew along.

"You know what I saw when I was playing with the dinosaurs outside?"

"Hmm?" Her nephew had only a fraction of her attention. Her concentration was diverted by the man who was now approaching the counter.

"It was way cool. There were funny noises and a guy dropped out of the sky. Then…"

The boy's words seemed to fuse with the scene at the counter, where the stranger was flashing a shield at the clerk. A sense of déjà vu hit Meghan in a nauseating wave, and for a moment she was deaf to Danny's words. Flight was the most primitive instinct known to man, and the urge to flee nearly overwhelmed her.

"…and then the first guy ran to the car…"

"We'll talk about it when we get home." Meghan's voice held an unusual edge, and the boy sent her a startled glance before falling silent. She didn't notice. Her focus was on the man, the *cop,* who'd just engaged another customer in a conversation she was too far away to overhear.

Placing one arm on Danny's shoulder, she guided him toward the door, disguising her haste behind a barrage of words. "We'd better check on our cab. We told the driver to come back in an hour, and I doubt he'll wait for long. Rush hour is the worst time to find another taxi."

She inched the boy closer to the door as she spoke. With every additional measure of distance placed between them and the policeman, the vise on her lungs eased slightly. Breathing a silent sigh of relief, she reached for the doorknob. Her fingers turned nerveless when a gravelly voice sounded behind her.

"Could I ask you a few questions before you leave, ma'am?"

Forcing herself to turn around she looked up, farther than she'd expected, to meet the enigmatic gaze of the man who'd stopped her. "I'm sorry." She managed, somehow, to keep her voice dispassionate. "We're in a hurry."

"This will only take a moment. Detective Connally, ma'am. CPD." The silver badge imprinted with the telling star was held out for her perusal. She didn't need the badge or his words to accurately guess the man's profession. There was cop in his eyes, in his voice.

The man's low bass somehow matched his brooding features. His short-cropped haircut accentuated the brutal lines and hard angles of his face. But it was his eyes that compelled attention. A pale color reminiscent of fine whiskey, they were trained on her now with the unblinking gaze of a hawk focused on prey. The utter lack of expression in them sent a chill chasing over her skin.

"A man wanted for questioning disappeared near here after some shots were fired. I want to talk to anyone who might have seen him."

Out of the corner of her eye, Meghan saw the cab pull up to the curb out front. Turning to her nephew she said, "Go tell the driver I'll be out shortly, will you?"

The boy opened the door and sped toward the vehicle. Gabe focused on the woman before him. It was no hardship. The bulky down coat she was wearing couldn't disguise the femininity of the form it enveloped. If he'd been a sucker for big blue eyes and delicate bones his professional objectivity might have suffered. As it was, he allowed himself only one brief mental lament over the capricious weather that still caused sensible people to bundle up, and kept his gaze trained firmly on her face.

"I don't think I can help you, Officer. I didn't notice anything."

"Detective."

"Pardon?"

There was confusion in her wide blue eyes. He noted that her nose was a trifle upturned, her lips perhaps a fraction too full, as if nature had been compelled to stop just short of sheer perfection. A wise move on Mother Nature's part, Gabe approved. Perfection was boring. Something told him that this woman was anything but.

"It's Detective Connally."

"Of course." The woman's smile appeared strained. "But as I said, I didn't see anyone. I was too involved looking at the merchandise."

Gabe nodded and raised his notebook, flipped a page. "And your name, ma'am?"

"My name?"

Pen suspended above the paper, he explained, "In case we should have additional questions to ask you at a later date."

Those full lips curved in a smile that tried to look casual. "Of course. It's Tina Wilder." He jotted down the name, as well as the phone number and address she gave him when pressed. And he wondered what possible reason this woman would have to lie to him.

A cop's experiences, hell, a *lifetime* of experiences had trained Gabe to recognize the subtle signals people gave off when they were straying from the truth. A tremor in the hands for some, eyes too fixed and bright for others. There were thousands of tell-tale signs, as individual as the people themselves. He wasn't even sure what tipped him off that Tina Wilder wasn't being completely forthcoming. Maybe it was her tone, just a trifle too polite, or her expression, just a little too impassive.

But then he looked into those big blue eyes of hers, eyes that could scramble the senses of a less wary man, and there he found his answer. Because behind her deliberately blank expression flickered an emotion much stronger. Even more intriguing.

Desperation.

Recognizing that emotion, he took his time drawing a card from his pocket. He handed it to her, watched carefully as she visibly tucked back her reluctance and reached for it. "In case you remember something later, ma'am. You can reach me at that number or leave a message if I'm not in. I'll get back to you as soon as I can."

When she nodded, he added, "I'd like to speak to the boy before you leave."

Her back stiffened, one vertebrae at a time. "He can't help you, either. He was much too interested in the toys to observe anything else."

He tried for a rueful tone, tough for his low timbre, to soothe the nerves he suspected she was hiding. "You're probably right, but I have to be thorough."

Her lips curved, and he mentally revised his earlier estimation. They weren't too full. They weren't *too* anything. They appeared to be…just right.

"I'll get him."

"Detective." The clerk's voice distracted him from her retreating form for a moment. "This gentleman thought he heard something earlier."

Gabe looked in the direction of the man the clerk indicated and said, "I'll be right with you, sir." Sending another glance outside, he gave a silent curse and yanked the door open, ran to the curb.

The cab was already pulling away.

"You gotta give me an address sometime, lady. This is costing you a fortune." The driver adjusted the mirror, his eyes meeting Meghan's. She hesitated, then recited her address. Her real address, of course. Not that of the fictitious Tina Wilder, which she'd manufactured for the detective.

She took a deep breath to calm her jangled nerves. Was there some sort of law against giving a false identity to a police detective? She was certain there must be. But like it or not, she was the only one Danny had left to protect him. And although the idea of her newfound guardianship could still lace her with mind-numbing fear, she'd do whatever it took to give the boy the stability that her own childhood had lacked. The stability his mother had failed to provide for him.

"Aunt Meggie?" She looked at her nephew, forced a

reassuring smile, one that faded as he continued. "You 'member that guy I told you about? The one in the alley?"

"Hey, I thought we were going to discuss your birthday." It was a topic guaranteed to shift Danny's attention.

"I'm going to have a real party, right? You promised."

His reminder was unnecessary, since he forced her to repeat the assurance several times a day. "I promised."

Once he was on this particular subject, Danny was extremely tenacious. "That means candles and cake. And friends. How many friends can I invite?"

Not for the first time since Danny had come to live with her, Meghan felt hopelessly out of her depth. "I'm not sure."

"How about six? That's fair, 'cuz I'm gonna be six."

Sheer terror seized her for a moment at the thought of dealing with seven six-year-olds. She drew a deep breath and released it. "I guess." His reasoning sounded logical enough. What did she know, after all, about what was "fair" when planning a birthday party for a child? What did she know about any child, and Danny in particular? The answers were depressingly obvious.

"Sweet!" He bounced up and down in his seat, testing the restraint of his seat belt. She'd successfully sidetracked his thoughts from the man he'd seen in the alley. And from the compelling detective who had questioned Meghan. She wished futilely that her own attention could be diverted as easily.

The sight of her apartment building had never been so welcome. Meghan punched her code into the security system, anxious to reach the privacy of her home. Her relief might be unfounded, but she would feel safe there from the shrewd gaze of the detective and from questions that she'd be better off avoiding.

"Aunt Meggie?"

"Hmm?" The door swung open, and she guided Danny into the foyer of the building.

''Why'd that taxi guy want your pants?''

Her gaze jerked to meet the boy's puzzled one. ''What?''

''The whole time in the taxi, he kept thinking he'd like to get in your pants. I don't see why. They wouldn't fit him, would they?''

A sheerly feminine response had her sending a fuming glance after the taxi, which was already driving away. Then reaction set in and closed like a fist around her throat. It took more effort than it should have to to keep her voice calm. ''Remember what you're learning about not walking around in other people's heads?''

He looked down and scuffed one foot along the floor. ''Yeah. But I didn't walk right in. It was more like he left the door open. I couldn't help seeing his thoughts when they were spilling out all over the place, could I?''

She studied the boy, little more than a baby really. The feeling of helplessness threatening to swamp her was all too familiar. Her sister, Sandra, had never mentioned Danny's father, but the boy was blond like his mother, like Meghan herself. Perhaps he'd gotten his coloring from her sister. Certainly he'd inherited Sandra's psychic ability. The same ability she'd alternately ignored or exploited all her life.

She pushed away the accompanying flash of guilt and kept her voice firm. ''You have to try. No mind games, all right?''

He nodded, his head still bent. Telepathic would be the best description of the infant ability he'd inherited from his mother, but Sandra had always called it mind games, as if the mental raids she'd made into other people's heads had been playful entertainment for all involved. As if her gift hadn't turned their childhood into a war zone.

As if it hadn't ended up getting Sandra killed.

When her doorbell sounded the next afternoon, Meghan glanced at the clock, faintly surprised by the hour. Her schedule had undergone major adjustments since Danny had

come to live with her. The only time she had in her home
studio were the hours he was at school. Every minute was
precious, especially with a deadline looming for her next
project. But it was almost time for Callie, who lived down
the hall, to drop Danny off. She must be running a little
early.

The bell rang again before Meghan reached the door and
pulled it open. "Boy, you're eager to get rid of him today.
Don't tell me he…" The rest of the words died in her throat
as she found herself face-to-face with two men; one a
stranger and the other all too familiar.

"This is Detective Madison, Miss Patterson." Her gaze
flying to Connally's, Meghan knew she hadn't imagined the
slight inflection he'd given her name. The smile he gave
her was humorless. "And I'm going to assume you remember my name, even though you had a little difficulty with
your own yesterday."

Her palms went damp, and she barely resisted an urge to
wipe them on her loose-fitting shirt. The force of his presence struck her anew. His eyes were hard and inscrutable.
They seemed to drill through her, effortlessly shredding all
pretense, all subterfuge. Somehow she'd never imagined
that Connally would bother to go to the trouble of finding
her. Of finding Danny.

It was that thought that had tension gripping her muscles.
Her chin angled up and she met his gaze. "Being a detective, you should have concluded that I gave you a false
name yesterday because I wanted to avoid just this kind of
harassment."

"Being a detective," Connally countered, "I get kinda
suspicious when people go to such lengths to avoid talking
to me. We had to trace you through the cab company you
used."

Meghan set her lips, but remained silent. She wasn't sure
what kind of tack to take with the detective. Defiance didn't
seem to work. Nor had her phony compliance yesterday. He

didn't appear to be a man who gave up easily. In contrast to his partner's lived-in face, with its homely charm, this man's features could have been carved from granite. She was beginning to believe that he had a will to match.

Surreptitiously, she glanced at her watch. Danny would be home in minutes. It was imperative that she get rid of the detectives before then.

"I'm afraid I don't have much time." Even as she spoke, Connally seemed to loom closer, and she retreated in immediate, involuntary response. Then somehow the men were standing inside her doorway, although she'd had no intention of letting them in. She thought she caught a flash of satisfaction in Connally's pale eyes before he closed the door behind him, and the sight of it stiffened her spine.

Her gaze swung to Detective Madison, who was speaking for the first time. "Sorry for the interruption. You didn't answer your buzzer, but the super told us that he hadn't seen you go out today. He let us in."

With a firmer grip on her composure now, Meghan pasted a polite smile on her face. "I'm afraid Detective Connally has wasted your time. I already told him yesterday that I hadn't seen anything while I was at the toy store."

"It's real important that we find the man we're tracing, ma'am." Madison's voice had a placating quality that his partner's lacked. "You left Favorite Things kind of suddenly last night. We just wanted to follow up to see if maybe you'd remembered something since then."

"Mind telling us why you were in such a hurry to get away?" Connally's gaze was directed above her head as he surveyed her apartment, before focusing once more on her.

She forced a casual shrug. "I'd arranged for the driver to come back for us. You know what it's like to find a cab at that time of day."

"That's sure a fact, isn't it?" Detective Madison's tone was understanding. "Last week I tried to take my wife out for a nice dinner and we had a devil of a time getting a taxi back home. She said it would have been more relaxing to stay in and cook.''

His easy manner should have disarmed her. There was something comfortable about the man, like a rumpled set of clothes kept long after they'd gone out of style. His thinning sandy-colored hair was brushed back from a broad forehead, and his slightly rounded shoulders made him seem smaller than his partner, although they were probably both over six feet. But the friendliness in his voice, in his pale-gray eyes, didn't eliminate her wariness. In her experience all cops wanted something. And some would go to deadly lengths to get it.

"Did you buy anything last night?" At the question she shifted her attention to observe Connally strolling around her living room. "It looked like an unusual place. I guess kids go nuts for that kind of thing."

"No, I didn't. And as I told you yesterday, I didn't notice the man you were looking for while I was in the store, either. Sorry I can't be of more help to you." Although her words were meant to bring a close to the conversation, neither of the men made a move to leave.

"What about the boy?"

The words hung in the air like leaden crystals suspended from a chandelier. She didn't answer; couldn't. Protecting Danny was her job now. And the threat these two men posed was nauseating in its familiarity. She wouldn't allow him to be used as his mother had been. She wouldn't risk his life the way Sandra had so carelessly risked her own.

When silence stretched, Madison said, "Detective Connally said you had a small boy with you, Miss Patterson. Maybe he saw something."

"My nephew was with me, yes. But he's only five. He isn't going to be of any help, either, I'm afraid."

The two men exchanged a glance. "We'd still like to talk to him. Could you arrange that?" Connally's words may have been couched as a request, but they were delivered in a voice accustomed to giving orders. And having them obeyed.

"No." Her voice was flat. The detective wasn't the only one who could be indomitable. "That won't be—"

The doorbell rang then, interrupting her. Frustration surged. Just five more minutes. That's all it would have taken to get rid of the men. The detectives were watching her expectantly. Mentally cursing the cosmic timing, she went to the door.

"Trying to pretend you aren't home won't save you." Callie's laughing words sounded above Danny's exuberant greeting. "Remember, I have a..." Her sentence trailed off when she saw the two men with Meghan.

"Hi, Aunt Meggie. I gotta go!" With a five-year-old's sense of urgency, Danny made a beeline for the bathroom.

"Ah...I'll catch you later. We're still on for tonight, right?" At Meghan's nod, Callie placed a hand on her son Alex's back to guide him toward their apartment. "Tell Danny I'll see him later." Meghan closed the door after them.

A compelling need to speak to Danny warred with an equally strong reluctance to leave the detectives alone in her living room, even for a few minutes. She didn't trust them. The last few months had destroyed any unquestioning faith she might have once had in the police. And Connally, especially, saw too much.

She didn't know which made her more uncomfortable—when his gaze raked over her home, her belongings, or when it fixed on her. Something about him caused a disconcerting awareness that was as unusual as it was unwelcome. Meghan flicked a glance at the two detectives. "If you'll excuse me for a moment, I need to check on my nephew."

Gabe watched her hurry down a hallway with a gait guaranteed to snag a man's attention and hold it. It sure held his.

"You're a card-carrying pervert, you know that?"

The words were pitched low. Gabe turned to his partner and lifted a brow. "What are you talking about?"

Cal made a sound of disgust. "You stared hard enough. Trying to get a complete description of her lingerie?"

"She's not wearing any, at least not on top. And noticing that doesn't make me a pervert." He crossed a few steps to the coffee table, which had some books stacked neatly on it. He picked them up one at a time, reading the titles.

"What's it make you then?"

"A typical red-blooded male." He gestured toward the books. "Look at these." Together the two men silently read the titles.

Your Extra Senses. Growing up Telepathic. Extra-Sensory Perception: Myth and Magic.

Cal lifted his gaze to Gabe's and shrugged. "So she's got an interest. You know, you should try reading more yourself. I've got a great book I'd like you to look at on homeopathic remedies for common ailments."

Giving a snort, he set the books down again. "Fat chance."

But Cal was nothing if not dogged. That quality of his was an advantage while working an investigation, but often a pain in the ass otherwise. "There's a great chapter on ways to quit smoking that you might find helpful."

Gabe threw him a dark look. "Thanks, buddy, but you've helped me in that area too much already." It had been Cal who'd suggested that he wear a rubber band around his wrist, and snap himself anytime he thought about taking a smoke. Called it aversion therapy or some damn thing. Gabe had given it an enthusiastic try once and discovered that the resulting sting hadn't appreciably lessened his desire for a cigarette. It had, however, given him a bone to pick with his partner. He was just waiting for the right time to pay the man back for his lousy advice.

Cal stiffened slightly, alerting Gabe that Meghan Patterson had reentered the room behind him. Not that he needed the warning. His instincts were excellent, and in her case they seemed to be unusually heightened. Turning, he found her standing with her nephew before her. Her hands were resting lightly on his shoulders, her stance protective. He wondered what it was she thought she was protecting the boy from.

Cal smiled at the boy, going down on one knee before him. Gabe made no move to follow suit. His partner was the natural one to put the kid at ease. Children and dogs liked him. And although Gabe didn't have anything against dogs, he'd be the first to admit that he didn't know squat about kids.

"Hi, I'm Detective Madison." He jerked a thumb in Gabe's direction. "That's Detective Connally. We want to ask you a couple of questions. Is that okay?"

The boy looked up at his aunt before giving an almost imperceptible nod.

Cal's voice was reassuring. "This won't take long. We just want you to tell us about your trip to the toy store last night."

Danny's words were hesitant. "I saw some dinosaurs. Electronic ones."

Cal gave a long whistle. "Dinosaurs, huh? That sounds exciting. The clerk said you took them to the patio in the alley to try them out. How'd they work?"

In his enthusiasm the boy was more forthcoming. "They were cool. They can roar and fight and everything. Aunt Meggie said maybe I can get two for my birthday."

Gabe entered the conversation. "While you were outside, did you hear anything, Danny? See anything?" The boy exchanged another look with his aunt. His answer was slow in coming.

"I...heard something. And then a man jumped out of the sky and ran to get in a car."

A car. Gabe thought quickly. Having a car waiting suggested that Lenny had been planning a quick exit from his apartment. What could have had him running so scared? Scared enough to shoot at them first?

He waited with barely restrained impatience while Cal smoothly extracted bits of information from the boy. D'Brusco must have jumped over the railing of the fire escape at the landing. The car he'd run to was black, according to the kid. Yes, the boy agreed, with Cal's coaching, the same color as the detective's belt.

"And he was real scared, too." Gabe noted the way Meghan's fingers tightened on the boy's shoulders, and Danny turned to look up at her. "He was, Aunt Meggie. Maybe 'cuz that other man was chasing him. Then they both got in the car and drove away."

Gabe squatted before the boy. "There was another man? Did they say anything? Could you hear them talking to each other?"

Danny seemed to get tongue-tied then. Or perhaps he was reacting to the death grip his aunt had on his shoulders. It took minutes of prying to elicit that the boy hadn't heard either man speak. Gabe visualized the dimensions of the alley and calculated that the boy wouldn't have heard anything below a shout, at any rate. The way the kid described the scene, he doubted whether there had been a chase in progress. More likely both of them had been in D'Brusco's apartment when he and Cal had knocked. He doubted the men had noticed the boy. If he'd been seated on the concrete patio, the wrought iron fence around it would have likely hidden him from view. With a bit more coaxing Cal was able to elicit a description that matched D'Brusco. He'd give a month's pay to know who the other one was.

"That's all the information my nephew can give you, Detectives." Meghan's voice was firm. "Now, if you don't mind, it's dinnertime, and we're on a schedule tonight."

Cal looked at Gabe, who nodded slightly. As they rose, he said, "We'd sure like to get an idea about the identity of the second man, ma'am. Could you bring your nephew in to look at some pictures?''

There was no mistaking the woman's reaction. Her spine went rigid. Voice tight, she said to the boy, "Danny, go in and get washed up for supper.''

"But I just washed my hands a minute ago.''

"Now, Danny.''

Apparently the boy recognized the steel in his aunt's words, because he turned without another word and trudged down the hallway. Meghan faced the detectives again and her tone went low and fierce. "Any further involvement of my nephew in your investigation is out of the question.''

Gabe tried to make his voice sound soothing, a difficult feat for his rumbling tones. "I don't think you understand, ma'am. All we're asking is…''

The look she shot him was as scathing as her words. "No, *you* don't understand. Whatever it is that you do, you'll do without Danny. The CPD has already cost my family more than enough already. Thanks to your department, my sister is dead.''

Chapter 2

"Uh-uh, buddy. It's my day, remember?"

Gabe scowled, his fingers poised on the handle of the driver's door. Heaving a matyred sigh he went around to the other side of the unmarked car and got in. Cal took cautious driving to new heights. Gabe had often thought if his partner entered a Daytona 500 held for females over ninety, every one of the little old ladies would be lapping him in seconds.

Once he'd eased the car into traffic, Cal spoke again. "What do you suppose Patterson's story is? She's sure carrying a whale of a grudge against the department."

Gabe loosened his tie and unfastened his top shirt button. The confining clothes he was forced to wear was one of the biggest disadvantages of having switched assignments three years ago from undercover work to his current position of detective in the Organized Crime division. In his opinion, neckwear should be outlawed as a particularly cruel and inhumane form of torture. He'd like to get hold of the guy who'd invented ties and beat an apology from him.

"Hard telling. Maybe her sister swore out a restraining order that went south." It happened, he knew, more often than they liked to consider. Domestic disputes especially could turn deadly. At any rate, after dropping her bombshell, Meghan Patterson hadn't wasted any time ushering them out of the apartment. Gabe decided he'd dig around a little and see what he could discover about the sister. Despite Meghan's hostility, the fact remained that they'd probably need to talk to her nephew again. Discovering the identity of the unknown man with D'Brusco just might be the key to blowing this case wide open. And the instant he had an inkling of who the guy could be, Gabe would be back on the woman's doorstep. He said as much to Cal.

His partner never took his eyes off the traffic. "We'll have to hope she changes her mind about letting her nephew cooperate."

"She'll change her mind."

Cal's brows rose at the certainty in Gabe's voice. "I don't know. She seemed pretty sure."

Reaching into his pocket, Gabe withdrew a package of gum and unwrapped a piece. He placed it in his mouth and chewed. It was a damn poor substitute for the smoke he craved, but it annoyed the hell out of Cal. That was powerful incentive. "I can be very persuasive."

Giving a hoot at that, Madison risked a glance at his partner. "You? Somehow I don't think the intimidation tactics you find so effective on street scum are going to be appropriate in her case. To handle a classy lady like that requires a certain finesse."

Just for the irritation value, Gabe cracked his gum loudly. "I've got finesse."

Cal was chortling now. "Boy, do you. I don't know what I was worried about. If the time comes, we'll just count on you to change her mind with your usual suave personality."

Gabe was undisturbed by his partner's gibes. "Don't discount my hidden charms."

"Yeah, your charms are well hidden, all right."

"Keep being mean to me and I'll tell Becky. She loves me. She'd kick your butt if she could hear you now." Becky and Cal had married the previous year, and Gabe returned the woman's fondness tenfold. She was upfront and plain-spoken, traits damn uncommon in the females of his experience.

A sudden thought occurred. "Speaking of your better half, why don't you give her a call when we get back to our desks. I was thinking of going out for a steak tonight. We could go together. My treat. I owe you for the last time you had me over. Or maybe for the last dozen times," he mused. "I lose count."

"Uh…" Cal cleared his throat. "I don't think so. Not tonight." He turned the car into the district parking lot and started cruising for a space.

Gabe looked out the window and spotted an empty slot. "There's a place. Up on your left." He shifted seamlessly back to the original conversation. "C'mon, think about it. How long has it been since Becky let you eat red meat? I could persuade her to let you order a steak. She's putty in my hands."

A dull flush had risen in his partner's face. He took even greater care than usual to park the car and switch off the ignition. "Actually, we have special plans tonight."

Gabe was perceptive enough to realize the plans weren't the sort his partner would want him included in. "Yeah, okay. Why don't you go on home and let me finish up the paperwork for today?"

"No, that's all right. Becky isn't expecting me until later, anyway."

The two men got out of the car and walked toward the building. Gabe threw a companionable arm around Cal's shoulders. "The trick to romancing a woman is to do the unexpected once in a while. Now you go on home and surprise Becky. Better yet, stop for some flowers and wine first.''

"Well…" Cal's hesitation was minuscule. "Okay. I'll owe you one.''

Gabe clapped him on the back. "Damn right you will. Oh, and give Becky a big kiss for me when you see her, would you? On the mouth.''

Cal shrugged off Gabe's arm and headed for his car. "You're depraved, Connally.''

"Yeah, I am. Forget it. I'll give it to her myself the next time I see her.'' He chuckled at the obscene gesture Cal made and entered the building.

Since it was time for a shift change, the halls of the Area One Detectives' Division were more chaotic than normal. Winding through the maze of desks and cubicles, Gabe exchanged greetings and one-liners with his co-workers and then dropped into the chair in front of his battered metal desk. Before getting to work, he shrugged out of his coat, pulled the loosened tie from around his neck, wadded it up and jammed it in the pocket of his sports jacket. Then he slung the jacket over the back of his chair, undid another shirt button and unfastened the cuffs, rolling the sleeves to his elbows.

"Connally, you savage. You're a little late to be the featured matinee,'' Detective Lydia Fredericks observed from her desk across the aisle. She raised her voice. "Hey, Connally's doing a striptease over here. Could we have a show of appreciation?'' There was a smattering of applause, and a wolf whistle from Lydia's partner, Marcy Rogers. Coins rained on Gabe's desk, courtesy of the detectives in the vicinity.

"Thank you, thank you. You've been a wonderful audience.'' He stood and did a quick shimmy, eliciting a heartfelt moan from Lydia and some more loose change. He scooped up the coins, frowning over the lone penny in the group. "Hey, who's the cheapskate? Fiskes?''

Detective Mark Fiskes grinned. "What can I say? You're a cheap thrill, Connally."

"Cheap, hell." Gabe slipped the money in his pants pocket. "I just made enough to drink all night. I'm thinking about taking a second j—" The rest of the sentence went unuttered, as the sudden studiousness of the other detectives tipped him off. He turned around, and his tone went abruptly professional.

"Afternoon, Lieutenant."

"Connally." The man nodded at a coin beside the desk that had been missed. "Taking up a collection?"

It wasn't uncommon for officers faced with Lieutenant Robert Burney's stern ebony mask to feel sudden, urgent needs to be elsewhere. Fast. But Gabe couldn't pass up the chance for a little retribution.

"You caught me, sir. I was just collecting my daily protection money from the others."

"Protection money."

Gabe propped his hips on his desk, crossed his arms over his chest and strove to make his tone earnest. "Yessir. The rest of the guys pay me to defend them from Detective Fredericks's compulsive stalking." Several of the men in the vicinity snickered, and Lydia invited Gabe to take a road trip to hell. He shook his head sadly. "She's getting bolder and bolder, sir. She follows us everywhere, making all kinds of lewd proposals. The truth is, the other guys are getting scared. I'm the only one brave enough to stand up to her." He turned to Lydia. "This is the last time I'm going to say it, Fredericks. Get help, for godsakes. You're getting pathetic." He dodged the pencil she threw at him, amidst guffaws from the surrounding detectives.

Burney's expression didn't change by as much as a flicker. "I'd like to see you in my office, Connally."

Gabe pushed away from his desk and followed in his superior's wake. When they reached the small office, he closed the door behind him and settled into a chair in front

of the lieutenant's desk. Burney lost no time getting down
to business.

"You and Madison make any progress today on
D'Brusco?"

"Some." Gabe stretched his legs out before him and
crossed one battered shoe over the other. "Best lead we got
was from a five-year-old kid who was in the alley when
Lenny took off." He filled the man in on their visit to
Meghan Patterson's apartment.

The lieutenant leaned forward, interested. "Any chance
you got a decent description of the second guy?"

"Well, the kid described Lenny pretty well, so he might
be useful if we get a lead on the other's identity. Said the
guy was thin, taller than me, and his face looked like a
skull."

Burney's weight shifted back in his chair, his disappointment obvious. "Great. The kid's memory is probably influ-
enced by a recent horror flick he watched."

Gabe lifted a shoulder. "Maybe. But the presence of a
second guy in the apartment would explain the shots fired.
That never did seem like Lenny's style."

"D'Brusco might have changed his style after his last
stint at Hill."

That was entirely possible, Gabe silently conceded. It had
been courtesy of Gabe that Lenny had been the state's guest
for a second time after Gabe had busted him for fencing.
D'Brusco had only been out for two years, and apparently
had changed his favorite con. He'd come to Gabe and Cal's
attention recently when they caught a money-laundering assignment he figured in. Gabe still had trouble believing that
Lenny had risen to such a level. Working with that kind of
money meant D'Brusco was playing in the big leagues. Apparently, he'd not only changed his habits, he'd also learned
some new skills in prison.

The lieutenant was speaking again. "Just be aware that

this case is attracting some attention from above. I fielded a call regarding it today from the deputy chief.''

Gabe's low, tuneless whistle conveyed his appreciation of the fact. Given the chain of command in the CPD, the deputy chief's inquiry meant that the interest was being generated several authority rungs higher, maybe even from the superintendent of police himself.

''Any clue what their interest is?''

''That wasn't shared with me. However, a private source informed me that Justice has been sniffing around the investigation.''

Gabe went still. ''Justice? Which agency?''

Burney shook his head. ''That I don't know. Just thought you should be aware that the case might be getting some profile.'' He stood, indicating that the meeting was at an end. Gabe's hand was on the doorknob before the lieutenant's wry tone sounded again.

''Oh, and Connally—'' he waited until the detective looked over his shoulder before finishing ''—you might want to rethink that second job. You know how the department feels about detectives moonlighting.''

Grinning, Gabe opened the door. ''If you say so, sir, but it seems a shame to waste a god-given talent. I figure I'm a natural.''

Too bad, he thought, an hour and a half later as he eyed the computer console before him balefully, that he wasn't a natural at technology. The damn thing had already eaten his report once, and he'd had to painstakingly retype it. Cal would have made some wiseass comment about garbage in, garbage out, but then Cal understood things like computers and DVDs, the new technology rage that he'd once tried to explain to Gabe. His efforts had been in vain. Gabe had considered it a major feat when he'd learned to program his VCR. His talents, he'd explained to his partner, time and again, lay in other areas.

Once he'd collected his hard copy, his attention shifted

to the woman who'd lingered in the back of his mind since she'd thrown them out of her apartment. Meghan Patterson. He typed her last name into the crime data base and waited for the computer to finish processing.

Despite his partner's assessment of his intentions, his interest in the woman was purely professional. Well, okay, he admitted, drumming his fingers lightly on the keyboard, maybe he'd admired her in a purely detached sort of way. He could only figure one good reason for a woman to scrape her hair up on top of her head the way she'd worn hers. He doubted very much, however, that she'd worn it that way with the intention of allowing a man to take it down, a pin at a time. He gave a purely masculine grin at the mental picture.

A good cop got to be an expert at sizing people up. It certainly didn't mean he was attracted to her, which was a good thing, because he had a long-standing distaste for dishonesty. Regardless of her reasons, Meghan had lied to him yesterday, and that alone was enough to keep him wary of her. There were, he'd found, simple facts in life that had to be accepted because they couldn't be changed. Trees had their leaves, oceans had their tides, and women had their secrets. He knew that. And knowing was reason enough to keep the females in his life at a comfortable distance.

The search yielded forty-seven Pattersons for whom arrest warrants had been issued or by whom complaints had been filed. He was unsurprised when he failed to find Meghan's name. He scanned each report, but could find nothing to match the little information she'd given them about her sister. He switched to the Internet and accessed the *Tribune*'s archives. He found several references to news articles in which Meghan was mentioned, and he went through them in reverse order, starting with the oldest.

The first he read had his eyebrows climbing. He hadn't realized the woman he'd spoken with this afternoon was part of the Tremayne dynasty. The connection implied old money, historic homes and very public divorces. Meghan's mother was the sole heiress to one of Chicago's wealthiest families and, from what Gabe could remember, had done her part to keep the family name in the news with the frequent breakups of her marriages.

It occurred to him then to wonder if Meghan had been married. He scrolled down the articles, but found no details to support the idea. Patterson had probably been her father's name.

He skimmed through several more clippings, most having appeared in the social registry featuring Meghan being escorted to lavish fund-raisers. It was interesting to note that none of the pictures showed her with the same guy twice, although they all shared a polished, worthless look that made them interchangeable.

He paused to read a couple that mentioned her career in the art world and clicked impatiently on the most recent selection.

The picture unfolded in slow-motion, which, given the age of the district's computers, was the way the Internet seemed to work most of the time. It was an invasive close-up shot, the kind the media was noted for, focused on Meghan, Danny and an older woman. The trio were dressed in black, and the photo had been snapped as they filed out of a church. Behind a casket.

The headline screamed at him, and he read the article quickly, his stomach dropping a little lower with each paragraph. He stared at the screen after he'd finished, absently rubbing a hand over his jaw.

Damn his luck. His earlier certainty about persuading Meghan to allow Danny to cooperate slipped several notches. He remembered the gist of the case involving Sandra Barton; who didn't? It had been splashed all over the news for weeks, and the only place news traveled faster than in the media was within the department itself. He now understood why Meghan might hold the police responsible for her sister's death.

On some level, he really couldn't blame her.

He'd lost his appetite for the steak he'd been promising himself all day, so Gabe got a couple of fast-food sandwiches before heading to Brewsters. The bar was a local hangout, its customers mostly cops, and a favorite of his and Cal's. Of course, Cal hadn't made regular appearances there since his marriage. Becky kept him on a pretty short leash, which was another reason Gabe steered clear of serious relationships. He had a long-held aversion to being confined.

He felt at home as soon as he pushed open the door and inhaled the secondhand smoke that all the ordinances in the world couldn't successfully ban. Returning the greetings of some of the regulars, he found a seat at the bar and signaled the bartender to bring him his usual.

When the bottle of beer was set before him, he took a comfortable swallow, before a man slipped onto the stool beside him. Casting a sideways look, he groaned aloud. "I'm here to relax, McKay. I don't want any hassle."

The blond man beside him raised his brows. "Hassle? Me? I was just hoping for some friendly conversation with one of CPD's finest."

Gabe took a long pull from his beer. "I heard a joke the other day that made me think of you. You know what you call ten thousand reporters at the bottom of the ocean? A good start." He chuckled at the other man's expression. "Present company excluded, of course."

"Of course." Dare McKay raised a finger, and the bartender slid an iced mug of beer toward him. "Besides, that joke is probably referring to the paparazzi, not to eminent investigative journalists such as myself. And speaking of investigating...I hear you caught the D'Brusco case."

Gabe shoved down his annoyance. The man's sources

were uncannily accurate. "I'm not giving out information so don't bother pumping me."

"Could be that I might be in a position to throw some information your direction as the case progresses."

Tipping the bottle to his lips, Gabe drank. "Don't do me any favors."

"Well, since you asked so nice...I'll be talking to you, Connally. Right now there's a blonde who craves my attention."

He slid off the stool and sauntered in the direction of a woman sitting at a table nearby, who looked distinctly happier to see him than Gabe had been.

Ordering another beer, Gabe listened with only half an ear to the guy on the other side of him bemoan the Bulls' chances of rebuilding another championship team. With one elbow resting on the bar, he let his attention drift as he studied the rest of the customers in the establishment.

Mostly regulars, he observed, people he knew by sight, if not by name. There were a few neighborhood faces, a few like McKay, who frequented the place trying to pick up information, but most of the customers were cops who enjoyed relaxing after the job with their buddies. He took another long swallow of beer, then froze in the act of returning the bottle to the bar. His gaze ricocheted to a table toward the back of the place, and he stared incredulously.

What the hell was Meghan Patterson doing in Brewsters?

What she was doing, he quickly concluded, was a damn fine job of distracting just about every man in the bar. His weren't the only pair of eyes trained in her direction. With that mass of golden curls spilling down her back, and her curves shown to advantage in the black sweater and skirt she was wearing, she looked as out of place in the slightly shabby tavern as a debutante at a cock fight.

His attention shifted to her companion and his brows drew together. Wattrel...Wadrell, that was it. His frown turned to a scowl. Fresh out of the academy, they'd been rookies in the same division years ago. The man hadn't made many friends then with his methods for cutting corners and currying favor with the brass. Based on what Gabe had learned recently, Wadrell hadn't changed much. Only the stakes had grown higher.

He brought the bottle to his lips and sipped, watching the couple unabashedly. Meghan's back was to Gabe; he'd recognized her only when she'd turned in profile for a moment. She slipped from her chair and headed in the direction of the rest rooms. He shot a glance to Wadrell. The detective watched her go, then reached for his drink with a self-satisfied smile.

Without further thought, Gabe grabbed his bottle of beer and slipped off his bar stool to wind his way to the back of the place. The rest rooms were located beside two pool tables, and from the looks of things the pool players' concentration had just been shot to hell by Meghan's appearance.

Loitering in the vicinity really wasn't difficult. The rear area was packed with players and spectators. A few made token attempts to hide their cigarettes, as if the smoke hovering below the hanging lights had appeared from nowhere. Gabe filled his lungs in vicarious appreciation.

When the rest room door opened, he shifted position so that Meghan could move only a few feet before finding her way blocked by him.

"Miss Patterson." Stunned recognition was in his voice. "I'm surprised to see you here."

She wasn't a good enough actress to hide her dismay at his appearance. Like this afternoon, she retreated a bit. Her response drew a different response from him this time, though. Earlier he'd been pleased that the distance had allowed him entrance to her apartment. Now he was fighting a compulsion to slide his fingers beneath her hair, around her nape, and haul her back to him, even closer this time.

He clutched his bottle tighter in one hand and jammed the other in his pants pocket.

"Detective Connally." She'd recovered quickly, but was still visibly eager to get away from him. Remaining planted solidly in front of her, he brought the bottle to his lips, took a drink.

"Given the high esteem you have for the CPD, this is a funny place for you and your date to show up. Of course—" a corner of his mouth curled "—guess it's also kind of funny that you'd be seeing a cop."

"I'm not 'seeing' him. At least, not in the way you mean. Could I get by, please?"

He obliged by moving a few inches. There was enough space for her to pass, if she didn't mind pressing against him, curves to angles, heat to heat. Her gaze measured the space and she remained still. Apparently she minded.

Her eyes closed for a moment in a gesture of pure frustration. "Look, I have business with him, okay? Business I'd like to finish so I can go home to my nephew."

"Your nephew lives with you?" The interest in his voice was genuine.

"I've been named his guardian." A less observant man might have missed the flicker in her eyes as she delivered the words. A less observant man also might not have focused on the way her blond waves framed her face or the interesting rise and fall of her chest as she breathed. Her blue eyes narrowed at him then, and he cleared his throat self-consciously. It was considered poor form for a trained observer to be caught staring.

"Yeah, I read about what happened to your sister. Sorry for your loss."

It was as though his words had pierced her with ice. Voice frigid, she replied, "Yes, everyone's *sorry,* Detective. But that doesn't make Sandra any less dead, does it?" She used her elbow to wedge her way past him and walked away, anger steeling her spine. Gabe watched her go, draining his beer musingly. His hope of gaining her cooperation in his current investigation seemed to be fading by the moment.

A few games of pool later, Gabe's mood was no better, and his pockets were considerably lighter. He handed his cue to a nearby man and shrugged into his coat, amidst some goodnatured jeering.

"Hey, Connally, you're a little off your game tonight. Must be worn-out from that second job you've taken on." Fiskes grinned at him from across the table.

"Yeah, but you wouldn't believe the benefits."

The other man laughed. The jeers were actually preferable to the truth, Gabe thought, as he wended his way to the front of the bar—that his concentration had been shredded time and again while he'd tried to keep an eye on Wadrell's table. He'd missed a crucial shot when he'd seen the man move his chair closer to Meghan's, put an arm around her shoulders. And it hadn't improved his game any to wonder whether she'd shifted away from the man purposefully, or if she'd really been reaching for her drink. At any rate his concentration hadn't improved in the twenty minutes since she'd left the bar, alone. Not while Wadrell was still sitting at the table, looking so damned pleased with himself.

Instead of passing the seat Meghan had vacated, Gabe pulled out the chair and sat down. "Wadrell, how's it going?"

"Connally." The other man's voice held an edge of wariness. "Oh...you know. Still chasing bad guys."

"Yeah, I heard about your big case." Gabe looked around, signaled the waitress to their table and ordered a couple of beers. "Got a lot of press on that one, didn't you?"

The man shrugged. "You know how the media is. Warring gangs are good for headlines, especially when drug dealing is thrown into the mix."

"Not to mention the sensationalism of using a psychic to

help round up the leaders." The waitress delivered the
beers, and Gabe nudged one of them toward the other man,
then handed the woman some bills.

Wadrell eyed him for a moment, then lifted the bottle to
his lips. "That didn't hurt any, of course."

"Yeah, that was a different angle." Gabe scratched his
jaw. "Can't say I've ever worked with one. Was she really
any help?"

There was still a note of caution in the other man's voice.
"Yeah, Barton gave us some good leads. She called in and
said she'd run into two of our guys in a dive they frequent.
She was referred to me and came up with a couple leads
about their activities that checked out. We started using
her." He shook his head and reached for a cigarette. "I
don't care if you believe in that kind of thing or not, the
broad knew things, okay? We'd run a suspect in, place Barton behind the one-way glass. She'd observe for a while,
give us some tips, and then we'd interrogate them. We put
away most of the members of the gang that way. Slick operation. With her help we nailed them in the questioning.
They never knew what hit them."

Gabe tried not to covet the cigarette the other man was
smoking. He failed miserably. "You're telling me she read
their minds or something?" He didn't bother to keep the
disbelief out of his voice. He'd never put much stock in that
kind of hocus-pocus. He still wasn't convinced that Wadrell
believed in it, either; he was just as likely to have grabbed
the opportunity to make headlines. "How do you suppose
the press caught wind that you were using a psychic? And
her identity?"

Setting the bottle down in front of him, Wadrell said,
"You know how the media is. Can't even call them leaks
when the department itself is like a sieve."

"Yeah, I know how it is. Just plain bad luck that the lady
up and died before you made cases on all the guys involved."

"Who, Barton?" Wadrell leaned back in his chair, visibly more relaxed now. "Yeah, too bad she bought it, but she really wasn't much help there at the end, anyway. The last few things she gave us didn't pan out. We'll round up the others. It's just a matter of time."

"That was her sister in here earlier, wasn't it? Meghan Patterson."

Wadrell's hand froze in the act of reaching for his bottle. "Yeah, so?"

Gabe lifted a shoulder. "Recognized her. She claim to be psychic, too?"

With a leer, the man said, "If she is, I hope she didn't read my mind tonight. You know what I mean?"

"Way I hear it, this Patterson's got a major beef with the department."

Wadrell nodded. "She's got some crazy notion her sister's car accident was no accident at all—that the gang we were busting set it up to get her out of the way. Nothing to that, of course, but she won't let it go."

Comprehension dawned, and with it, a shimmer of anger. "Oh, so that's the angle." At the man's silence, Gabe lowered his voice conspiratorially, buddy to buddy. "C'mon, Wadrell, you gonna pretend you're cherry on this? You're stringing the sister along like you might be able to get more information on the accident for her, all the while hoping she'll throw a little action your way."

The smirk that settled on the man's lips was an open invitation to a clenched fist. "Well if there's any action to be thrown, I'm gonna be the one to catch it. That is one fine piece of woman."

Gabe leaned back in disgust. "Yeah, and why wouldn't she be interested in a prince like you? Did you have something going with this Barton, too?"

The other man drained his beer, and set the bottle back on the table. "Naw. Not that she wasn't a looker. But there was a hard edge to that one, you know? Compared to her, this Patterson is a babe in the woods. The sister was downright spooky.'' Catching the scowl the bartender was aiming at him, he ground his cigarette out in the ashtray.

A few more minutes convinced Gabe that Wadrell had no more information that was of interest, which was good, because his tolerance level had lowered alarmingly. Gabe threw a couple bucks on the table and rose. Self-serving jerks like Wadrell gave him the heaves. There was no doubt in his mind that the other detective had been the one to alert the media, anonymously, of course, that a psychic was helping with his case. Wadrell would hand over his grandmother to get some exposure. It had been unprofessional and, once the media had dug up Barton's identity, downright dangerous for the woman. With guys like Wadrell in the department, it was no wonder Meghan was down on the CPD.

He pushed open the door, the cold slap of wind in his face a wicked contrast to the heat in the bar. Given the circumstances, he could understand why Meghan was convinced Wadrell's suspects had arranged to get rid of her sister. It could have happened just that way. But according to the detective, it hadn't.

There was a movement to his left, alerting him to the figure huddled against the building. He took his time reaching into his pocket and unwrapped a piece of gum.

''Buses stopped running a couple hours ago.''

Meghan pulled the collar of her coat up closer around her throat and refused to look his way. ''I've got a cab coming.''

''It must be taking its sweet time. How long have you been waiting?'' He figured it had been at least a half hour since she'd left the bar.

Determinedly she kept her gaze fixed on the street. ''I've called twice. It won't be much longer.''

Resting his shoulders against the brick building, he studied her. ''Be a lot warmer to wait inside.''

Finally she turned to him. Even the darkness couldn't

prevent him from noting that her gaze wasn't friendly. "I'm fine out here. I don't need company. You're free to be on your way."

Those words were delivered with just the right amount of haughtiness—duchess to serf. He supposed with her background she'd grown up giving orders. Too bad he'd never learned to take them.

"I've got my car. I could give you a lift home if you want."

She'd returned to face the street. "That won't be necessary."

He nodded. "Your choice. Hope for your sake that cab arrives soon, though. Some men might be forgiven for thinking that your hanging around out here means you've changed your mind about ending the date so soon." He heard a slight sound in the darkness that he fancied was her teeth clenching together.

"It was not a—"

"Date. Right. You said that." Giving a shrug, he pushed away from the wall. "Well, if the cab doesn't show, I'm sure Wadrell would enjoy escorting you home."

He started in the direction of the parking lot. He'd gotten only a dozen steps when he heard her voice again.

"Wait. Maybe…maybe you're right."

He looked over his shoulder. The frigid breeze was combing reckless fingers through her hair, and she pushed it back over her shoulder with an impatient hand. "Those are words every man likes to hear, ma'am. Exactly what was I right about?"

Her chin lifted to an imperious angle, and it took little imagination to guess the effort it took to keep her tone civil. "I guess I will take that ride, after all. That is, if you're sure it won't take you out of your way."

He masked his surprise at her sudden change of heart and dug in his pocket for his keys. Risk management, he figured, silently leading her to his car. She'd considered her options and decided that at the moment he presented less of a threat than Wadrell. He wasn't sure whether to be amused or offended. But he'd seize the opportunity to spend some time with her. He didn't mind driving a few extra miles, especially if it got him closer to gaining her trust.

He was truthful enough to admit, at least privately, to a fascination for the woman; an interest in more than her cooperation. But that was as far as it would be allowed to go. Work came first with him, it always would. And if the unlikely day ever came that he actually got serious about a female, it wouldn't be one with shadows in her eyes and secrets on her lips.

He didn't have to be psychic to realize that a woman like Meghan spelled the kind of trouble he'd spent a lifetime avoiding.

Chapter 3

It was a mistake. Nerves scrambled in Meghan's stomach. In her eagerness to avoid Wadrell, with his increasingly slick lines and smooth advances, she'd considered Connally the lesser of two evils. Too late she'd remembered all the reasons she would be wise to shun his presence, as well. In the shadowy interior of his car, on the near-silent ride to her apartment, he exuded a danger all his own.

His voice rumbled out in the darkness, startling her. "Who's taking care of your nephew tonight?"

With effort she kept the anxiety from her words. "My neighbor, Callie."

"The woman who came to the door this afternoon?" He glanced her way, caught her nod. "Is she your baby-sitter?"

"Her son, Alex, and Danny are friends. We trade off duties. That way each of us can get away when we need to."

"Sounds handy."

That deep bass of his sounded even more gravelly in the shadowy interior of the car. His natural timbre was low, always sounding as though he'd just awakened. That thought elicited an accompanying mental image of him just rousing from sleep, his hard jaws shadowed and those whiskey-colored eyes still drowsy. She could feel her cheeks warm at the intimate thought of him, and turned her face to the window, glad that the darkness would hide her reaction.

She could blame the odd path her thoughts were taking on the upset she'd had earlier today, and then again tonight. She didn't normally spend much time thinking about men's voices. And especially not a man who was intent on pulling her nephew into the middle of a criminal investigation.

The memory firmed her earlier resolve. At all costs Connally and his partner had to be kept away from Danny. The boy was too young to be well schooled in keeping secrets. And Meghan was determined Connally would never learn about his ability.

The rest of the ride passed in silence. When he pulled up in front of her apartment, she lost no time exiting the car. "Thank you for...what are you doing?"

Gabe put the car into park and turned off the ignition. He didn't answer her until he'd rounded the vehicle and cupped her elbow in his hand. "Walking you up to your apartment."

She tried, in vain, to pull away from him. "That isn't necessary. Besides, you left your car in a no-parking zone."

His teeth flashed in the darkness. "Don't worry. I know someone who can fix tickets for me."

"An admission of corruption," she muttered as he steered her toward the door of the building, "from one of CPD's finest. My, my, how surprising."

"I can also spring that security code for you if you're not going to punch it in. Lose your key? The inside lock will take ten seconds, tops." He gave a shrug. "Some talents never leave you."

She gave him a sidelong glance as she tapped in her code on the security panel. "Rather odd 'talents' for a detective to admit to. Did you pick them up from your days in the academy?''

He scanned the street quickly, then opened the door and ushered her inside. ''No, from my days as a delinquent.''

His answer succeeded in keeping her silent all the way up to the fourth floor. Knowing it would be fruitless to try and leave him at the elevator, she suffered through having him accompany her to her door, take the key from her and open it.

''Thank you. Again.'' She snatched the key away from him and dropped it back in her purse. There was no gratitude in her tone, and she was certain he realized it.

His lips quirked slightly. ''No problem. Again. Where's Callie live?''

''Why?''

His smile grew wider at the thread of caution in the word. ''That's where Danny is, right? I figure she wouldn't leave her son and maybe her husband to come over here and sit, so Danny must be over there.''

She heaved a sigh. It had been an impossibly long day, and this man was partly responsible for that. The sooner he was on his way, the sooner she could get her life back to normal. Or what passed for normal these days.

''She just lives a few doors that way. Now if you...'' Her words tapered off as he began to stride in the direction she'd indicated.

She trailed in his wake like an obedient puppy and didn't care for the feeling. ''Detective, I've thanked you for the ride, but it's time for you to leave.''

''The kid's probably asleep. You shouldn't be carrying him. Which door?''

''I'm perfectly capable of carrying him—no, God not that one.'' Meghan managed to catch his arm before he could pound on Edna Hathaway's door. ''All you're liable to find in that apartment is a seventy-eight-year-old lady with an eye for expensive vodka and anything in pants.'' The warn-

ing wasn't exaggerated in the slightest. "I heard that it took
three days to resuscitate the last man who went in there."

He grinned at her over his shoulder. "Sounds interesting." He'd managed to surprise her. He could see it in her
eyes and the way her mouth tilted in response. He watched
closely, wanting, more than he should have, to see her smile
break free. And then he stared, staggered when it did, lightening her expression and softening her eyes. His stomach
jittered oddly, and he couldn't take his gaze off her, not
even when her smile faded to be replaced by her earlier
coolness.

She moved past him to a door on the opposite side of the
hall and tapped lightly. A few moments later it opened and
a woman Gabe recognized from that afternoon appeared in
the doorway. "Hi. I thought you'd be later. I went ahead
and put Danny down on the couch. They begged to stay in
Alex's room but I knew my chances of getting them to sleep
there were nonexistent."

"It didn't take as long as I thought." Meghan moved
through the doorway, with Gabe right behind her. Spotting
the boy curled up on the couch, he crossed the room, bent
down and lifted him easily in his arms.

"He gave me a ride home…it's a long story," he heard
Meghan murmur to her friend.

"Well," Callie replied, turning to follow the three to the
door, "you can tell me about it tomorrow. *All* about it."
As the door closed behind her and Meghan hurried to catch
up with Connally's long strides, she tried not to imagine
the conversation she was going to be in for the next morning.

She caught up with the detective in her living room,
where he was waiting patiently for her. "Which is his
room?"

"Really, you've done enough. If you'd just put him
down…" When the man continued to stand there, clearly
with no intention of complying, she gave in with ill grace

and led him down the hallway. She picked up his treasured Pokémon backpack and tossed it to the end of the bed, before pulling the covers down. Connally moved past her without a sound and gently laid the boy down on the lower of the two bunk beds.

Pulling the covers up and tucking them around her nephew, Megan paused an instant. His breathing was even and deep, and there was a slight flush on his face, which still held some baby fullness. There was an unexpected catch deep in her chest, and in an unconscious gesture, her hand reached out, hovered.

"He's a good-looking kid."

The deep voice rumbling in her ear made her start, and she snatched her hand away. Putting a finger to her lips, she walked to the door and waited for Connally to follow. Then she flipped on the hallway light, being careful to leave Danny's door open. By the time she'd led him back to the living room she'd run out of both patience and composure. "It's been a long day. I'm going to follow Danny's lead and retire soon myself."

Her attempt at a dismissal failed sadly. Connally's mouth quirked. "Could I get a glass of water before you throw me out?"

"I'm not—" Pressing her lips together midprotest, Meghan turned and marched to the kitchen. There was something about that man, she fumed, snatching a glass from the cupboard and waiting for the water to run cold, that had her stuttering and stammering like an adolescent. She seemed to have difficulty finishing a sentence around him, and she suspected that he deliberately tried to keep her off balance.

When she returned with the glass, Connally wasn't where she'd left him. Instead, he'd poked into her study, and seemed quite at home surveying the works in progress she had tacked up on the walls.

The sight stoked her temper further. She'd never enjoyed

having people look at her work before it was finished. Even her agent didn't see her sketches until she'd painstakingly redone them to her satisfaction. Privacy was something that had been hard fought for, hard won. She didn't relinquish it easily.

"Your water, Detective." Her voice was several degrees cooler than the liquid in the glass. He didn't turn at her voice. He was shaking his head slowly.

"Wow. These are yours, right?"

The admiration in his tone slightly soothed nerves that were scraped and raw. "Yes. I'm currently working on illustrations for another Milton Cramer book. It's about a lonely monster who's looking for friends, but I'm going to have to scale some of these drawings back. I'm afraid they might give the children nightmares."

Gabe walked from one large sketch to another, studying each carefully. "You're probably right. They kinda give a chill." He sent her a measuring glance. "I read you had something to do with art, but I figured maybe one of those high-priced galleries or something. The ones where they hang pictures that don't look like anything."

Her earlier calm shattered as she grasped the meaning behind his words. "You 'read'?" He'd used those same words earlier, she remembered, when he'd spoken about Sandra. Her eyes narrowed. "Am I correct in assuming you've been checking up on me?"

He seemed unfazed by the fury on her face, in her voice. "Hazard of the job." He approached her and took the glass from her hands and drank. "You didn't seem to want to explain any further about your sister, so I did a little checking."

The ease with which he explained away prying into her life, her *family,* with all its twisted, dysfunctional fragments, made her shake with anger.

"Well, I have to hand it to you, Detective. You move fast." She went toward the door, her movements jerky, and yanked it open. "I'm sure they have quite a file on Sandra at CPD. The cops always liked to do a background check before they decided to use her in any way they could."

He sipped from the glass and watched her, his pale eyes giving nothing away. "If there's a file, I haven't seen it. I pulled up the *Tribune*'s archives. You've gotten a fair amount of press yourself over the years."

His words were like a blade, tearing through the fragile shroud of privacy she'd sought for so many years. Seclusion had always proved elusive for her family. The huge gates around the family estate had seemed more effective at keeping them in, than in keeping the rest of the world out. Her hand clenched on the knob, longing to slam the door shut with a resounding bang, preferably on him.

"You're mad."

"It must be your excellent deductive skills that earned you the rank of detective." He didn't appear about to leave. When a neighboring tenant walked by the open door and glanced in curiously, Meghan swung it shut, wishing the detective's big foot were caught in it.

"I can understand why you might blame the department for what happened to your sister."

She regarded him warily from her position by the door. For some reason she was loath to get any closer. "Thanks. You can't know what your validation of my opinion means to me."

He thought it wise to ignore her sarcasm. "I've pieced together enough to figure out how it went down. Your sister offered to help Wadrell with his investigation. Word somehow got to the press that a psychic was being consulted. The media dug up her name and that was made public, too. Your sister wound up dead and you think the gang Wadrell was investigating is responsible." He watched her soberly. "And you blame the police."

The brief dispassionate narrative made Meghan's mouth go dry. The words, honed with truth, arrowed with painful accuracy. "They didn't protect her. She put herself at risk to help them and then ended up with her name in headlines. It was an open invitation for those thugs to go after her."

Interest flickered in his eyes. "Do you know for certain that she was threatened?" Wadrell, when pressed, had claimed otherwise.

Meghan looked away. "Sandra didn't mention anything, no." In masterful understatement she continued, "But then, we weren't particularly close."

He was silent for a moment. "In any case, I think you had a legitimate fear. One that deserved to be looked into."

"According to your department, it was looked into. Are you going to spew the party line, too, and tell me that her car accident was just a coincidence?"

Her words were delivered like a dare. Because he recognized the pain underlying them, he kept his tone even. "Is that what you were told?"

Voice brittle, she said, "I was assured that a thorough investigation of the accident was conducted. Sandra supposedly went over that embankment because she misjudged the curve, not because the car had been tampered with. It was just plain old bad luck, but gee, the department sure regrets our loss." She stopped then, and pressed her lips firmly together.

"But you don't believe that."

"Would you?"

He set the glass down on a nearby table and then straightened again. "If I were in your shoes? Probably not."

Her gaze swung back to him. She'd expected him to ridicule her beliefs, or to hotly defend his department's ethics. His failure to do either took her off guard. "What's that supposed to mean?" He unzipped his battered leather jacket and slipped his hands in the pockets. His stance drew her eyes to the width of the shoulders, the narrow waist and lean hips. The body was as impressive as the face. He radiated strength, determination and heat. She had no doubt that countless women had been attracted to that combination, had sought to warm themselves with his fire. She was equally certain that each of them had ended up badly burned.

He shrugged, snagging her attention again. "Since you're blaming the department for your sister's name being made public, you'd be apt to question the investigation of the accident." Taking a step backward, he leaned one shoulder against the wall. "I'm still having trouble trying to figure out why you'd go to Wadrell for help with this. I'd think with the grudge you're carrying, he'd be the last one you'd trust, seeing that he was primary detective on the case your sister was involved with."

Because he owes us!

The hot words blazed across her mind, but remained unuttered. She had no intention of explaining herself to this man. "Yes," she replied flatly. "He was."

She crossed to the couch and sank down on it. She didn't like the way Connally watched her, as if he could read her emotions, the jumbled pain, anger and regret, all too clearly. His scrutiny made her uncomfortable, although it shouldn't have. She was a master at shielding her thoughts. She had her childhood with Sandra to thank for that.

"Detective Wadrell naturally feels badly about my sister's death." Only the slightest hint of irony tinged her words. "He's offered to look into the accident report himself, double-check the conclusions by running them by another investigator he knows."

Connally said nothing, only continued to watch her. A sense of unease slid down her spine. There was a stillness about the man that had her nerves prickling. All his concentration, all his considerable energy was focused on her, and the intensity was unsettling. She wondered if he used this brooding contemplation to effect, when staring down a suspect. There was something about the simmering silence that made her want to fill the void with words, though she'd never been one to babble.

With effort, she glanced away, crossed one leg over the other and smoothed her skirt. She'd expected the detective to chide her for her lack of faith in the CPD, rather than express understanding. But it didn't matter. Nothing he could say would sway her from her goal, at any rate. She'd use Wadrell just as he'd used her sister. There was no question of feeling guilty about it. The cost of Sandra's cooperation with the department had been high. Danny had lost a mother. Meghan had lost a sister. She'd never believe that a simple accident was the cause. Nothing about Sandra had ever been simple. Certainly not her death.

"Is Wadrell hoping you'll take your sister's place in his investigation?"

Her head jerked up. Gabe's expression was inscrutable. "No. Sandra's ability isn't exactly something that runs in the family, like blond hair." She held her breath, wondering if he'd accept the blatant untruth.

He nodded, and she breathed a little easier. She doubted whether he was convinced of the authenticity of Sandra's talent, at any rate. He struck her as a very pragmatic man. He'd believe only what he could see, could prove.

"Wadrell's a decent cop, but there's not a considerate bone in his body. I can only think of one other reason he'd offer to help. And that's to get close to you."

"Do you think I don't know that, Detective?" It was her turn to surprise him. She took a grim satisfaction in his reaction. "I'm not naive. I know exactly what motivated your buddy's offer of assistance. And I don't care what his intentions are, as long as I get what I want."

With slow, deliberate movements he pushed away from the wall and approached her, one methodical step at a time. He set the glass down and braced his hands on the coffee table. Face close to hers, he murmured, sotto voce, "He's *not* my buddy."

His proximity leeched the air from her lungs. She'd underestimated the man. His presence was even more compelling up close, close enough for her to see the flecks of gold in his pale eyes, near enough for her to reach up a hand and trace every hard angle of his face.

Her fingers curled into her palms. She refused to let him see the effect he had on her, the cost of her careless shrug. "Sorry. From what you said it sounded like you knew him well."

He gazed at her a moment longer, then slowly straightened. Her strangled lungs drew in much-needed oxygen. "I know him well enough to realize he's not the type to do a favor without expecting something in return."

He wasn't saying anything she hadn't already figured out for herself, but the words, spoken out loud, made her hesitate. She'd taken grim satisfaction in the idea of using Wadrell to answer the questions she still had about the accident. It was, she'd thought, no more than was due them. And if he expected more than she was willing to give in return, rejection was exactly what he deserved. Although, she remembered, with a faint shudder, having to dodge his interest tonight had filled her with nothing short of revulsion.

"I can handle Wadrell," she said with more assurance than she felt. Her words clearly failed to convince Connally. He was regarding her with something like derision in his eyes.

"I guess it depends on your definition of the word. From where I sat tonight it looked like you were the one being handled."

Meghan flushed. She looked good with temper flaring in her eyes and coloring her cheeks, Gabe decided. She wasn't as emotionless as she would have him believe. Why that should matter to him he didn't know, except that it would have been a shame if a woman who looked like her was really as cold and as closed off as she pretended to be.

He folded his arms over his chest. "Let's look at your

options here. As far as the department goes, your sister's accident is a closed case. You said yourself Wadrell's motives are suspect. Why would you trust him to follow through on his promise?''

"Are you worried about me, Detective?" Her voice was mocking. "Don't be. I learned a long time ago that the only person I can trust is myself."

Her statement hit him with the force of a punch. He could have echoed the words himself; certainly he believed the same. But he knew the kind of knocks it had taken to shape his cynical point of view. For reasons he couldn't explain, he didn't like to consider the kind of experiences that might have shaped hers.

He perched on her coffee table, retaining a position close to her. "There's no use taking stupid chances if you don't have to. Wadrell's a slime. You know he's more interested in your body than in your sister's death."

Her chin angled and she met him stare for stare. "Why do you care?"

Their gazes battled for long moments before Gabe finally answered. "Let's just say that I don't like to see people taken advantage of. And I've never been a fan of Wadrell's."

Meghan looked beyond his shoulder to the clock on the wall. It was after ten. Early, really. But all of a sudden she was weary, clear to the bone. The time she'd spent with Wadrell had put her on edge. She still didn't doubt her ability to keep him at arm's length, but she was beginning to question the wisdom of her plan. She would have only the detective's word, after all, that he'd actually conducted another investigation into the accident. She'd have no reason to believe him. And no choice not to. When Danny was old enough to be given the details, the very least he deserved were the facts involved in his mother's death. All of them.

She glanced at Connally again. Sitting atop her table, he

was much too close. Much too...physical. He was big enough to project a subtle threat sheerly through his stature. The breadth of his heavy shoulders blocked her view of the room behind him, and the broad chest beneath his crossed arms depicted a certain power. In a studiedly casual move, she settled more deeply into the couch cushions. It was ridiculous to feel that the slight movement had put some much-needed distance between them. Ridiculous, because there was nothing about his actions or his expression to suggest she had anything to fear from him.

Except that he was a cop. He was in her apartment, and he was intent on dragging Danny into the middle of a police investigation.

"I have another option for you to consider." His voice, coming after a minute of silence, seemed raspier than usual. "Forget Wadrell. Let me help you instead."

She looked at him as if he'd lost his mind. Maybe he had. He'd never be considered one of those white knights charging to rescue ladies in distress. He found jackets and ties confining enough; armor would be murder.

He shook off the fanciful thought. "You want something. So do I. I'll take another look into the accident for you. In return, you'll cooperate by allowing Danny to assist us in any way we need him." As if sensing the protest she was about to utter, he went on quickly, "You get what you want, I get what I want. It'll be strictly business." Her cooperation would make his job easier. He didn't want to chance her sabotaging him at every turn, maybe even coaching the boy to tell them nothing. He needed every lead he could get on this case.

Everything inside Meghan recoiled from accepting his offer. For different reasons, she was even more loath to spend time in his presence than she was in Wadrell's. And there was no way, absolutely none, that she would let Danny get embroiled with the police. She knew nothing about raising children. But the one thing she did know was that her psychic ability had ruined Sandra's life. If she could spare Danny only one thing, it would be that.

Connally was speaking again. "Of course, maybe you have other reasons to want to stick with Wadrell. Maybe you really wouldn't mind if you and he..." He made a gesture with his hand which, along with his tone, made his message clear.

Meghan's indignation overcame her caution. "Believe me, I find cops eminently resistible. For that matter, how can I be sure that I wouldn't have to fight off *your* advances?"

He didn't appear to take offense. "'Cause I make it a point to steer wide of your type. So if we partner up for a while, you won't have to worry about me coming on to you."

He watched her intently, but when she failed to respond, he said, "If you need convincing..." Before she could guess his intention, he leaned forward in one smooth movement and covered her mouth with his own.

Shock held Meghan motionless. The man was completely outrageous! She managed to raise her hand to his chest before her bones began to take on the consistency of warm wax. It was like kissing a flash of lightning, she thought fuzzily—all sizzling heat and banked strength. There was an unexpected measure of wildness to his taste, layered beneath a hint of tightly harnessed control.

He wasn't a man to ask permission, and there was no entreaty in his touch. Her hand lingered, forgotten, on his chest as he angled his head and pressed her lips open. His tongue boldly swept in, exchanging her flavor for his own.

Her heart spun once, then kicked a faster beat. He tasted foreign, and primally male. His hand cupped her jaw, his fingers caressing her throat, and the dual assault made her shiver and want, with a suddenness that was all the more frightening for its being completely unfamiliar.

His mouth lifted from hers a fraction, lingered a moment, then eased away.

She stared at him, stunned. "Just what was that supposed to convince me of?" Her voice was threadier than she would have wished, but at least it was steady.

Gabe reached for the glass he'd set down, and brought it to his lips for a long swallow. His eyes avoided hers. "Just proving my point. Neither of us is attracted to the other. That kiss left you cold, right? Me, too."

Cold? Numb, maybe. Achy, certainly. But cold? A sheerly feminine ire fueled her next words. "The next time you try conducting a little experiment like that you'd better be wearing protection." She left no doubt that she wasn't referring to his gun. "The only point you convinced me of is that I'm no better off with you than with Wadrell."

He looked impatient at her words. "Use your head." Holding up his fingers, he enumerated, "One, I'm not the detective you hold indirectly responsible for your sister's death. Two, I outrank Wadrell and I'm better liked. I've got guys who'll be willing to do me favors when I poke into the accident investigation. I doubt Wadrell can get his own mother to invite him to Sunday dinner. And three, we've just shown that physically we don't do a thing for each other."

She crossed her arms over her chest to keep from strangling him.

"You won't have to worry about me making moves on you, because I like women with more obvious…uh… charms." He cocked his head, pretending not to see the simmer of latent temper in her eyes. "Unless…you can't do that little tassel trick I've seen, can you? You know—" his index fingers circled in the air in front of his chest "— the one where you get them going in opposite directions?" When she didn't respond, *couldn't,* he shook his head. "I didn't think so. So as near as I can tell, us matching up would be perfect. There'll be no personal interest on my side, and if you can promise the same there won't be any complications at all.''

The deep-breathing exercises learned at Miss Devain's School of Deportment had never been more necessary. The actual physical effort of filling her lungs with oxygen almost took Meghan's mind off the shockingly primal urge to knock that complacent expression off Connally's face. The strength of the temptation was shocking. Civility was a quality not only valued by her family, but demanded. Tremaynes didn't indulge in spectacles. There had been no public displays of temper or of affection. Every conversation, every cutting remark, was made in the same chillingly dispassionate tone. The genuine lack of emotion displayed by her mother and grandparents had confused and saddened Meghan by turns.

However, it wasn't a lack of emotion that was bothering Meghan right now, but the imminent volcanic eruption that this man was close to eliciting. Her gaze narrowed at his bland expression. He was goading her; he had to be. Surely no one could be that irritating, unless by design. What he was suggesting was out of the question. There was no way she was going to shackle herself to Connally willingly, no matter what he promised to do for her.

When she didn't respond, he shrugged and rose. ''Let me know if you change your mind. I've got one piece of advice for you, though. Stay in public places when you meet with Wadrell. You'll be safer there.''

His words triggered the memory of what she'd gone through to avoid Wadrell's touch earlier that evening, and a renewed shudder of revulsion prickled her skin. Connally was right about one thing. She didn't relish having to fight off the other detective's smarmy advances.

She glanced at Connally, reconsidering. She could make Danny's cooperation dependent upon him showing her evidence of a renewed look at Sandra's accident. She'd get what she wanted up-front, and that would be the end of their agreement.

Because of course she had no intention of going through with her side of the arrangement.

Ruthlessly she brushed aside a whisper of conscience. She didn't owe anything to this man, especially after his recent display. And the CPD certainly didn't rate her honesty. The only one she owed was Danny. And the sister who would never know the lengths to which Meghan had gone to make amends for a lifetime of estrangement between them.

"You may have a point." His hand on the knob of the front door, Gabe looked back at her words. She moistened her lips nervously. "You understand that I'll require something solid to convince me that you actually followed up on the accident."

He regarded her soberly. "And you understand that I'll hold you to your end of our bargain."

It took effort not to reveal the direct hit his words had scored. "Of course."

He gave a short nod. "I'll be in touch, then." He opened the door and advised, "You'd better lock this after me."

She approached silently. Gabe gave her a long look, then she swung the door shut on him. He stood, listening to the sound of her securing the dead bolt. Then he released a long breath and started down the hall, feeling as though he'd just run a marathon.

He was a master at getting what he wanted, but he'd have to admit that this was the first time he'd had to deny any attraction to a woman in exchange for her cooperation. It had taken a lot of talking, and more, to convince Meghan that she had nothing to fear from him physically, that he didn't want her, on any level. The words had been easy to say, easier to mean...until he'd tasted her and felt a surge of violent emotion that proved otherwise.

He gave an involuntary look upward. Lucky for him that God didn't smite down bald-faced liars. He'd have been a goner.

Chapter 4

Gabe hunched over the steaming cup of coffee on his desk, wishing he could just inject the caffeine into his bloodstream without the necessity of actually swallowing the stuff. It was the unwritten rule of every squad room he'd been in that the coffee had to be as thick and black as sludge, and just as tasty.

In front of him was the report from D'Brusco's parole officer. According to it, Lenny had lined up a job shortly after his release from prison. As manager of Ultimate Video, he was in charge of a full half-dozen branch stores in the city. That a convicted felon would be put in charge of any business involving cash was in itself cause for suspicion. He was dying to ask Lenny's superior how the ex-con had come to be hired. But they hadn't caught up with the guy yet. Supposedly he was out of the country.

The smell of the coffee beckoned, promising a caffeine jolt that Gabe badly needed. He used to do his best thinking over a morning cup of coffee and a cigarette. The nicotine was out, and after the restless night he'd spent, the coffee was his only hope. Wincing a little, he lifted the cup to his lips and manfully took a gulp.

"Yech!" The acrid brew seared its way through his system. He could almost feel his stomach lining peeling under its impact. "You'd think someone around here could learn to make decent coffee."

"I think they just warmed up yesterday's," one of the other detectives offered. Grimacing, Gabe took another swallow.

Cal looked up from the report he was reading and frowned disapprovingly. "You can't believe how much better I've felt since I gave up caffeine."

Gabe sipped again, more carefully this time. "Yeah, I was there when you were going through withdrawal. You were in prime shape, all right."

"The cravings don't last long. And the organic juices that Becky buys aren't that bad. Once I started drinking them, I felt fitter and stronger almost immediately."

"I liked you better when you were weak and unhealthy." Gabe hadn't even gotten over his urge for nicotine yet. The thought of giving up caffeine, as well, had him raising the mug again. The coffee might not have been so critical if he'd gotten a decent night's sleep. But memories of that brief kiss he'd shared with Meghan had been annoyingly persistent. Mere seconds shouldn't have left him with such exquisite recall of the taste of her mouth, silky and warm, or the touch of her skin, almost unbearably soft. Her scent curled through his memory, a drift of something mysterious and alluring. It was unusual for him to lose sleep over any female. It was even more unusual for thoughts of a woman to tangle in his mind, refusing to be shaken.

A small eraser whizzed past his face and narrowly missed landing in his coffee mug. Cocking a brow, he looked at Cal. "Those juices haven't improved your aim any."

"And the caffeine hasn't improved your listening skills. I asked you what you thought of bringing the kid in and having him look at some pictures, try to ID Lenny's friend. Get your mind off spending the upcoming weekend with your flavor of the month and concentrate, will you?''

Slouched in his chair, legs propped on his desk and crossed at the ankle, Gabe still managed an indignant expression. ''I'm *trying* to concentrate. But you keep interrupting me.''

Cal rolled his eyes. ''Yeah, I forgot. Genius at work always looks like a nap in a hammock.''

''Just so you recognize the genius, pal. And we're not going to pull the kid in just yet.'' He reached forward, set the mug on his desk.

''Don't tell me you're beginning to doubt being able to work your magic on the Patterson woman? Could it be fear that the mighty Connally charm will strike out?''

Gabe linked his hands behind his head. ''My lifetime batting average notwithstanding, it's too early to play that card.'' The fact that he had to bribe Meghan to get the boy's cooperation wasn't something he wanted to share with his partner. ''We'd just be fishing at this point, anyway. We haven't come up with any KAs that match the description the kid gave us. When we bring him in, I want it to count. His aunt still isn't real happy about his involvement in this case. I doubt we'll get more than one shot with him.''

Looking doubtful, Cal said, ''Maybe we shouldn't count on being able to use the kid at all. Patterson didn't look like the type to change her mind.''

''She already has.'' Gabe didn't attempt to keep the smugness from his voice. ''We've reached an agreement. She'll let the boy help, but it's not a card I want to play until we have to.''

Uh-oh. He'd said too much. Cal's eyes narrowed speculatively. ''You and she reached an agreement.''

''Yep.'' The phone on his desk rang then, and he reached for it in gratitude, strangely unwilling to share all the details of the arrangement he'd made with Meghan. After a few moments he dropped the receiver in its cradle and looked at his partner. "That was Parker at the twenty-first. He mentioned a few places we could look for Siemons." Eddie Siemons had been the informant who'd been responsible for bringing D'Brusco's activities to the attention of the police. He'd been dubbed Fast Eddie by vice detectives for the swiftness with which he offered up information in return for a blind eye being turned to his own activities. It was he who had shared some details about D'Brusco in an effort to get Parker to drop a pandering charge against him. The tip had been passed on to the organized crime unit and landed in Gabe's and Cal's laps. Since Lenny's disappearance, they had a few more questions for the man.

Gabe swung his feet off his desk, but Madison didn't move. "So you saw Ms. Patterson last night? And you managed to convince her to allow the boy to help?" Gabe rose and shrugged into his rumpled suit jacket, jamming a hand in one pocket to pull out an equally crumpled tie, which he slipped on and knotted. The action succeeded in switching his partner's focus. "When's the last time you had that jacket dry-cleaned?"

Donning his leather coat, Gabe lifted a shoulder. "What difference does it make? It's not dirty."

Cal slipped his parka over his muted gray suit coat. "A good pressing wouldn't hurt it."

Tone lofty, Gabe informed him, "I'm not interested in making a fashion statement."

"The way you dress you're more like a fashion tragedy." Gabe waited until his partner had started away from the desk, still detailing Gabe's failures in the fashion department, and then stealthily slipped open his middle desk drawer and reached nimble fingers inside.

"And you never did explain how you happened to see Ms. Patterson again last night." Cal swung around. "I hope you didn't—"

Suspicion stamped Cal's face as Gabe froze. "What are

you doing, Connally? Do you have *cigarettes* in there?'' He rapidly retraced his steps.

"Of course not.'' Indignation threading his voice, Gabe withdrew a pen and held it up for his partner to see. "I was just getting my lucky pen.'' He slammed the drawer shut before Cal rounded the desk. "You're getting to be a real nag, you know it?''

Cal's gaze traced between the closed desk drawer and Gabe's face, before he gradually relaxed. "I'm just trying to help you quit.'' The two men made their way through the maze of desks while Cal embarked on yet another of his endless sermons on the hazards of smoking. Gabe's concentration drifted. He'd heard it all before. He had more important things on his mind, at any rate. There was Siemons to find and work. He still needed to get someone lined up to look into Barton's accident for Meghan. The sooner he fulfilled his end of their agreement, the sooner she'd let the kid cooperate.

And then he needed to find a different hiding place for his last stash of nicotine. A bloodhound had nothing on Cal.

In the car Gabe gave his partner an abbreviated version of his meeting with Meghan last night, leaving out the details of their arrangement. Conducting a private investigation of a closed case wasn't exactly against department regulations, but it usually didn't earn one any friends, either. Gabe didn't doubt his ability to discreetly get the information he needed, but decided against burdening Cal with all the facts. His partner had a way of asking way too many questions.

They tried all the locations Parker had mentioned, but were unable to find Siemons. Finally they parked outside the man's shabby duplex and prepared to wait for him.

"You ever figure how much time we spend sitting in a car waiting on some punk?''

"Yeah.'' Cal's voice sounded odd. Gabe slanted a look

at him. "I wonder sometimes what it would be like to work a nine-to-five job. Someplace you just punch out and leave the work at the office."

"Becky after you to quit the force?"

The other man caught his partner's gaze on him and said hastily, "No, of course not. But things change after you get married, you know? You start to imagine what it would be like for your wife to open the door to a pair of uniforms, knowing they're there to tell her you bought it in the line of duty."

"I guess." It *was* different for Cal, Gabe acknowledged, because now the man had someone to consider besides himself. And he recognized the unspoken truth in the man's words, as well. In the event of Gabe's death, there'd be no address to send the uniforms to. His foster parents had retired five years ago and moved to Florida.

"The thing is—" Cal stared out the window "—we've kinda been thinking about having a baby. Guess you could say we're in the planning stage."

Nothing he could have said would have shocked Gabe more. Clearing his throat, he searched for an appropriate answer. "Yeah? That's great. I mean…good luck with that."

His partner shrugged, embarrassed. "Well, now you know what made me start thinking. Not that I'd ever quit the department, but a man has to consider his family's security."

"I guess." What Gabe knew about family, the kind of family Cal meant, wouldn't fill a thimble. He could admire his partner for his ambitions in that direction while shying away from the idea himself. There was something to be said for having only yourself to consider. There was no one to disappoint then, because no one was relying on you. And if alone sometimes meant lonely, that could be dealt with. The thought of making the kind of commitment Cal was talking about terrified him.

To break the monotony and distract them both, Gabe leaned forward and reached into the glove compartment, withdrawing a cellophane-wrapped package of cream-filled snack cakes.

Immediately Cal groaned. "Oh, no. Don't tell me you're actually going to eat those. Why don't you just inject poison into your veins and be done with it?"

"Somehow I don't think it'd be the same."

His partner watched, half reproving, half envious. "Those things are filled with cholesterol. Do you even know what your cholesterol level is? I'll bet it's through the roof. Do you realize what that means?"

"That I'm filled with buttery goodness?"

"No, that you're a heart attack waiting to happen."

Gabe waved the remaining cake in front of Cal's face. "This one's got your name on it, buddy."

The man looked away. "The difference between the two of us," he began, "is willpower. I've got it, you don't."

"Smell the fragrant junk-food aroma." Gabe continued to dangle the snack in front of Cal's face. "Think of the burst of flavor, the sugar high, the empty, delicious calories." He barely finished the words before his partner grabbed the snack from him and devoured it in three quick bites.

Cal looked at Gabe, who was convulsed with laughter. "You know how many miles on the Stairmaster it's going to take to undo this one moment of weakness?"

"Forget that. I'll bet Becky will be able to smell the junk food on your breath." Cal blanched, reached in his pocket for a breath mint. "I'm gonna have to tell her that you snuck it despite all my efforts to stop you." His partner's retort was stemmed by Gabe's next words. "There he is."

The detectives got out of the car, and Eddie spotted them immediately. He ran the last few feet to the steps in front of his duplex, and took them two at a time. Gabe and Cal made it to his door seconds behind him.

"Hey, I got nuthin else to say to you guys."

"Let's go inside, Eddie. Get off the street."

The man ignored Gabe's suggestion. "I done my part. That charge was dropped, and now I'm square with the system. I don't have to tell you nuthin' else."

"You want to have this conversation out here?" Cal inquired. "We don't care. Broad daylight, in front of your friends and neighbors...if you don't mind being seen with us, that's fine."

Considering his options, Eddie sucked in his bottom lip, making his receding chin all but disappear. A curious passerby who looked their way seemed to make up his mind. "Yeah, okay. But let's take it away from here."

Dejectedly, he walked back to the car and got in. Gabe turned on the ignition and pulled away from the curb. "You know what you just did back there?" Eddie demanded. "Man, in this neighborhood if a guy's seen talking to the likes of you he could be killed."

"We've got a little problem with that information you passed on to us." Gabe adjusted the rearview mirror to catch Eddie's reflection. "D'Brusco has disappeared."

"Yeah, that's a problem, but it ain't my problem, you know?"

"It is now." Cal said, turning in his seat to face the man. "Give us some ideas about where he might have gone. Names of people he hangs with."

"Oh, man, you guys never give up!" Eddie hunched down in the seat.

"You said you were tight with D'Brusco in the old days," Cal reminded him.

"That don't mean I know nuthin' about him now." He caught Gabe's stare in the mirror. "Yeah, okay, so we ran into each other that once. Had some beers, talked about old times."

"And he told you he was smurfing for some bigwig

whose name wasn't mentioned." Gabe's tone was impatient.

"And he was getting rich doing it. 'Course, that might not have all been from his salary."

"What's that mean?"

Eddie swallowed and wished Connally would just concentrate on driving. That glare of his made him damn nervous. "Well, he mighta said something like he was starting his own private account."

"You mean he was skimming from the take?"

"I don't know. Maybe. We were both wasted, all right? Now let me out here, I'll catch a bus home and we'll call it even."

They didn't do as he requested until after some more lengthy questioning, but they got nothing else of value from the man. He couldn't, or wouldn't, give them any ideas as to where D'Brusco had gone and claimed he had no ideas about the identity of the man Lenny had left his apartment with. Finally Gabe dropped him off in front of a bus stop, and Eddie climbed out of the car with undisguised haste.

"You know, with all the time we spend with punks like him, it's a wonder we have any faith left in humanity." Gabe steered the car into a small break in traffic.

"You see that van behind you, don't you?" Cal began. With one look from Gabe he went silent. Safety with his partner at the wheel was a chancy thing, but it was even more dangerous when Gabe argued with him. The man had a hair-raising habit of taking his eyes off the road while he was trying to make a point.

"Not to mention saints like D'Brusco," Gabe continued. They'd spent several days watching the man, whose only real job in the outlets had seemed to be to collect the daily take and deposit it in a bank. He'd used a different bank for each branch of the store, but that in itself wasn't unusual. Cal had followed him inside a few of the banks, lingering nearby while the man conducted his transaction. He'd been obviously well-known each place he went. At each a teller would address D'Brusco by name.

Trouble was, none of the names he'd been addressed by were his own.

"He had a pretty good scam going," Gabe mused. "Video rental businesses are an ideal sink—just feed cash into the system. Nobody's gonna spot an additional five hundred or a thousand coming in daily through the tills if it's done gradually. Lenny was in charge of cleaning up someone's extra cash. He just put the money with the daily take and deposited the whole thing in the bank."

"According to Eddie D'Brusco had decided to start taking a little something extra for himself," Cal said. He never took his eyes from the road, as painful as it was to watch. He preferred to know when his time was coming.

Gabe gauged the upcoming traffic light and decided he had time to make it across the intersection. The sound coming from his partner's side of the car had him grinning. "Ol' Lenny had really hit it big this time."

"Gives a whole new way of looking at his disappearance, doesn't it?"

"Way ahead of you, Cal. If someone else got wind of his private account, could be Lenny didn't escape with a friend of his after all." The two men exchanged a glance, sharing the unspoken thought. One rule of money laundering was that constant control had to be maintained over the entire process. Theft of the money couldn't exactly be reported to the police.

If their informant was correct about Lenny's secret fund, it was increasingly likely that the guy who left D'Brusco's apartment had been sent there to eliminate him.

"How do you think he's doing?"

As the woman turned the question neatly back on her, Meghan glanced over her shoulder before replying. Danny was safely out of earshot, playing contentedly with Legos in the corner of the office. "I'm not sure. He seems better. I mean, there haven't been any more outbursts."

Raina Nausman regarded her with the aura of serenity that was so much a part of her. That was the first thing Meghan had noticed about the woman upon meeting her for the first time two months ago. There was a timelessness in the woman's eyes that belied the soft wrinkles on her face, the whiteness of her hair. And the serenity was coupled with a keen insight and wisdom that had been Meghan's savior many times in recent weeks.

"So the new school continues to be a good fit."

Meghan nodded. "You were right about the small class sizes being less stressful for him. I haven't had any complaints from his teachers at all, and I've been monitoring his progress regularly."

"So, yes." Raina patted Meghan's hand as she spoke, her accent giving a lilt to her words. "We work well together."

Meghan managed a smile, but worry was still uppermost in her mind. "I just want things to be as normal as possible for him. I don't want him growing up...different."

Raina surveyed her steadily. "But he is different, Meghan. I can teach him shielding, so he will not feel bombarded by others' thoughts and emotions. I can teach him to respect the mental privacy of others. But he will always be different."

Feeling the subtle censure in the woman's voice, Meghan bit her lip, the familiar guilt and anxiety warring inside her. "I understand."

Relenting, Raina said, "As do I. You do not want Danny to make the mistakes his mother did, is this not true? And together we can prevent that. By giving him the understanding that was absent in your sister's younger years."

Understanding. Meghan met the woman's calm gaze with her own. No, there had been no attempts by her mother or grandparents to recognize the burden Sandra's ability must have been for her. Meghan was only recently coming to understand it herself. She'd been years younger than her sister; vulnerable; easy prey for the psychological ambushes Sandra had delighted in. She'd learned to fear her sister's gift and later to prevent those mental invasions. But she'd never sought to understand it until Danny.

Her gaze shifted to the boy again. He'd concocted some sort of flying machine and had it swooping through the air, making the appropriate noises. He wasn't as quiet as he'd been when he'd first come to live with her, when they'd each walked on eggshells for fear of upsetting the other. He was becoming less like the sad, too-wise wraith who slipped into and out of rooms silently, and more like a normal five-year-old boy. Some of the credit for that was due to exposure to others his age, and even more was due to the woman across from her.

Desperation had led Meghan to Raina Nausman, coupled perhaps with a touch of divine intervention. Unprepared to handle any child, Meghan had been especially ill equipped to deal with Danny. She'd thought she'd been doing the right thing entering him in school for the first time. The private kindergarten she'd carefully chosen was supposed to be one of the finest in the city.

But the problems had started almost immediately. There had been arguments and tantrums at school, and Meghan had been called on an almost-daily basis. More and more frequently the otherwise quiet little boy had engaged in outbursts at home, refusing to go back to school. Unsure of whether she was encountering a burgeoning discipline problem, delayed grief or something else, Meghan had sought help. And her search for someone to assist her in understanding the special little boy in her care had led her, eventually, to Raina.

The retired parapsychology professor had the necessary background to help Danny. And if Meghan suspected that Raina's empathy for the boy came from more than intellectual learning, she was grateful enough for the woman's help to shunt aside her own personal fears.

"He seems happy."

Meghan's gaze sought the older woman's. "Do you think so?"

Raina patted her hand again. "I do. Although he misses his mother, I believe he has adjusted well to the stability you represent for him. Children need structure."

"I suppose." There had been plenty of structure in her own childhood, Meghan recalled, in the form of edicts on behavior befitting a Tremayne, but it hadn't equaled stability. Her mother's frequent marriages, the endless parade of nannies and the upheaval Sandra had taken pleasure in causing had created chaos in her childhood. Meghan relied on common sense and advice from Callie to fashion a home life for Danny that was as normal as possible. Certainly she had nothing in her own experience to draw from.

Meghan glanced at her watch and rose to leave. Her twice-weekly visits with Raina always seemed to pass too quickly. "Danny, it's time to go. Get your coat." To Raina she said, "Thank you. Talking to you always helps me bring things into perspective."

"And what about that police detective you mentioned? Have you put him into perspective, as well?"

Meghan paused in the process of putting on her coat. With more confidence than she felt she said, "I have that matter under control."

When she'd told Raina of the incident in the alley, the woman had gently questioned the boy. To Meghan's dismay, he'd perceived some thoughts from one of the men. What he was able to relate, however, barely made sense. It was sheer rationalization, but Meghan was certain that even if they could afford to share the information with Connally, it would make little difference.

"What will you do if he should find out about Danny's ability?"

"That's exactly why I plan to keep the detective as far away from the boy as possible," Meghan said firmly. But the woman's question had caused an undeniable chill. "I don't anticipate any real problems. Detective Connally isn't really the type to believe in psychics, at any rate." Meghan tried for a smile. "The two of us make an odd pair. He wouldn't put any stock in Danny's ability, and I dwell too much on it."

"And yes," Raina said, in that gentle voice of hers, "you are perhaps worse than a nonbeliever of the phenomenon, Meghan, you are a victim to it. In the end, your barriers are more formidable, I think, than those of your detective."

Meghan faced the contents of her refrigerator unseeingly, Raina's words echoing in her mind. She welcomed the woman's familiarity with Danny's abilities, but it was distinctly unsettling to have that calm equanimity turned on her. Forcing herself to concentrate, she focused on dinner possibilities. In the past she would have been satisfied with salad or a bowl of soup, but felt compelled to offer more nourishment to Danny. Not that the boy had an exceptionally developed palate. The only things he ate without complaint were peanut butter sandwiches and pizza.

The buzzer rang, indicating a visitor outdoors. Crossing to the intercom, she pressed the button. "Yes?"

"Buzz me in, Meghan."

There was no mistaking the low timbre of that voice, just as there was no mistaking its immediate effect. The raspy tone was like a long sensuous stroke down her spine. The prickle of awareness that followed dismayed her.

"Meghan." A hint of demand had entered his voice. "I need to talk to you about our arrangement."

She didn't answer; she couldn't. No man in her dismally limited dating experience had prepared her for dealing with Gabe Connally. Frost didn't work with him; he simply ignored it. And her aloof distance that other men had complained of, some bitterly, appeared just as ineffective. With his focused intensity he was proving about as avoidable as a battering ram, and having that single-minded attention turned on her was more than a little unnerving.

Their kiss, heated and uninvited, had managed to undermine her earlier certainty about using the man and skating away unscathed. But where it had shaken her, it had left him unmoved, a fact she found both irritating and relieving. The incident had proved that she could use him for information and not worry about the consequences of unwanted attentions. Ignoring the sly inner voice questioning just how unwanted those attentions would be, she pressed the button to allow his entrance.

Minutes later she was pulling the door open to face Connally, his hands full of small covered cartons. She blinked at the incongruous sight. He walked past her through the apartment and into the kitchen. "I called earlier, but there was no answer. I figured it was early enough that you probably hadn't eaten. This Chinese place was on my way over here."

"Yes, we were out," she murmured, watching in mingled fascination and annoyance as he set the cartons on the table and started pulling open cupboards and taking out dishes. "I was just about to fix something for Danny and myself."

"No need." He set three plates on the table and began to rummage in drawers for silverware. "I brought plenty."

"Is there something I can help you with?"

Her saccharine tone was wasted on him. He didn't even look up. "No, I think I found everything. On second thought, what do you have to drink?"

"We have milk."

Both adults turned to find Danny standing in the doorway of the kitchen, looking at the large detective with wide eyes. "Aunt Meghan says you should drink milk with every meal. It's good for your bones."

Gabe quirked a brow at the boy's solemn tone. "Milk it

is, then.'' Meghan crossed the kitchen in time to prevent him from searching through her cupboards for glasses.

''Do you mind?'' she muttered through her teeth. Gabe cast a look at her and a corner of his mouth lifted.

''Not at all.'' He stood aside while she took over.

''Where's your gun?''

Gabe's attention returned to the boy. ''Locked in the trunk of my car.''

''What if you meet some bad guys on the way home?''

Pretending to give the question consideration, he said, ''Well, I guess I'd have to take them with my bare hands.''

This seemed to satisfy the boy for the moment, so Gabe shifted his focus back to Meghan. The table before him had taken on an elegance he rarely encountered outside of restaurants, complete with place mats and napkins. The cartons had been moved to the counter, where she was emptying their contents into serving bowls. ''You didn't have to go to all this trouble for me.''

The look she sent him over her shoulder was scathing. ''Don't worry, I wouldn't.''

''A nice table helps us remember nice table manners,'' Danny parroted, clearly entertained to have a guest. ''But you don't have to worry about spilling. Aunt Meggie never gets mad about spills.''

''Good to know.''

The boy looked at the dishes Meghan was placing on the table and wrinkled his nose. ''What's that? I don't like it.''

''How do you know, if you don't know what it is?''

Ignoring Gabe's words, Meghan told Danny firmly, ''You like rice and you like chicken.'' She scooped some of each onto his plate. ''Try a little bit and see.''

While the boy slowly did as he was bid, she slipped into a chair that seemed much too close to Gabe's. Surreptitiously she inched a fraction closer to her nephew and tried to make sense of the scene. Gabe Connally had bulldozed his way into her apartment, again, and was sitting at her table, as if he had every right to be there. As if he belonged there.

Firmly she avoided his gaze as she handed him one bowl after another. He seemed to shrink the small kitchen with his presence. Had she not had Danny's eating habits to distract her, she doubted she'd be able to eat at all. As it was, nerves were dancing in her stomach.

"Have you ever shot anyone?" Danny asked Gabe as he picked at the unfamiliar food on his plate.

Gabe's gaze went to Meghan first, then trained on the boy. "Yeah. I've shot some p—crooks."

The boy's eyes grew wide. "Did you kill anyone?"

Taking his time chewing, Gabe finally answered, "When cops have to fire their guns we usually try to wound the person who's shooting at us." His words seemed to satisfy the boy, but a sidelong glance to Meghan proved that his subtle verbal maneuver hadn't been lost on her. Her lovely profile could have been etched from glass. He gave a silent sigh. Clearly the conversation wasn't one that was going to inspire any additional faith in the police.

"If I eat one more bite can I have a peanut butter sandwich?" Danny wanted to know.

"Five more bites," Meghan said firmly.

The boy cocked his head, apparently in familiar territory. "Two more."

"Four."

"Three."

"Deal." She rose and made the sandwich while Danny attacked the food on his plate. When he finished, his attention shifted to Gabe again.

Searching for a subject to divert him, Gabe said, "You go to school?"

Danny nodded. "A new school. It's better than the first one Aunt Meggie made me go to."

Meghan turned quickly and slid the sandwich on Danny's plate. "There you go, buddy. Eat up."

His curiosity slightly roused, Gabe inquired, "You've been in two different schools since you came to live with Aun—your aunt?"

His mouth full of peanut butter, the boy bobbed his head in lieu of an answer. Taking a large gulp of milk, he said, "I didn't like the other one. There was too much thinking. It made my head hurt."

Gabe grinned, but his smile quickly faded as he observed Meghan's reaction to the boy's words. Her expression had stilled. When Danny glanced at her, he froze for an instant, his sandwich halfway to his mouth.

"I'm sorry, Aunt Meggie," he whispered, his voice miserable.

She flashed him a smile that was obviously forced and said, "You know what? Since this is your TV night I'm going to let you finish eating in the living room."

By the boy's incredulous expression it was apparent that this was a rare treat, indeed. He lost no time bolting from the room, plate in hand. Moments later the sounds of an animated television show drifted into the kitchen. Gabe finished eating slowly, his gaze watchful. He wasn't sure what had just passed between the two, but he was certain that something had. And although his curiosity was roused, it would be a waste of time to question Meghan about it. She was a long way from trusting him, and for some reason he was reluctant to put her in the position of lying to him again.

She got up and started clearing the table. When she reached for a dish near Gabe, his hand shot out, clamping around her wrist. Meghan hesitated, shooting him a startled look.

"Give that a rest for now. Don't you want to know why I came by?"

"I am interested in this aversion you seem to have for the telephone." With a discreet tug she freed her wrist. She curbed the urge to cover the spot he'd touched, trapping the heat that lingered there. She walked to the chair Danny had

vacated, the one safely across from the big detective—sa
and eyed him coolly.

He pushed away from the table. "I told you, I calle
earlier. I took a chance that you'd be home around dinner
time. If you hadn't been—" here a large shoulder lifted
dropped "—I would have called again later."

"That would probably be best." His steady stare was a
trifle unnerving. Meghan cleared her throat. "I mean nex
time. If there is a next time."

Gabe hooked one ankle over his knee. "There'll be a
next time, Meghan. We're partners, remember? You agreed
to that, last night."

She didn't need the reminder. Her decision had neve
seemed more foolhardy. When she'd agreed to the arrange
ment, it had seemed simple to keep Connally at a distance
She would extract the information from him easily, while
keeping Danny's secrets. But nothing about the man seemed
easy. She had a nagging suspicion that she'd seriously over
estimated her ability to handle Gabe Connally.

"I tracked down the location of your sister's car," Gabe
stated baldly. "It hasn't become scrap metal yet, so a me
chanic friend of mine is going to go look it over. If there'
something there the investigators missed, he'll find it."

"I...thank you."

He watched Meghan carefully, noting the barely percep
tible tremor in her hand as she smoothed one edge of the
place mat on the table before her. "It's pay-up time
Meghan." Her gaze jerked to his, held. "I kept my word
It's time to keep yours."

"Not quite." Her voice admirably steady, she never too
her eyes off his. "I told you I was going to need proof tha
you actually followed through before I allowed Danny t
cooperate."

His gaze narrowed. "I have to provide you with proof
but I'm to take your offer of cooperation on faith, is tha
it?"

"Exactly."

He let loose a breath that was half frustration, half disbelief. "You don't want much, do you?"

She pressed imaginary wrinkles out of the place mat with quick, nervous movements. "Those are the terms." She held her breath, a part of her almost wishing he'd refuse. Surely there must be an easier way to get what she wanted without having to deal with this man. She gauged his reaction carefully, noted the inscrutable expression on his face.

"Let me get this straight." Was that sarcasm she heard in his voice? "You're saying that I just have to trust you?"

She met his gaze squarely and pushed back the mingled dread and guilt his words elicited. "Yes. That's what I'm saying."

Danny's attention strayed from the TV to the murmur of voices coming from the kitchen. He wondered if Aunt Meggie was mad that he'd talked about his old school in front of that detective. He tried hard to remember what he could say and what he was supposed to keep quiet. It made him tired sometimes, trying to keep it all straight. But he hoped Aunt Meggie wasn't mad at him.

He sat really quiet on the couch and turned the TV down with the remote, but he still couldn't hear what the grown-ups were talking about. He didn't know why the big detective was at their house. He wasn't like the men who had come to see his mom sometimes. And Aunt Meggie didn't laugh a lot and talk loud like his mom did around those men, either. Sometimes he thought she really didn't like the man much, and other times he thought she might be scared of him. But he didn't try to check for sure. Raina told him it was cheating to peek in people's heads.

Meggie. That was what his mom had called her, Danny remembered. But she'd said it in a voice that was hard and kinda mean. He didn't know how anyone could be mean to Aunt Meggie. She was nice and never yelled.

Scrambling off the couch, he took his plate and set it carefully on the table with the lamp on it. There were only a few crumbs on the couch, so he pushed them onto the floor. Then, with a glance at the kitchen door, he climbed back up on the couch and turned to look at the TV again. But he wasn't really thinking about TV.

Danny wondered if Aunt Meggie and the detective were telling secrets. The thought made his stomach feel funny. He didn't like secrets. His mom had told him one, and then she got dead.

He stared hard at the TV, but tears burned his eyes anyway. His mom would be mad if she knew he hadn't told Aunt Meggie the secret by now. He grabbed the remote and turned the volume way up, but the noise couldn't drown out the worried thoughts that crept like shadowy animals in his mind. He was supposed to show his aunt what his mom gave him. That's what she'd said.

But he hadn't told, and it wasn't an accident, either, like sometimes when he forgot things. He hadn't told on purpose. Because the secret had made his mom dead. He didn't know how he knew that, but he did.

And telling Aunt Meggie the secret just might make her dead, too.

Chapter 5

"Geez, the mope was living like a king." Gabe prowled around D'Brusco's apartment, using one gloved hand to pick up a small gold, sharp-edged blade. "You see this? He used solid gold to run his lines to fry his brains with. Sure a long ways from the cockroach-infested life he was leading the last time I busted him."

Cal glanced over and grunted. "Has he always been a user?"

"Yeah." Gabe replaced the blade next to the tell-tale white substance on the table. "Smack was his choice a few years ago, but he must have acquired a different taste. Looks like he was interrupted before he got to enjoy the private party he had planned."

They proceeded with the search, pulling out drawers, painstakingly going through the contents, examining furniture. Gabe left his partner to do a quick search of the kitchen. There wasn't much food in the refrigerator but the imported beer and expensive wine kept there had to have set D'Brusco back a bundle. Again, Gabe was struck by the heights to which the punk had risen. Quite a step up for a former fence. He let the refrigerator door swing shut and rummaged through the cupboards for a few minutes. When he moved to examine the sink, he hit pay dirt.

Cal heard his whistle of discovery and called from the living room, "Whaddya got?"

Gabe went into the living room, holding a large freezer bag aloft. "Pretty clever guy. Had his dope stashed in the garbage disposal. Guess we can figure he didn't eat in a lot."

He placed the bag into evidence, then watched Cal grapple with the entertainment center. "You want to give me a hand here?" his partner finally asked. "I think this front panel is false." Gabe got on the other side of it, and together the two men wrested the paneled piece off the furniture.

Eyebrows skimming upward, Gabe murmured, "Lenny is just chock-full of surprises isn't he?" He watched Cal reach in and pull out bundle after bundle of bills. He joined him in counting the piles, then they looked at each other. "Damn near thirty thousand dollars. Hell of a nest egg."

"Whatever he was up to, he was getting paid pretty damn well for it," Cal said.

"Or else this is the private stash Eddie was talking about."

They moved into the bedroom, and a broad grin split Gabe's face. "Hey, Cal, isn't this the honeymoon suite you brought Becky to?"

"Ah, the famed Connally wit," Cal retorted. "Immature, and yet...not funny."

The room was decorated in a style reminiscent of early American brothels. The mirrored ceilings and heavy drapes lent an even tackier air to the tasteless artwork that adorned the walls. Assuming—Gabe squinted at the naked forms frolicking in one of the paintings—they would qualify as art.

The two men worked silently. Gabe pulled the drawers

out of the dresser, riffled through them, then checked inside the bureau itself. A pleased sound escaped him. "Looks like Lenny forgot all about laws prohibiting felons from owning guns." He released the heavy tape securing a Sig revolver from its hiding place, and held it up for Cal to see.

"The protection wasn't going to do him much good kept in there."

"Probably a second piece. And from the kind of money he was running with, he needed it."

The rest of the room turned up little more than D'Brusco's fetish for exceedingly raunchy porn. They moved to the closet, and Cal shook his head in disapproval. "Even money can't buy him taste, can it?" The suits the man favored featured eye-popping colors and loud patterns. Grateful for the gloves he wore, Gabe gingerly checked the pockets of the suits and trousers.

"Look at these."

Gabe turned to look at the wallet his partner had drawn from one of the suit jackets. Inside it was an Illinois driver's license in D'Brusco's name, and a half-dozen others with the man's likeness, imprinted with phony names and addresses.

"You know, I'm quickly losing my faith in the rehabilitative nature of prison. Lenny seems to have picked up all kinds of bad habits there."

"Pretty good forgeries, too," Cal noted, dropping the wallet into the evidence bag. "Those don't come cheap." He rubbed his hand over his face. "All these stripes and plaids have me seeing double. Have you run across anything else?"

"Just this." Gabe held up a matchbook advertising the Sunrise Lounge. "Heard of it?" When the other man only shook his head, Gabe flipped the cover open. "Looks like a telephone number scribbled on the inside. Cross your fingers. Maybe we'll get lucky."

"Maybe. We're due a little luck in this investigation."

*   *   *

It sounded as though a demented logger was using a battering ram on her door. Meghan jerked, and the pen she'd
been using to list donors for the battered women's fund-
raiser slipped from her fingers and rolled across the floor.
"What in heaven's name…" She left her studio and crossed
rapidly to the front door. Old-fashioned caution had her using the peephole, and a sound of dismay escaped her. A
microsize Gabe Connally filled her vision, and the expression on his face was pure menace.

She stood undecided for a moment, creasing and recreas-
ing the paper she'd carried with her. When he'd left here
last night he hadn't been happy with her. She'd refused to
back down from him, and something told her that he was
unused to the experience. But certainly he hadn't left in a
state that would warrant hammering her door with what
looked like lethal intentions.

The pounding came again, awakening her from her leth-
argy and fueling a delayed sense of ire. Releasing the locks,
she threw the door open and glared at Gabe, barely regis-
tering Madison's presence at his side.

"Your social habits are deteriorating even further, Detective, if you've now decided to ignore the buzzer, as well
as the telephone."

"Since you seem to be ignoring both today, I had the
super let us in."

The super, she seethed silently, was going to get an earful
from her. When she was working she often ignored any and
all interruptions, letting her answering machine take messages she could return in the evening. But she could hear
the callers speaking. She had to take the precaution in case
an emergency arose with Danny. There was no way she
would have missed Connally's rasping tones. But he hadn't
bothered, apparently because only a face-to-face meeting
would satisfy him.

Grasping the edge of the door in her hand, she watched

him warily. She masked the trepidation spreading in the pit of her stomach with flippancy. "So, what is it now? You have an overwhelming urge to share lunch with me this time?"

"No," Gabe answered grimly, placing the heel of his palm on the door and shoving it wider. "I just had an overwhelming urge for the truth."

Meghan stepped out of his way, his words painting her insides with a glaze of panic. There was no way he could know about Danny, she reassured herself. No way at all. But she watched him, wide-eyed, as he strode into the middle of the room and then turned his steely gaze toward her again. Swallowing hard she gave the act of closing the door more attention than it warranted. She'd known Connally would make a formidable opponent, but faced now with that menacing expression, she was certain that she'd underestimated him.

Her chin angled up in an outward show of defiance. "I don't know what you mean."

"Well the thing is, Miss Patterson..." Both Gabe and Meghan acted as though they hadn't heard Cal's diffident words.

"I'm talking about D'Brusco and your sister. What was going on there? Did they have a relationship?"

The questions, and their rapid-fire delivery, left her speechless. Incomprehension warred with relief. Danny's secret was safe. For now. "Who's D'Brusco?"

"One of the men your nephew saw outside Favorite Things."

She heard Cal's words, but they clarified nothing. If anything, her mind grew more muddled. "What would he have to do with Sandra?"

"Exactly what we'd like to know," Gabe said. "Why don't you enlighten us? We found your sister's phone number scribbled on the inside of a matchbook in D'Brusco's apartment." He watched closely, but could see no reaction on her part other than confusion. "So how did they know each other?"

Meghan walked slowly to the couch and sank down on it. "I have no idea."

Keeping a watchful eye on his partner, Cal approached her. "Did your sister ever mention someone called Lenny? Was she seeing anyone in particular?"

"No. I mean, I don't know."

"You don't know." Gabe's words were imbued with disbelief. "Are you saying you don't know if she mentioned him, or you don't know if she was seeing someone?"

The derision in his tone ignited irritation. Shoulders stiff, she retorted, "Both."

"The thing is, Miss Patterson—" Cal sat down in the overstuffed chair next to the couch and leaned toward her "—finding your sister's number in D'Brusco's things was pretty unexpected. Anything you can tell us about your sister's life those last few weeks, anything at all, might end up being really helpful to our case."

Focusing on Madison's sincere expression was a way to block out Gabe's far more formidable one. "I wish I could help. I just don't know anything."

"Let's start with what brought her back to town." The emotion in Gabe's voice was tightly reined in now. "I seem to recall the newspapers saying she'd been living somewhere in the South."

Meghan traced the floral pattern of the couch with one index finger. "I really can't say."

With two quick steps Gabe was at the couch, and when he sat down he was far too close to Meghan for comfort. "Can't? Or won't?"

"Can't!" she snapped. She hated this line of questioning, and she hated him for pursuing it. There were few things she detested more than dwelling on her relationship with her family. Any of them. "I don't know where Sandra was before she came back to Chicago, but she never stays in one place for very long. I didn't even know she'd returned until that news article was published about her involvement with Wadrell's investigation.''

The silence that stretched after her words was almost worse than the questions themselves. She'd prefer to deal with the detectives' disbelief than the speculation that would surely arise after her outburst.

''You're saying that you and your sister were estranged.''

Meghan glanced at Detective Madison, tempted to laugh. *Estranged.* What a dispassionate word for a relationship fraught with conflict. With resentment. With fear.

''Yes.'' She was aware of the irony lacing her voice, but was helpless to prevent it. ''I only spoke to her once after the article came out.'' She'd gone to Sandra's apartment. It wasn't until later that she'd thought about how easy it had been to discover her sister's address. And how easily others could have discovered it, too, others with far more nefarious purposes in mind.

She shook off the memory when Gabe spoke again. ''So you did speak to her once. What'd you talk about? Did she mention anyone in particular to you?''

''Our conversation didn't last long.'' Just long enough for Sandra to laugh at Meghan's concerns about her involvement with the police. Just long enough for her sister to taunt her with reminders of how useful her talent was…didn't Meghan remember how much she'd enjoyed mind games when they were kids? And then they'd been interrupted when a boy had entered the room, a little boy with golden hair who was unmistakably her sister's son. The wonder of the discovery had been shattered with Sandra's offhand introduction.

You'll like my kid. He's a freak, just like me. And we both know how you feel about freaks, don't we, Meggie dear?

The memory, coupled with Gabe's proximity, drove her to move. To give herself time to calm her jangled emotions, she crossed to the table where she'd left her purse, and slipped in the fund-raising sheet. But Gabe's next words did nothing to ease her anxiety.

"Seems odd that you ended up as guardian to your nephew," Gabe observed. "What with you and your sister not being close and all."

Because it was far easier than confronting old ghosts, Meghan retreated emotionally. Barriers, long ago constructed, clicked neatly into place. "There's no one else."

"What about your mother?"

Cal slid a quizzical gaze at Gabe, one that was ignored.

"Based on previous history, I suspect my mother is prowling Europe, on the hunt for husband number six. At any rate, the courts thought Danny would be better off staying with me, so that's the arrangement we arrived at."

Gabe listened to her words, but it was what she didn't say that intrigued him. There was far more to Meghan than she was willing to share, and despite his dislike for secrets, he had a healthy respect for privacy. He, better than most, realized how deep some wounds could scar.

So instead of pushing further, he said only, "Do you have a picture of your sister?" When she just looked at him, he explained, "Whether you know anything about it or not, we've got to investigate what connection D'Brusco had with her. We have to pursue all angles."

After a moment Meghan rose. "I'm not sure how recent it is, but I have a Polaroid shot I can let you have." She strode across the room and disappeared into her studio. Without a thought he followed.

Three photos were pinned to a cork board on the wall, beneath which sat a canvas. Meghan reached up and released one of them and turned to find Gabe there, staring hard at her half-completed work. "Here," she said stiffly, thrusting the picture at him.

He took it, but his gaze never wavered from the unfinished portrait. "I guess that's your sister."

Meghan's gaze followed his, then flicked away. "Yes.

Danny's birthday is coming up. Portraits aren't really my thing, but I thought it would be nice if he had something for his room to remind him of his mom.''

"Yeah. Probably.'' Looking carefully at the photos, he compared them to the work in progress. His first thought was that Meghan was being kind for the boy's sake. Her rendering of her sister was far softer than the woman in the photos. Wadrell had said Sandra Barton had possessed a hardness, and that edge was apparent in the likenesses captured by the camera. And then in the next thought he wondered what it had been like for Meghan to find herself suddenly saddled with a kid she'd barely known; the son of a sister, who, from all appearances, she hadn't cared for. What kind of woman would be able to get beyond old resentments and care about the feelings of the kid in question?

He didn't know the answer to that. But he couldn't deny a growing desire to find out.

"You'll need to leave now.'' Meghan led the way back to the living room, and Gabe reluctantly followed. "It's my turn to pick Danny and his friend up from kindergarten, and I don't want to be late.''

"Do they both go to the same school?'' Gabe asked. His mouth quirked. "The one with less thinking?''

Her gaze flashing to his, she remembered the careless remark Danny had made last night and her reaction to it. "No, Danny goes to a private school, but Alex's is in the same neighborhood.''

She offered the information with little thought to the words; her attention was focused instead on the way the half smile transformed Connally's expression. She'd seen him look forbidding, inscrutable and charming, by turns, and each persona of the man held a certain fascination for her. A fascination that tempted further exploration. One she would be wise to avoid.

"We'll be on our way then, Miss Patterson. Thanks for your time. And for the photo.'' Cal's words jolted the other two from their silent exchange. Gabe joined his partner at the door.

She waited with a sense of relief as the men prepared to leave, and then Gabe turned to address her. "I'll be in touch."

As the door closed behind the two detectives, she hugged her arms across her chest in an unconsciously defensive gesture. She should have interpreted the man's parting words as a threat.

Instead, they seemed imbued with a hint of promise.

Gabe ignored his partner's methodical driving for a moment as he rifled through the glove compartment in vain. "Damn." He slammed the compartment door shut. "Stop at a gas station, will you? I'm out of gum."

Reaching into his pocket, Cal withdrew a package of breath mints and handed them to his partner. "If you have to have some sort of oral fix, try these."

"You wouldn't happen to have any with nicotine added, would you?" He raised his brows at the swift look Cal shot him. "Hey, just kidding." And he was. Sort of. He took the package with a long-suffering sigh and withdrew a mint, popped it into his mouth and dropped the package into his pocket. Morosely he considered the difference of flavor between the mint and the smoke he craved. They didn't even begin to compare.

"So do you want to tell me what that was all about?"

At Cal's question, Gabe shrugged. "I never should have let you talk me into giving up smoking. Gum and breath mints just don't cut it."

"Nice try, Connally. I'm talking about Meghan Patterson, and you know it. What was that she was saying about you and lunch?"

"You know there's a minimum speed limit, don't you? Driving too slow is just as dangerous on these streets as excessive speed." His words affected neither Cal's driving nor his stoic expression. Recognizing the corner he was backed into, Gabe finally answered. "I took some Chinese over there last night. No big deal. I told you I'd be working on gaining her cooperation."

"Couldn't have proved it by the way you went after her this afternoon."

Gabe considered the scenery that wasn't flashing by nearly as quickly as he wished. "What are you talking about?"

Hands on the steering wheel at a precise ten and two position, Cal snorted, his eyes never leaving the street. "You jumped all over her at first, practically accused her of lying to us. I wouldn't have been surprised if she'd kicked us out of the place. Maybe after kicking you first."

"She wouldn't have done that," Gabe disputed, not nearly as sure as he sounded.

"It lacked your usual finesse. Mind telling me what was going on?"

Gabe drummed the fingers of one hand in a restless tattoo on his thigh. "It looked like she might have been keeping something from us, okay? Admit it. You were as stunned as I was when we traced that phone number to Sandra Barton."

"That's a twist in this case, all right."

"So, I just thought Meghan…Miss Patterson, might know more than she said at first."

"But you believe her now when she claims she didn't know much about her sister's life at all?"

"Yeah." He believed her, at least about this. It wasn't something he could put into words, but it was something he recognized. Family didn't mean connection. Relationships didn't mean intimacy. He knew that better than most. He recognized an aloneness in Meghan, a wariness that mirrored his own. And he observed the ability she had to shut others out, including him. Although he understood that quality, his reaction to it was totally unfamiliar. He wanted to shred those barriers she erected so effortlessly, to smash through them and bare the essential, fundamental woman inside. And the violence of that particular urge wasn't something he was willing to discuss with his partner.

"So you thought she was keeping something from us. That's hardly unusual in our line of work. Still doesn't explain why you went off like that."

Cal was right. For most of the people they encountered on the job, lying was habit. It was their task to rip away the lies they were handed and find the real answers beneath. For some reason he'd overreacted when he'd thought Meghan had deliberately withheld information from them. And he didn't want to consider the reasons for that too closely.

"Why don't we head over to the Sunrise Lounge and see what kind of response we get by flashing D'Brusco's and Barton's pictures around."

Obediently Cal turned at the next corner and headed across town to the address on the front of the matchbook cover. "You wanna know what I think?"

Wearily, Gabe slouched down in the passenger seat, tipped his head back and let his eyes slide shut. "Yeah, I'm fascinated by what you think."

Ignoring the sarcasm in his partner's voice, Cal continued, "I think I witnessed...a thing...between you and this Patterson."

"A thing."

"That's right, a thing. Don't act stupid, Connally, you know exactly what I'm talking about. I had a hard time for a while, there, figuring whether I was going to have to stop you from arresting her or ravishing her."

"Ravishing? You've been reading Becky's romance books again, Cal."

But the man wouldn't be swayed from his argument. "I'm beginning to think you have more of an interest in the woman than gaining her nephew's cooperation."

Without opening his eyes, Gabe replied, "And I'm beginning to think there's something seriously wrong with your imagination." Meghan had promised to provide access to her nephew, who might be able to identify the guy with D'Brusco. And if they discovered a connection between Sandra Barton and D'Brusco, Meghan would be indirectly involved herself. That was as far as his interest in her went. As far as he would allow it to go. He had plenty of commendations in his attaboy file to credit his bravery on the job. But he tended to minimize risk-taking in his personal life. That's why he stuck to women who were simple, uncomplicated.

And Meghan Patterson had *complication* written all over her.

The Sunrise Lounge was a trendy bar in a fashionable downtown neighborhood. Gabe followed Cal into the establishment and scanned his surroundings. A high-class strip joint, he surmised. The stage and runways were giveaways and from the decor it appeared that the usual customers would be more likely to wear suits than denim.

The place was nearly deserted. The men headed toward the bar, where the bartender slowly straightened from his conversation with a customer to watch their approach.

Although he knew they'd already been made as cops, Gabe pushed aside his coat to reveal the shield clipped on his belt. "Detectives Connally and Madison. We've got a few questions to ask. Are you the only employee here?"

The man shook his head. "Yvonne's in back. Most of the others won't show for another hour or so."

"Then I guess we'll start with you and Yvonne. Why don't you get her out here?" suggested Gabe.

Instead of leaving the bar, the man turned his head and shouted, "Yvonne!" He turned back to the men and returned their regard stoically.

"Interesting technique," observed Cal.

"Crude but effective," Gabe agreed.

An attractive dark-haired woman came through the swinging door in back of the bar, saying, "I swear, Jack, if you don't stop screaming for me…" The rest of her words tapered off as she saw the detectives. "Well, hello, gentlemen. What can I do for you?" Her walk transformed into a glide as she approached them. As she leaned forward against the bar, the detectives were treated to an eye-popping amount of cleavage.

"Your name, ma'am?"

Heavily mascaraed lashes fluttering, the woman purred, "Yvonne Basily. I'm the hostess here. Whatever you gentleman need, I'll do my best to oblige you."

Gabe reached into his coat pocket, withdrew the photos of Lenny and Sandra, and tossed them on the bar. "Oblige us by taking a look. Have you ever seen either of them?"

Yvonne studied each photo in turn, then tapped a long bright red nail against Lenny's. "He's a regular. Comes in every week or two. I've never seen the woman before."

Gabe transferred his attention to the bartender. "How about you?"

He stepped forward for a closer look. "Same here. I know the guy."

"Do you know him by name?"

"Lenny," the woman said, and the bartender nodded. "Didn't know his last name, but I knew him to say hello to."

"When's the last time you saw him?" Cal questioned.

The woman pursed her glossy lips for a moment. "I'm not real sure. Not this week, for certain. But last week…" She glanced at Jack and he shook his head.

"I haven't seen him for over two weeks."

Further questioning provided very little additional information. Neither of them knew Lenny well, nor could they remember ever seeing him with anyone.

"He'd invite one of the girls over to sit with him, sometimes, buy her a drink after her act, something like that," Jack said. "But he always came in alone."

"Where'd he usually sit?" asked Cal. "At the bar here, or at one of the tables?"

"Depends on if the shows were on," Jack said. "When they were he was always at a table right up front."

"What about your wait staff?" If Lenny had been a regular, Gabe figured, the waitresses might be more familiar with him. "When do they come in?"

"Most of them won't be here for another forty-five minutes."

Resigning himself to the tedium ahead, Gabe said, "We'll wait."

Yvonne exchanged a look with Jack. "Things start to get busy in here about that time. It'd probably be better if you came back near closing time."

"We hate to put you out, ma'am," Gabe said sardonically. "But I know you'll want to help us get this job done as soon as possible. What with you being so obliging and all."

It was close to an hour before they were able to interview the first of the wait staff. And from the looks of most of the women, they pulled double duty, both on the runway and in the bar. After another hour of questioning, Gabe was ready to call the lead a dead end. Most of the women admitted knowing Lenny, at least by sight. None recognized the picture of Sandra.

While they waited to question the last waitress, Gabe made a sound of disgust. "Well, this was a dead end. All we've found out so far is that D'Brusco was a major lech."

"Like we didn't already know that after tossing his bedroom." Cal glanced at his watch. "If we're going to be much later, I need to give Becky a call."

"Got another special occasion planned?" Gabe ribbed his partner, enjoying the immediate flush that crawled to the man's cheeks.

Cal moved uncomfortably on his chair, directing his gaze past Gabe. "Every night's a special occasion when you have someone to go home to, you know?"

"Sure," Gabe agreed, turning his head to watch the next waitress approach them. But in truth he didn't have a clue. And he doubted he ever would.

Tracie, with an *ie,* she informed them breathlessly, looked all of about nineteen. Without the heavy makeup, she'd look even younger, Gabe figured. He waited silently as Cal explained their purpose and showed her the photos they'd brought.

"That's Lenny D'Brusco," she said, tapping one long bloodred nail against the photo. "He was in here all the time. Kind of a sweet guy, you know? Always kidding around with the girls."

"How well did you know him?" Cal asked.

She lifted one bared shoulder above the skimpy waitressing costume she wore. "Like I say, I talked to him when he came in sometimes."

Pushing the other photo forward, Cal asked, "What about this woman? Have you ever seen her before?"

Tracie glanced at Gabe, and then over her shoulder to the bartender who watched them. She shook her head. "Nope, I just know Lenny. Everyone knew him. I never noticed anyone with him."

"Got any ID, Tracie with an *ie?*" Gabe asked in a deceptively soft voice.

The woman darted another glance at him. "Not on me. Why?"

"'Cuz maybe we'd like to look at it. Maybe we'd like to check your birth date."

Her face stilled, and she shot another look toward the bar. "I'm plenty old enough for whatever you guys have in mind."

"I'm betting not," Gabe disagreed mildly. "What do you bet, Al? Fifteen? Sixteen?"

"I'd bet ten she's sixteen." Cal followed his partner's lead with smooth precision. "If that."

Wetting her lips, Tracie lowered her voice. "C'mon, guys, whaddya want to hassle me for?"

"I can't speak for my partner here, but I'm willing to hassle you because I have the feeling we've been getting jerked around for the last couple of hours."

"And I'm getting hungry," Cal continued. "I always get ornery when I'm hungry."

"So how about it, Tracie?" Gabe turned his attention back on the young woman who looked ready to flee. "Want to be the first one in this joint to stop yanking us around, or should we call the juvies?"

The threat of the juvenile authorities was the first crumble in Tracie's wall. "Hey, I'm six weeks away from my eighteenth birthday, okay?"

"And the way you spend those six weeks is up to you."

Faced with Gabe's implacable mask, Tracie shot a beseeching look at Cal, who regarded her steadily. Shaking her head for the benefit of her audience at the bar, she murmured, "Okay, I saw her a couple times, all right? She was in here for a while one night, and Lenny invited her to his table."

"They didn't come in together?"

"No. But the next time I saw her she went to where he was sitting and joined him right away." Her gaze flickered to the bar, where Yvonne had joined Jack. "And I don't know nothing else."

"How long ago was this?" Gabe asked.

Tracie screwed up her brow. "A long time ago. I don't remember exactly. At least three months ago."

Gabe watched the woman get up from their table with barely disguised eagerness and walk rapidly away. Then his gaze met Cal's. "I pulled up the file on Barton the day we interviewed Meghan Patterson. She died a little over three months ago."

Cal rubbed his jaw as he considered this information. "So Barton meets D'Brusco a couple of times in this place, and a few days later she winds up dead. Coincidence?"

"Yeah." Gabe rose and waited for his partner to do the same. "I'd say that's one helluva coincidence."

Chapter 6

"Meghan."

"Hm-m?" Still half-asleep, Meghan sat up in bed, clutched the telephone receiver to her ear.

"Are you still in bed?"

For some reason the question seemed imbued with a hint of intimacy and chased away any lingering sleepiness. She grabbed the bedcovers and pulled them up to her chest, as if to protect herself from the vision of the man on the phone. "I'm awake. What do you want?"

He was silent for an instant, long enough for her to regret the phrasing of her statement. "What did you do with your sister's effects? The things you cleaned out of her place after her death?"

The low tones were like sandpaper dragged over velvet, and the effect elicited an unexpected, unwanted response. She shook her head to dislodge the fog that was suddenly hazing her mind. "Why?"

She expected the impatience in his response but not the hint of amusement beneath it. "Can't you ever just answer a question? I'd like to go through them. See if I can find a clue that will give me an idea of your sister's last days.''

It took concentrated effort to ignore the insidious heat that was drifting through her limbs. There was something curiously intimate in talking to him like this while she still lay in bed, half-dressed. His raspy tones could have been coming from beside her, a drowsy male just rousing from sleep. The mental image flushed her cheeks and made her voice sharper than she intended.

''Don't you think I've already thought of that, Detective? I've been through her things over and over again. There's nothing there to give the slightest hint of what she was involved in. All I know about her activities I read in the paper.''

''You've been through her stuff—a cop hasn't. I might see something you overlooked. Might find something you didn't think was important.''

''I don't see the point.'' More than stubbornness drove her. It had been hard enough to go through her sister's things the first time; to sort through the curiously scant belongings and imagine what importance they might have had in Sandra's life. Like Meghan she'd had a generous trust fund, one that would have enabled her to live comfortably. But Sandra hadn't wasted much money on furnishings and the kind of momentos that made a house a home. Meghan suspected that she'd moved too often for that. Each succeeding time she'd searched through them had gotten increasingly painful. How strange that she would have to peruse inanimate objects for some hints into her sister's life. And how unbearably sad.

''I heard from the guy I had look at your sister's car. He couldn't find anything to suggest it had been tampered with. But...yesterday Cal and I did find out that Sandra and D'Brusco knew each other. They'd met, at least twice.''

His words had the effect of a one-two punch. Dread circled in her stomach. She'd gotten her second look into the accident, but closure was elusive. Finding a link between Sandra and the detective's current case meant that it would be harder to shake Connally; harder to dodge his insistence to draw Danny, and perhaps her, into the investigation.

Her voice sounded strained even to her own ears. "I don't see what that..."

"It means D'Brusco was one of the last people to see your sister alive." His blunt pronouncement hung between them, thrumming with tension. "You want answers about your sister's death, Meghan. The second look into the accident didn't bring any. Maybe this will."

Her fingers clutched tightly at the comforter around her waist. "I stored most of her things away. I didn't know what Danny might want. I mean, when he gets older."

"You can take me there tonight after work." His voice had gone low and persuasive. "Want me to bring dinner? We can eat first."

"No." She was in a sudden hurry to end this conversation, as if by doing so she could sever her connection to Connally. Barring that, keeping him at a distance was the wisest course of action. He was offering to provide her with the answers she had regarding Sandra's death, but he was only a means to an end. She'd be wise to remember that. "After I feed Danny I'll meet you there." She recited the address of the storage unit she utilized. "I probably won't make it until seven o'clock."

"Seven o'clock is fine." There was a long pause, and then he said, "You're doing the right thing, Meghan."

The right thing. She regarded the receiver in her hand after the conversation had ended. Further involvement with the detective could prove to be the right thing for putting Sandra's memory to rest. It may well be the right thing for Danny, if it answered the questions the boy was liable to have when he got older.

But she was certain that it was the absolutely worst thing she could do for herself.

* * *

"You're a slippery guy to get hold of, Mr. Jamison."
Gabe ignored the plush, leather chair offered him by the
CEO of Golden Enterprises and roamed the well-outfitted
office.

"I'm a busy man, if that's what you mean."

Gabe lifted the blinds away from the window with one
finger and peered out. The view offered a magnificent view
of the lake. He let the blind drop and turned back to the
man. "Yeah, that must be what I mean."

The immaculately clad blond man watched the detectives
from behind an acre of polished cherry. "I hope you haven't
been too inconvenienced by my absence. When I heard
there were detectives asking to speak with me, I wrapped
up my business in Zurich as quickly as possible."

"What can you tell us about the operation of Ultimate
Video?"

"Well, it's one of Golden Enterprises's vast array of
holdings. Exactly what is it that has you interested?" He
countered Gabe's question with one of his own.

"We're trying to locate one of your employees. He was
the manager for Ultimate Video. Lenny D'Brusco."

Todd Jamison spread two well-manicured hands in a gesture of bewilderment. "Your interest mirrors my own. I'm
told the man hasn't shown up for work for the past few
days. It seems we'll be looking for a replacement."

"Another ex-con?" Gabe inquired.

Jamison's expression blanked. "I beg your pardon?"

"Did you know Lenny D'Brusco is a convicted felon?"
Cal asked. When the man didn't respond he continued, "I'll
take your silence as a no. See, that was one of the questions
we had. Seems unusual for an ex-con to be placed in a job
that would enable him to handle sums of money like he did
at the video outlets. Just how is it that D'Brusco came to
be working for one of your companies?"

The congeniality had vanished. Jamison's face was hard.

"Gentlemen, I hire people to take care of those sorts of chores for me. I agree with you, someone wasn't doing his or her job when D'Brusco was hired. I intend to get to the bottom of that matter."

Gabe looked at the man consideringly. Jamison would look at home on the cover of one of those magazines, he thought, the kind that purported to be for men but that no man Gabe had ever known would be caught dead reading. Tan, polished and glib, maybe Jamison was CEO material. That didn't mean he wasn't up to his neck in something dirty.

"How long have you been CEO of this outfit?"

Jamison folded his hands before him like an altar boy about to recite a well-practiced prayer. "Just over a year. Why?"

"Looks like it'd be a demanding job."

"Yes, it is." He gave a thin smile. "Fortunately however, I'm up to it."

"Know who held this position before you?"

"I don't recall."

Dropping into one of the chairs opposite the man, Gabe regarded him shrewdly. "How closely do you follow the daily operations of all the holdings of Golden Enterprises?"

"I have managers for that sort of thing. I wouldn't impugn their skills by attempting to micromanage, if that's what you mean. It'd be counterproductive at any rate. My responsibility is to keep an eye on the performance of each of the businesses. Since Ultimate Video was performing well, it warranted no close attention from me. Are you saying it should have?"

Gabe cocked a brow. "Not necessarily. Just trying to get a feel for the chain of command in this outfit. You answer to someone, too, don't you? Or is CEO a fancy name for owner?"

Jamison adjusted the lapel of his Armani suit jacket. "Somehow I believe we've veered from your original concern. I'm afraid I can't give you any information on D'Brusco, but I do wish you well in your endeavors.'' He rose, and slowly Gabe and Cal did the same.

"If you find him, Detectives, you can give him a message for me.'' He waited for the two men to turn back to him. "You can tell him that he's fired.''

"So what was your take on this Jamison?'' Lieutenant Burney faced the two detectives in his office an hour later. "Do we like him for being involved in the laundering scam?''

"I wouldn't cross him off our shortlist,'' Gabe responded. He reached into his pocket and thumbed another mint from the package Cal had given him yesterday. Its taste didn't improve his mood any. His mouth was as fresh as a damn wintergreen forest, whatever the hell that was, but it didn't appreciably lessen his craving for a cigarette. "Hell, he's the CEO, isn't he? Could D'Brusco be running the money exchange without him knowing about it? How would he get it past accounting?'' He threw the crumpled wrapper into the wastebasket beside the lieutenant's desk.

"He didn't particularly want to answer any questions about Golden Enterprises itself,'' Cal said.

"Did you let him know what your interest was?'' the lieutenant asked, his ebony eyes intent.

Gabe shook his head. "Just that we wanted D'Brusco. He never asked why.''

Lieutenant Burney nodded reflectively. "Put a time line together of D'Brusco's activities while you were tailing him. Then concentrate on the pictures you took while you had the outlets under surveillance. Maybe we can work a clue that way.''

The problem with the lieutenant's advice, Gabe thought hours later, was they'd snapped hundreds of pictures while Lenny had been inside the stores. Trying to match customers that had been seen more than once at the same store was a tedious process. Identifying them once a match had been made was damn near impossible. And even if they were identified, chances were each would turn out to be a retired schoolteacher with a passion for old movies.

His eyes were starting to cross, so Gabe decided it was time for a break. There had been something nagging at him since their visit with Jamison, and he wouldn't rest until he'd checked it out. Going to the computer, he logged on to the Internet and started looking through the database of local property transactions. He found what he was looking for in about ten minutes, and his eyes widened. ''Hey, c'mere a minute.''

Cal looked up from the pictures he was poring over. ''What are you doing, sluffing off? Get back to work.''

''Come and look at this. Didn't you wonder about the ownership of Ultimate Video?''

With a long-suffering sigh, his partner got up and rounded the desk. ''We already know it belongs to Golden Enterprises. What's the surprise?''

''Look who sold it to that corporation a few years ago.'' Gabe tipped back in his chair so his partner could lean closer to the screen.

''Victor Mannen used to own it?'' Cal's voice was filled with distaste. ''Now there's a scumbag of the highest order.''

''Yeah, a powerful scumbag. Maybe beating that murder rap cost him big time and he had to sell the video place to raise the dough for those fancy lawyers of his.'' Years ago the man had faced a federal trial for murder. Two weeks before the trial was to begin, all but one of the witnesses were massacred while in protective custody. The survivor, not surprisingly, hadn't stuck around to testify. Finding Mannen's name attached to this investigation, no matter how remotely, was jarring.

Gabe checked his watch, relieved to see that it was close to five already. The events of the day should have kept thoughts of Meghan at bay, but mental pictures of her had insisted on lingering, dancing at the fringes of his consciousness. It had taken effort to ignore persistent images of her in bed when he'd called her, heavy-eyed and half-asleep. It had taken even greater effort not to picture what she'd been wearing, what she'd been thinking when he'd heard that slight catch in her voice.

His imagination was working overtime today. He'd never seen her bedroom, but he thought it would be lacy and delicate, the kind of room that would make a man feel awkward and out of place. But it wouldn't be his surroundings he'd be concentrating on if he were there. His attention would be focused on Meghan. Familiarizing himself with the softness of her skin, with every scented curve and hollow of her long, lithe body.

Logic reared and reminded him of all the reasons for the inappropriateness of his mental wanderings. He'd made a promise to her at the beginning of their relationship, one he meant to keep. It wasn't her fault if he couldn't bring himself to mean the words; if they'd taken on a sense of falseness the moment he'd uttered them. There were many reasons why he needed to avoid a closer relationship with Meghan Patterson. His promise was only one of them.

"You've got a visitor, Gabe." Cal's quiet words succeeded in shaking Gabe from his reverie, and he looked up, half expecting that his thoughts had conjured the very woman who dominated his thoughts. Then reality slapped at him. His voice expressionless, he said, "Ma."

Joyce Reddington smiled tentatively at her son, that half hopeful, half scared kind of smile that always managed to make Gabe feel annoyed and guilty by turns. She clutched her glossy leather purse, the one he'd sent her for her birthday, and her fingers twisted nervously on the handle.

"Gabriel." She took a couple of steps closer to his desk, then stopped again and fixed the smile that threatened to waver. "How are you?"

"I'm good." Gabe looked around, noted the studiously turned heads of his colleagues that couldn't disguise their heightened radar, and rose. "I'm gonna use the coffee room."

Cal nodded, although he knew the remark had been directed at everyone in the room. "Yeah, okay."

Rounding the desk, Gabe took his mother's elbow in his hand and guided her away from listening ears and prying eyes, wishing the whole time that he was on the other side of one of those desks. Grimly he pushed the door open into the empty room and ushered his mother inside. "Coffee?"

"Oh, no." Joyce shook her graying head. "I don't drink coffee anymore. Butch says it's bad for my health, and he's probably right. He knows about that stuff."

Gabe pulled out a chair for her and propped one hip on the table, facing her. "Yeah, Butch is a real expert on a lot of things."

At his terse words, her fingers worked the purse's leather strap more vigorously. "I wish you understood him better. He's a good man. Been real good to be me, better than I deserve."

Because he didn't want to focus too much on what she deserved, on what either of them deserved, he changed the subject. "So what brings you into the city? You don't often leave the suburbs."

"We were at a big revival meeting they had downtown at one of them fancy churches. You should have seen it. Everyone was singing and clapping...we heard lots of real good preachers, too."

That would explain, Gabe thought dispassionately, why Joyce had been allowed to leave the domains of the suburbs. The only things that would bring Butch to the city was booze or Bibles. Both of which, in that man's hands, were equally dangerous.

"And where is Butch?"

One hand fluttered nervously. "Oh, he's waiting for me while I run some errands."

Meaning of course, that he was skulking in a corner tavern nearby while Joyce did his bidding. The scene had been replayed too often for Gabe to mince words. "What's he want?"

"Oh, nothing. Not a thing." She shook her head to underscore her words. "You've been nothing but kind to us. We wouldn't think of asking you for—"

"Ma."

At the edge of impatience in his tone, Joyce stopped and pressed her lips together. "Well, the thing is, I wanted your advice on something. You know that house you bought me is just the best place ever. I figure it's the nicest place I've ever had to live. But it's really too big for Butch and me. I don't know what we need with two bedrooms. And the yard—" Her words stumbled, and she visibly fought to recover "—we really aren't gonna want to worry about yard work as we get older." Her smile now seemed more like a grimace. "Not that we don't appreciate all you've done for us."

"I didn't buy the house for Butch, I bought it for you." Gabe made no attempt to curb his bluntness. "And it's in both of our names for a reason. So tell Butch to forget about selling it and pocketing the money."

He could tell by the flicker in her eyes that he'd guessed correctly, and not for the first time he cursed the man his mother insisted on staying with. "Ma." He forced his voice to a gentler timbre. "You love that house. And your garden."

"I've never had either one before, that's true enough. I do like to putter around in the yard." As if the enthusiasm in her voice was a betrayal, she immediately shifted back to her earlier recitation. "But we really could use a smaller place…an apartment maybe."

"Tell Butch I said no." His tone brooked no argument.

"If the yard and house get to be too much work for you, I'll spring for someone to help out."

An odd look of pride crossed her face at his words. "Well, Gabriel, if you aren't the best son a mother could want." The statement told him better than words that it hadn't been her idea to come here, hadn't been her idea to sell the first home she'd had in years.

He shifted away from the hug she would have pressed on him and opened the door. "Let me know if you need anything. You know I've got a grocery account set up for you at the Safeway in your neighborhood."

"I do know. A mother just couldn't ask for more." An uncertain expression crossed a face that had once been pretty but now bore the ravages of her past. "It sure would be nice to see a little more of you. Maybe you could come to dinner sometime?"

The timid tone, the commonplace remark, stirred old feelings in Gabe, feelings best kept tucked firmly away. "Yeah, maybe. I'll let you know."

She got to the door and hesitated, looked up at him. "Well, bye, then, Gabriel."

His hand propped on the doorjamb, he watched her walk away, weaving through the maze of desks and tables overflowing with caseloads. He wished he could feel something normal, something that didn't summon old resentments and regrets.

Cal came by, his parka in his hand. "I'm heading out. How about you?"

"Yeah." Grateful for the diversion, Gabe stepped out of the room and headed toward his desk. "I think I'll head out, too."

"Everything okay?" Cal's diffident tone indicated a man who knew he was tiptoeing in a minefield.

"Yeah." Gabe slipped his coat from the back of his chair and shrugged into it. "Everything's great."

* * *

The knock on her car window caught Meghan by surprise. The figure that bent to peer in, didn't. She collected her purse and got out of the car, pressing the automatic lock. "I didn't see you drive up."

"Must be my years of undercover work. Sneaking up on people was my specialty."

She shot him a look as they started across the street to the large rental storage units. "Your years undercover…or your years as a delinquent?"

He didn't spare her a glance. "Probably both."

She studied him carefully as they continued in silence. It didn't take any special intuition to perceive that he was in a fractious mood tonight, with an edginess layered beneath simmering temper. She wondered what had caused that mood. What would it take to ruffle Gabe Connally's customarily stoic demeanor? And why should it matter to her?

"I've brought a flashlight," she finally ventured, almost trotting to keep up with his pace. "It's lit inside but at this time of the evening it will be hard to see."

His attention shifted to her, and she almost wished she'd kept quiet. "I hope you're not telling me you've been here at night before."

"Not at night, no." She pulled her identification tag from her purse to show to the watchman at the door, and he waved them both in.

"But you have been here alone? In the evening?" He made a sound of irritation. "You've gotta know that's just plain stupid."

"Thank you very much for your unwanted commentary on my intelligence," she snapped. Now it was she who strode ahead, leaving him trailing in her wake. "Somehow I've managed to muddle along in life without your brilliant advice."

"You've been lucky," he commented flatly. They entered an elevator, and Meghan stabbed a finger at the button marked for the third floor. The door slid closed. "A woman has to be careful where she goes in this city."

"I've been moving about in this city on my own quite successfully for a number of years."

He regarded her profile in the confines of the elevator compartment. He'd gotten her in a snit somehow, without even half trying. Something lightened inside him a fraction. She looked good with storm clouds brewing in her eyes and temper heightening the color in her face. A measure of tension began to seep from his limbs.

"Excuse me, ma'am. I didn't mean to impugn your intelligence."

The apology lacked sincerity, and she rightly chose to ignore it. "Impugn? Vocabulary word of the week, Detective?"

Damned if she didn't have him dead to rights. The elevator door opened, and he followed her out, taking advantage of his position to watch that shapely behind. "Learned it today, as a matter of fact. You learn the damnedest things on the job."

He thought he heard her mutter something about manners not being one of them, and he grinned. It occurred to him that it was easy to be around Meghan. Too easy.

Following her across the dimly lit building, he felt another urge to admonish her for ever coming here alone. He now knew better than to give voice to it. But these places were notorious for housing vagrants who managed to sneak past the guards, something that wouldn't have been too difficult, given the attitude of the watchman who'd let them in. Thieves, too, targeted places like this. Once inside, a metal saw or wire clippers gained them access to just about anything that caught their eye.

Their footsteps echoed in the cavernous corridor. Built much like a parking garage, the place was lined on both sides with separate spaces enclosed with wire fencing. Gabe scanned the area. It appeared empty except for the two of them.

Meghan stopped before one of the enclosures and fitted a key into the padlock securing the door. Unlocking it, she swung the door open, and Gabe entered, looked around. "Is this it?"

She took the flashlight from her purse and flicked it on. "All of Sandra's furniture was rented. I packed up her clothes, took Danny's stuff to my house and just boxed up the rest."

Meghan looked at the five lonely boxes stacked neatly in the corner and thought again that it was a sad sum of a person's life. But she refused to dwell on the welter of old regrets that threatened to well up within her. Sandra had left more than this—she'd left Danny. And through her son the mother would, in a way, live on. It was more than some people ever had.

Gabe went down on one knee and pried open the flaps of one of the boxes. "What all is stored here?"

"I told you before there wasn't much. There are some things of Danny's that he outgrew...toys and such. Things she kept on her dresser. Albums...old pictures."

But Gabe had already found those on his own. He drew out a couple of photo albums that dated back to Meghan's childhood and began to flip through the pages. Without a word he reached out to take the flashlight from her, directing its beam over the pages. He paused over one page, studying it. "That's you, isn't it?"

"Yes," she said shortly. There were few pleasant memories associated with any pictures from her childhood, one reason she'd chosen to store these away. She'd spent years trying to forget many of the events pictured; she certainly didn't want to relive them now, with Gabe at her side.

He put the album away and reached for the rest of the contents of the box. Recognizing the scrapbooks in his hands, Meghan steeled herself for the questions they would surely elicit.

The only sound in the enclosure was the whisper of paper rustling as he silently turned pages filled with newspaper clippings. Sandra had meticulously collected every article ever written about her, and since she'd made her ability very public whenever the mood suited her, the scrapbook was thick.

His words, when they came, seemed innocent enough. "So I guess that investigation with Wadrell wasn't your sister's first venture into the public eye."

It was difficult to speak around the knot in her throat. "Not exactly."

Page after page of newspaper clippings were jammed with articles featuring Sandra, even including one magazine cover proclaiming her as one of the leading psychics in the country. The real story, however, was what was missing from the scrapbook. The periods of time during which Sandra had been sent away to school, only to return, dismissed and rebellious. The times when her sister had appeared to conform, only to seek headlines months later.

It was easier from the perspective of adulthood for her to understand Sandra's motives a bit better. The headlines had provoked reaction from their mother and grandparents, and perhaps Sandra had been willing to accept their censure, as long as it was a response. It wasn't a method Meghan would have embraced even if she'd been able. Her chosen strategy for dealing with her family had been to stay invisible. The times when Sandra would carelessly divulge her secrets, the attention of her family would be focused on her, and the consequences were still painful to recall. Her only outlet, the only thing Sandra hadn't been able to spoil for her was her art, and Meghan had pored everything she had into it.

Gabe was studying the last page in the scrapbook, the one depicting CPD's use of a psychic in a gang investigation. Missing was the one that released her name. Meghan

wondered if that was an oversight on Sandra's part, or if
she'd finally recognized the danger of the situation she'd
involved herself in.

To her relief he put aside the scrapbook without further
comment, and together they emptied the contents of another
box. They sorted through old toys and abandoned treasures
of Danny's. Meghan was struck, not for the first time, by
how meager his belongings had been, as well. Sandra had
traveled light, she imagined, and Danny had been forced to
do so, as well.

"What's left?" he asked, when she started on the fourth
box.

"More of the same. Like I told you, there wasn't much.
Some of Sandra's personal belongings that I thought Danny
might want someday, a few more pictures, odds and ends."

"Any embarrassing photos of you when you were
young? I didn't get a chance to look too closely at the al
bum."

"Hardly. Just a few more Polaroids like the one I gave
you. They were the only recent pictures I found. When I
decided to do that portrait for Danny I came down here and
went through them, keeping the best shots of the two of
them. I left the rest of them—" She made a sound of dis
covery, pulled a handful of the photos from the carton.
"Here they are."

Gabe checked his watch. "Well let's finish these last two
boxes, and then I'll follow you home, make sure you get
there safely."

Despite knowing he wouldn't be able to see the gesture
she rolled her eyes. "That's hardly necessary, Detective."

"Humor me. I like to—" His words stopped abruptly.

"I told you earlier, I've been taking care of myself for a
long time." Longer, she supposed, than he imagined. "I
don't need—" Two fingers pressed against her lips, stem
ming the rest of her statement.

Her first thought centered on the heat radiating from his

ouch, the way her lips seemed to swell in response beneath it. Curiosity followed a distant second. She remained silent, at first to humor him and then because she was listening as hard as he was.

There was a scraping sound, like a boot on cement, and then, silence. After a few more moments Meghan pushed Gabe's hand away. "You're jumpy tonight."

He rose silently and moved to the door of the enclosure. "Someone else is up here."

"So what? Lots of people have a right to be up here—namely, everyone who rents a space on this floor. There's no need to be paranoid...."

As if to negate her sentence, the lights abruptly went out. Swiftly Gabe snapped off the flashlight, backed up a few steps and pulled her to her feet. "Keep this." His voice was a mere thread of sound in her ear. "But don't turn it on unless I call to you." He walked her backward a few steps and pressed a hand on her shoulder, forcing her to sit among the boxes. "Stay down."

Then he melted into the darkness. And it *was* dark. Despite her earlier assurances to him, without the dim lighting the interior was filled with an inky blackness that was absolute. Straining her ears, she could hear nothing. The lack of either sight or sound lent an eerie quality that began to play on her imagination.

The sound of her own breathing seemed as loud as a siren in the stillness. It occurred to her that the entire floor would be filled with hiding areas. The compartments were all rented out, and most were stuffed with boxes, suitcases and furniture.

Minutes stretched, with only the occasional whisper of sound reaching her ears. Then a clattering noise split the darkness like a shot. Meghan's pulse froze in her veins. She heard footsteps running, in the direction of the exit.

Anxiety pumping, she rose and went to the doorway of the enclosure, uncertain about her next move. If Gabe was

following an intruder downstairs, she wouldn't be close
enough to hear him if he needed help. Even as she had the
thought, a figure loomed out of the darkness, and she gave
a startled exclamation. ''Gabe?'' The flashlight in her hand
swung upward to identify him, but midmotion the figure
swung its arm, and Meghan felt a crushing blow to her head.
She crumpled to the floor, the flashlight falling from her
hands. She had an instant to register the feel of the cool
cement beneath her cheek before the darkness swallowed
her completely.

Chapter 7

The key sounded in the lock, and Danny's stomach lurched in response. Then the doorknob turned and he launched from the couch, unmindful of Callie's warnings.

"Hey, champ."

He didn't pay any attention to the big detective's words, either. He barreled up to the couple and wrapped his arms around his aunt's knees.

"Hey." Her voice was weak, but she still sounded like his aunt Meggie. "You should be in bed."

He just clung tighter, barely hearing the murmured explanation Callie offered. He'd felt something was wrong, long before he'd heard the phone ring in Callie's apartment, before he'd ever seen the worry on her face.

"Your aunt needs to go to bed. Bet that's never happened before, huh? Your aunt going to bed before you?"

Danny loosened his arms a little bit and tipped his face up to the detective's. "Is she gonna die?"

"Of course not. I bumped my head and Detective Connally made me have a doctor look at it." Danny stepped back now, so he could see his aunt's face. Her voice sounded kinda funny. Maybe she didn't like doctors. Maybe one gave her a shot. He didn't like shots, either.

He stepped back and watched as the detective walked Aunt Meggie through the living room to the bedrooms. Callie tried to convince him to let her help him into bed, but he'd refused, and finally, after a whispered conversation with his aunt, she left.

Danny sat on the edge of the couch, thinking what to do next. He was glad, real glad, Aunt Meggie was all right. She had a big white bandage on her head, and her hair looked like there was blood in it. Once he'd bumped his head, really hard, but it hadn't bled. He didn't think Aunt Meggie could have bumped hers hard enough to make it bleed.

He thought about that for a while, then slipped from the couch and walked to her bedroom. His aunt and Raina said it was wrong to peek into people's minds. Even a little bit. But if he didn't, how could he know if Aunt Meggie was gonna be all right?

Standing in the doorway, he thought how the detective looked funny in her room, like he was too big to be in there with Aunt Meggie's things. Her things broke real easy, Danny knew. He hoped the detective wouldn't break anything.

He watched Meghan hard, letting the sensations that were pouring off her wash through him. Her head hurt. He winced in sympathy. And she was kinda mad and kinda tired. And a little scared. He wondered what had made her afraid, and knew that if he asked she wouldn't tell him. But sensing her fear made him afraid, too.

"Best thing for her now is sleep," Gabe said. He pulled the covers up to Aunt Meggie's chin and joined Danny in the doorway. "Whaddya think, champ? Lights out for her?"

Danny cocked his head, pleased to be consulted. "She'll feel better in the morning."

"My thoughts exactly."

"This conversation is not over, Connally." The words sounded as though Meghan was uttering them from between clenched teeth.

"It is for tonight." He reached out, flipped off the light switch. "We'll talk in the morning."

With a hand on the boy's shoulder, Gabe guided him from the room, pulling the door shut behind him, pretending he didn't hear the words she was muttering in the darkened room. He knew women well enough to know when he should play deaf.

It wasn't until he and Danny were standing in the middle of the living room that the full weight of responsibility hit him. Meghan needed someone to watch over her tonight. He didn't care what that quack intern had said. Head injuries could be funny. He looked at the boy, who was regarding him somberly. There was the kid, too. No way was Meghan in any condition to care for her nephew.

"So." Because he could think of nothing else to do with his hands, he jammed them in his pockets. "I guess you should be next in bed, huh?"

"You got blood on your shirt."

"What?" Gabe looked down, for the first time fully aware of the scarlet stain across his shirt front. *Meghan's blood.* His stomach clenched, and it was too easy to recall his terror when he'd found her, unconscious and bleeding, near the storage compartment. Too easy to remember cradling her limp body while he punched in the emergency number on his cell phone.

Undoing the buttons, he shed the shirt and wadded it in one hand. Blood wasn't something that normally got to him, but under the circumstances it was having a decided effect. He looked at the boy. "Where can I go and wash up?"

Danny turned on his heel and led him down the hallway to a bathroom and then watched silently while Gabe rummaged for a washcloth, wet it, then swiped it across his torso. Abandoning it in the sink, he found a towel and dried himself, his brisk actions gradually growing slower before finally stopping altogether. Silent disapproval was coming off the kid in waves. "What?"

"You gotta hang up your washcloth or it won't get dry. You don't want Aunt Meggie to get more mad at you, do you?"

Fighting an uncustomary smile, Gabe murmured, "God forbid."

Obediently he hung up the cloth and towel and turned back to the boy. "Okay, let's get you to bed."

Danny shook his head. "I have to stay up and take care of Aunt Meggie."

Something in the boy's manner caught at Gabe, held. The tone, the sentiment, seemed oddly adult. For just a moment he had an unsettling flash of déjà vu. Shaking off old memories, he steered the boy out of the bathroom. "That's not your job, kid."

"Then who's gonna do it?"

After a brief inner battle, one too weak to even constitute a struggle, he hauled in a breath. "Me, I guess."

"Oh." The boy considered the prospect for a moment and then seemed to approve it. "You could sleep on my other bunk. Alex sleeps there sometimes when he stays over."

Gabe had a brief mental image of trying to fit his large frame in the child-size bed. "The couch will do fine." Under the circumstances it was definitely the most appealing option. Well, he mentally amended, that wasn't quite right. The most appealing option would be to curl up beside Meghan where he could keep watch over her during the night. Somehow he didn't think she'd be too pleased with the prospect of finding him in her bed in the morning. He, on the other hand, found the image all too tempting.

Given his vastly limited experience with kids, he thought later, as he leaned against the kitchen counter, he'd had no idea what he'd been volunteering for. Meghan, despite the running litany of protests she'd put up since she'd regained consciousness, had been easier to get to bed than the five-year-old boy. Danny was seated at the table, legs swinging, as he enjoyed a double scoop of fudge ripple ice cream.

"Are you sure your aunt lets you eat ice cream before bed?"

"I eat ice cream most every night," the boy assured him.

Gabe stared hard at the kid, figuring he was being scammed, unable to be sure.

"You could have some ice cream, too," Danny offered, not for the first time. "Aunt Meggie eats some with me sometimes."

"Yeah?" Gabe tried to imagine Meghan sharing a bowl with her nephew. She didn't look as though she indulged in many caloric vices. She was slender, almost too much so. In his arms tonight her body had seemed slight, weightless. Although she'd stirred before the ambulance had arrived, he'd forced her to stay still. And suffered for it, he recalled, when her verbal ability had made a remarkable recovery.

"Now I have to wash my face." Danny slid down from the chair and went to the sink, scrubbing his face on a towel hanging from a drawer handle. Gabe watched, brows raised. "I can go to bed now," he pronounced, turning to consider Gabe. "But first you have to read me a book."

"You're out of luck, pal," Gabe replied, trailing behind the boy down the hall and to his bedroom. "I don't do bedtime stories." When the boy had crawled into bed, Gabe flicked off the light. "G'night." He started out the door, pulling it closed behind him.

"Don't close the door!"

The very real panic in the boy's voice froze Gabe in his tracks. "Aunt Meggie always keeps it open. With the hall light on."

Gabe pushed the door ajar. "Hey, it's no problem." He

didn't move; he was listening to the sound of strangled breathing trying to smooth out. Long moments passed.

"I wasn't scared."

Without really thinking about it, Gabe approached the bed. "I didn't think you were."

"Really?" A healthy dose of skepticism mingled with the alarm that was still apparent in Danny's tone. "Alex says only babies sleep with lights on."

"Yeah?" Gabe sat on the foot of the boy's bed, met his solemn regard. "Well, Alex is full of—" almost too late he caught himself "—misinformation," he concluded. "Lots of people sleep with the light on. If you get up in the middle of the night, you have to be able to see where you're going, right?"

"Yeah." It was clear that the explanation appealed to the boy. "Detective?"

Gabe crossed his arms over his chest and leaned against the footboard. "Under the circumstances, I think you should just call me Gabe."

"Is that what Aunt Meggie calls you?"

"No, she mostly calls me…other things." She had been quite inventive with some of those things earlier this evening, when she discovered he was determined that she go to the hospital and be checked out by a doctor. Her creativity had been further stoked by the fact that she'd been forced to ride in the ambulance. His quick grin at the memory faded just as swiftly. No, he couldn't remember a time when Meghan had called him by name. As a matter of fact, she seemed to go out of her way to avoid addressing him at all, as if by failing to do so she could keep a greater distance between them.

It shouldn't matter. And it certainly shouldn't make him long, quite violently, to rectify that situation. To hear his name on her lips, uttered in impatience. In anger. In desire.

"Are you sure you don't know any bedtime stories?"

Danny's question shattered the wholly inappropriate train

of thought, and probably none too soon. "None suitable to tell you."

"Well, what do you know?"

Gabe pursed his lips. What did he know about that could be shared in the middle of the night with a scared little kid? "I know about trains," he said finally.

That seemed to spark some interest. "What kind of trains?"

"All kinds. Mostly model trains, though, the kind you run in your house. Haven't you ever had a train set?"

The light spilling into the room from the hallway was enough for Gabe to see the boy shake his head. "Well, you'd probably like them. You hook a bunch of train cars together, see, and lay the track on a big piece of plywood. You fix the plywood up so it looks like the train is running through a city or country scene."

The topic of conversation managed to leech the last bit of tension from Gabe's limbs, and he settled more comfortably against the footboard. And as the minutes ticked away he found himself explaining his passion to a willing audience. He talked about prototypes and drive units and constant lighting circuits. When he was midway through a comparison between 1:32 and 1:22 scales, he realized the boy's breathing had grown slow and even. He stopped, more than a little amazed at his own verbosity. He'd talked more in the last hour than he usually did in an entire evening. It seemed to be a night of firsts for him.

He reached up and grabbed the pillow off the top bunk. Leaving the room, he was careful to leave the door open. It was late. After the events of the night he was suddenly dog tired. But instead of making his way to the couch, he found himself instead going to Meghan's door. Entering silently, he approached her bed, more than a little relieved to find her breathing as deeply and steadily as her nephew.

A sliver of moonlight graced her cheek, highlighted her lips. Because the opportunity rarely arose, Gabe stared his

fill. Sleep freed her face of that careful guard she normally
wore. Except for a few glimpses, Gabe had rarely seen her
without it. Now, stripped of reserve, she seemed vulnerable.
Certainly she'd already raised his fiercest protective instincts.

It was unusual for a woman to elicit much emotion from
him at all, outside the most obvious one. And because he
wasn't completely comfortable with the unfamiliar feelings,
he turned and exited the room, with undeniable haste. Away
from that bed and away from the woman lying in it.

The wind whipped whitecaps over the darkened lake and
sprayed an icy mist across the deserted wharf. The man in
the shadows cursed, pulled his collar up to protect his neck.
His clothes would be ruined. The fretted suede coat and
leather pants had been manufactured more for style than
practicality. He hadn't planned on being here this long,
hadn't figured on being kept waiting an hour beyond the
agreed upon time. The slight rankled him, but his pride
wasn't a factor when dealing with his superior. Staying alive
was.

A black limo rolled out of the darkness without lights to
herald its approach and pulled to a soundless stop on the
wharf. Familiar with the drill, the man remained where he
was while the front passenger door opened and a hulking
figure emerged.

"Raise your arms, Shadrach." The man obeyed, submit-
ting to a body frisk that was professional and insultingly
familiar.

"You're pretty good at that." He would never have dared
address the boss in such a tone, but his bruised self-respect
demanded some type of retribution. "You get to feel guys
up all day, I bet. Bet you like it, too." His snicker turned
into a wheezing gasp when a hamlike fist plowed into his
stomach and doubled him over.

Before he'd recovered, one huge paw grabbed his hair

and pushed him toward the vehicle. He sprawled to his knees on the wet boards, his breath sawing in and out of his lungs like a jagged blade.

The back door of the limo opened, but no tell-tale light went on inside. Their business was the kind best conducted in shadows.

''That display was unfortunate, Shadrach.'' The cultured voice inside the limo was reproving. ''A man at the mercy of his impulses will certainly be destroyed by them.'' As if to prove the truth of the words, the huge figure moved closer, and Shadrach huddled into a protective crouch.

''Sor...ry,'' he wheezed. In misery he registered the contemptuous snort, before the threat moved slowly away.

''You continue to disappoint me.''

The dispassionate words cut through the pain and humiliation with razored precision. ''No, sir, I don't think—''

''Thinking isn't something you do especially well. Your *thinking* has a way of calling unwanted attention. Tell me that attention is going to dissipate.''

Shadrach straightened but remained kneeling. The position of supplication wasn't lost on the man in the limousine. ''I think I got it taken care of.'' Nerves stretched in the resulting silence, encouraging a looser tongue. ''I mean I know I do. I been watching that spook's sister on the sly. She don't know nothing.''

''Your logic is as poor as your grammar. She must know something. You told me she's been seen with a *cop*.''

His life seemed to dangle by one precarious thread. ''Won't do her no good. There's nothing can link me and Chafe to Barton.''

''You've taken care of the loose ends?''

He thought of his mission a few hours earlier and felt a measure of relief that he could answer truthfully. He'd had an incredible bit of luck tonight that just might end up saving his life. ''Yessir. I got the pictures back.''

''Give them to Peter.''

The large man loomed over him, and Shadrach crouched protectively, holding the photos in the air. He didn't breathe until Peter had taken the pictures and stepped away again.

"That's all of them?"

He hesitated for a moment. He didn't remember how many pictures there were, but it made sense that they'd all be in one place, wouldn't it? "Yeah. Yeah, that's all of them."

"And there are no more loose ends?"

Forgetting the darkness for a moment, Shadrach shook his head vigorously.

"I hope, for your sake, that you're a better judge of these things than your friend, Chafe. He sent you a message, by the way." As if on cue, the hulking figure reached into the car, withdrew a bundle and tossed it on the wharf. It skittered across the boards to bump up against Shadrach's knee.

"You may open it."

With trembling fingers he unwrapped the damp cloth, straining to see in the darkness. He identified the item by touch first, a palm, five ragged digits, before horror and revulsion overtook him. He thrust the item away and turned to the side, retching.

"I'm afraid Chafe won't be around to give you a hand anymore. Pity. But he did a little too much thinking on his own when he chose to involve that Barton woman in our business. Only a fool would make the same mistake."

Car doors slammed, and the limo glided away, leaving the huddled man to empty the contents of his stomach on the water-slicked boards.

The driver of the vehicle was well away from the dock before he turned on the headlights. "Home, sir?"

"Not quite yet. I promised to join some friends, and I'm frightfully late already."

"Did you enjoy the opera, sir?"

The man in the limo straightened his cuffs and ran a meticulous hand over the satin lapel of his tux. "The tenor was a bit pretentious, I thought, but one can hardly expect more from an American production." He turned on a light and checked his appearance in the fold-down mirror. Every silver hair was in place. "Peter?"

The large man riding with the driver answered. "Sir?"

"I think we need to be looking for a replacement for Shadrach. He's outlived his usefulness."

Meghan opened her eyes in the darkness with an odd sense of disorientation. Her head was pounding. Her hand went to investigate and encountered the bandage. Snippets of memory floated across her mind. Gabe had forced her to go to the hospital, despite her vehement protests. Traveling there in an ambulance had heaped mortification on reluctance. There had been no reasoning with the man. She hadn't been surprised to discover that he was as unrelenting as a brick wall when he'd made up his mind.

Carefully she sat up, relieved when the throbbing in her temples didn't intensify. Gabe had refused to discuss her attacker; he'd been oddly intent on her well-being. He had, in fact, been giving orders in a terse, hard voice unlike any she'd heard from him before.

And then the events of the night dimmed in importance as she thought about Danny. She remembered how tightly he'd grasped her legs, and she knew he'd been thinking of his mother. And how one night she hadn't come home. Meghan hadn't been able to spend much time reassuring him before Gabe had bullied her into bed.

Swinging her legs over the edge of her bed, she rose gingerly and found the headache had abated a bit. She needed to check on her nephew. Callie wouldn't have left without making sure he was tucked in bed, but Meghan was familiar with the fears that could keep the boy awake.

She padded down the lit hallway and peeked into the boy's room. A few seconds' observation assured her that he was asleep. She made her way to the kitchen for a glass of water and stopped short halfway through the living room.

Asleep on her couch, looking decidedly out of place and distinctively uncomfortable, was Gabe Connally. Eyes huge, she approached him silently. His torso was bare. In a flash she remembered the state his shirt had been in, covered in her blood. Undoubtedly it had been ruined.

Logic was replaced by a visceral curl of feminine appreciation. It may have been shock that had pulled her to the couch, but it was definitely something else that kept her rooted to the floor, staring at him. She would have expected sleep to soften that hard jaw, to lend an ease to his features that wasn't normally seen there. It didn't. He looked much the same as he did when he was awake. Restless, faintly impatient and a little rough.

And half-naked. He was even more powerfully built than she'd realized, with muscles that begged to be stroked, kneaded. Her fingers itched, and traveled in his direction of their own volition.

Her wrist was caught midair in a hard grasp that had her bones aching and the breath hissing out of her lungs. With a quick yank, she was pulled across his chest, his other arm snaking out to keep her immobile. She gasped and found her face very close to a shadowed jaw, firm mouth and narrowed, flinty eyes.

"Meghan. Christ." He released her wrist and shoved his hand in his hair, as if he could push back the street reactions that even in sleep always hovered just below the surface. "Sorry. I wasn't expecting…" He stopped, his gaze going to the bandage on her head. "What are you doing out of bed?"

"Checking on Danny and getting a drink of water." She was amazed at the steadiness of her voice, given the fact that she was still sprawled intimately atop him. "What are you doing on my couch?"

He rubbed at his jaw, averted his eyes. "Didn't want to

leave while you were still out. I figured I'd stick around until you were back on your feet.''

Both spoke just above a whisper. Although no one could ever describe Gabe's low, rumbling tones as anything so delicate. She'd wondered once what his voice would sound like upon awakening, and now she knew. Whiskey rough, like a callused palm smoothing down her spine, leaving prickles of awareness in its wake.

Neither of them spoke for a moment. The arm keeping her pressed against him hadn't loosened, and for some reason Meghan couldn't find the will to struggle. ''Your bed partners must find your reactions upon wakening somewhat alarming.''

She could scarcely believe the words had come from her mouth. It didn't seem wise, under the circumstances, to refer to any of Connally's girlfriends. And it especially didn't seem wise to provoke this reaction from him. His eyelids grew heavy, and he stared at her with an intensity that stole the breath from her lungs. One didn't have to be overly experienced to recognize the emotion in his eyes. *Hunger.* Naked and hot, it fired an answering emotion. The blood in her veins went hot and molten, and her heartbeat stuttered, before slowing to a steady, primal beat.

''Is that what you're thinking about, Meghan? My bed partners?''

Wetting her lips, she shook her head, but the look in his eyes told her he didn't believe her. His hand slid into her hair, tangled from sleep, and cupped the back of her head. The gradual pressure he exerted was more than matched by her own craving. When their lips met it was with mutual longing.

His mouth tasted at once familiar and foreign, welcome and forbidden. She recognized the effect he had on her system, the slow roll in her stomach, the tripping of her pulse. But there was something present in his kiss that had been absent that earlier time. Before she could identify it, reaction crashed over her, sweeping aside reason.

It was like being caught in a current, swift and strong. She was carried along by the pleasure that came from the deft expertise of his touch. But it was that hint of wildness that pulled her under, that tempted her to dive recklessly into uncharted waters. He had the taste of a man who was straining at the reins of control, and the resulting reaction was devastating.

Gabe's lips twisted against hers in a burst of ravenous hunger. The taste of her was heady, long awaited. He recognized the quick punch of desire from the last time he'd kissed her, but this greed was startling. It sliced through him with ruthless claws, whipping passion to an abrupt churning point.

He pressed her lips apart, demanding entrance. Her tongue stroked his in welcome, a long velvet glide, and her flavor raced through his system. He could taste her response even as he fought with his own, and identifying it only stoked his own reaction. A dizzying burst of need licked down his spine and exploded in his blood.

He wasn't a reckless man and he didn't take impulsive chances. Risks were calculated, odds weighed. But the risk here, in his arms, was immeasureable. Distance was impossible, and control was rapidly spinning out of reach. He could only think of Meghan, and the feel of her pressed against him. The silky fabric of her nightshirt glided over his heated skin. Her curls were tumbling over her shoulders, brushing his chest. He was swamped in sensation, steeped in pleasure that could have only one outlet. Only one conclusion.

He dragged his mouth from hers and released a shuddering breath. He wasn't a particularly kind man, but he tried his damnedest to be an honest one. And if Meghan was going to give herself to him, it wouldn't be because desire had outpaced logic. It would be a conscious choice, rationally made.

"Open your eyes. Look at me." The command in his voice was tempered with passion. Her eyelids fluttered, and he felt as if he'd taken a quick jab in the gut. Her eyes were dazed, and need had deepened their hue to the color of a shimmering pool. Her lips were only a fraction of an inch from his own and presented a temptation that made him edgy.

"I told you at the beginning that I didn't want you. It'd be simpler if that were true." His stomach muscles clenched at the hint of feminine satisfaction in her eyes. Her gaze dropped to his mouth, and it took every ounce of determination he had to keep from grinding his lips against hers again.

"If you stay out here with me, it's because you choose to. No excuses. No regrets."

But he was the one to experience regret. For comprehension dawned on Meghan's face, mingling with the need that had been stamped there earlier. And because he recognized the expression of uncertainty that followed, he sat up and put some much-needed space between them.

It would have been easier if she had said something. But she only stared at him, eyes huge in her pale face, her lips still damp and swollen from his own. Though unspoken, her answer was clear.

There was a primitive force inside him that demanded he reach for her, follow her down on the couch and allow the resurging pleasure to change her mind. But he didn't play that way. Life itself sure as hell wasn't fair. He tried to do his best to be.

Frustration roughened his voice. "Go back to bed, Meghan."

For a moment he didn't think she'd move. For the space

of an instant he was convinced that she was rooted in place, and his already tattered control began to fray.

Then belatedly his words seemed to register and she fled. Gabe was left alone to stare into the darkness and curse chivalrous instincts better left denied.

Chapter 8

The living room was empty when Meghan got up the next morning, but voices drifting to her from the kitchen shattered her cowardly hope that Gabe had already left. She stopped, drew a deep breath. She owed him a vote of thanks for the opportunity he'd given her last night to come to her senses. However, she wasn't feeling particularly grateful. It would have been so much easier if she hadn't had to face him this morning, if she'd been allowed time and distance to gather senses that had scattered beneath his touch. But life, in her experience, rarely worked out to be easy.

She forced herself to move again and entered the kitchen where Danny was seated at the table chattering nonstop, and Gabe...well, Gabe was making a mess.

With raised eyebrows she silently surveyed the area. The burned remains of some mysterious substance was heaped on a plate beside the sink. Plops of runny goo were distributed on the counters and ran over the side of the bowl Gabe was holding. If she wasn't mistaken, a matching streak was smeared across his chest. Which was still bare. Still broad. Still devastating.

Her gaze raced over his form. His hair was damp and recklessly combed. An intriguing stubble shadowed his jaw. He was wearing the pants he'd had on last night and he was barefoot. For a moment she wondered which was the more incongruous: finding a half-bare man on her couch or finding one in her kitchen. With a quick flutter her pulse decided. The sight had similar effects regardless of the vantage point.

Gabe poured some of the stuff into the pan he held in his other hand, and belatedly, Meghan understood. Pancakes. No doubt her nephew had prevailed upon the man to fix his favorite breakfast.

Meghan leveled a look at the culprit in question. Danny was at the table standing on a chair, scrutinizing Gabe's actions. "Don't make them too big this time. They'll just burn up again."

"You're supposed to burn the first batch," Gabe informed him. "It gets the pan warmed up."

"Really?"

"Yeah." He tossed the boy a quick grin and saw Meghan in the doorway. His smile quickly faded. The familiar, impassive mask slid over his features, and the contrast seized her heart. He hadn't been guarded last night. She'd seen his face stamped with passion, felt his control begin to shred. But she'd made her choice then, and it had been the right one. Gabe Connally was the last man she should get involved with. He was a cop. He was intent on pulling her nephew into the middle of a police investigation. And he seemed to put a high value on honesty. That was something she couldn't afford to reciprocate.

"Okay, here you go, ace. Pancakes à la Connally." With swift, economical movements Gabe produced a plate with a flourish, atop which sat a misshapen and slightly singed-around-the-edges pancake.

Danny eyed it critically. "It looks funny."

"That's because it doesn't have syrup on it yet. And because you're looking at it from a height." With one arm, Gabe scooped him up and deposited him in a chair. "Pancakes are best surveyed up close." He slid the plate in front of the boy and reached for the syrup, making a big deal out of pouring it to Danny's specifications.

Meghan's chest tightened when her nephew laughed at Gabe's antics. Where had this casual ease between the two of them sprung from? Danny's customary reserve with strangers was understandable, considering everything he'd experienced in his young life. But it hadn't taken long for his fascination for the detective to overcome his usual reticence.

"Morning." Gabe's expressionless voice had her attention shifting, and she met his too-observant gaze. "Head still hurt?"

Unwilling to give voice to the pain that still sliced at any careless movement, Meghan lifted a shoulder. "Not bad."

Danny looked up with a mouthful of pancakes. "What happened to your Band-Aid?"

"It came off in the shower." And it had, with a little help from her. She wasn't about to walk around for the next few days looking like a crash survivor. Her still-damp hair covered the stitches well enough. It was obvious from Gabe's scowl that he disagreed.

"That intern specifically told you not to get the Band-Aid wet."

She found it more comfortable to avoid his eyes, so she went to the cupboard and took out a glass. "It'd be a little tough to wash my hair without getting it wet."

"You don't take orders very well."

"I don't take orders at all." Pouring orange juice into her glass, she finally turned back to face him. "I thought you'd be gone when I got up." When she realized how the words sounded, she flushed. "I mean, I thought you'd have to get to work."

"I do. Cal's bringing some of my stuff over so I don't have to drive home first. And then he can update me on what he found out last night. I called him before the ambulance arrived. I wanted him to get a look at the scene before the uniforms showed up."

As if on cue, the buzzer rang. Gabe padded out of the kitchen to the intercom mounted beside the front door. After a terse exchange he turned back to Meghan, who had followed him. "He'll be right up."

It occurred to her that he had a way of taking charge, even in her apartment. But she swallowed her protest. At last it seemed as though she'd get some answers. Gabe had been maddeningly elusive when she'd questioned him last night.

"I'm done." Danny scrambled from the chair and headed toward them. "I can get ready for school now."

"Not so fast." With effort Meghan pulled her thoughts from last night and focused on her nephew. "I don't suppose you had a bath last night?"

His head started to bob, then, catching Gabe's eye, turned into a negative shake. "Then I'll go in and run the bath water. You can't go to school covered with syrup."

Gabe watched the pair walk toward the bathroom. The boy's words drifted behind him. "You make me take too many baths. My skin's gonna get soaked off. I'll just be bones."

Meghan's response reached Gabe just before the taps turned on. "Think how cool you'll look then."

A corner of his mouth lifted. He could almost imagine the kid's response. The boy seemed to have a macabre interest in things like that. He didn't know why he was so surprised that Meghan realized it. It was obvious she was devoted to her nephew. Sometimes, though, he thought she was as guarded around the boy as she was with Gabe.

A knock sounded, and he pulled the door open and let Cal in. "Thanks," he said, taking the hastily packed bag from his partner. "I would have hated to have to fight the traffic all the way home and then back to district headquarters."

"No problem." Cal's attention was fixed on Gabe's state of undress. "I didn't realize just how desperately you needed a change."

Gabe laid the bag on the coffee table and unzipped it. Peering inside, he pulled out a pin-striped shirt with a scowl. "What'd you bring me this one for? I hate this shirt."

"Which probably explains why it was the only decent one in your closet. God, Connally—" Cal walked over to the couch and sat on it "—your clothes are just a cut above the ones we found in D'Brusco's closet."

Leaving the shirt half-unbuttoned, Gabe glared at him while he exchanged his pants for the ones his partner had brought. "There's nothing wrong with my clothes."

"Nothing a good rummage sale wouldn't fix."

"Listen, pal, you weren't exactly a fashion plate yourself until Becky took you in hand."

"Then it's time you were taken in hand. Got someone in mind for the job?"

Gabe chose to ignore the speculation in his partner's voice. Meghan had returned to the room and was watching him with huge eyes. He shoved the tails of his shirt into his waistband with barely controlled violence. If the woman was intent on keeping their relationship platonic, she damn well ought to stop staring at him like that. A man could be forgiven for mistaking that look for something else. Like wanting. Hunger. The kind he'd had a taste of last night. The kind he was itching to taste again.

He zipped his pants and buttoned them, keeping his gaze firmly trained on Cal. "Why don't you tell us what went down when you got there last night?" Meghan sank into one of the easy chairs flanking the couch, and he took the other.

"Actually, I got there right after the ambulance pulled away, about ten minutes before the uniforms. Found the watchman on the floor of his station. He was just coming around."

"The watchman?" Meghan's attention jerked to Gabe who nodded.

"I figured as much. The punk must have knocked him out after gaining access. Any chance the guard can ID the guy?"

Cal shook his head. "He never knew what hit him. There was a door in back that had been jimmied open. The intruder probably entered there. How about you? Did you get a look at him?"

Gabe made a sound of disgust. "Not enough for a description. Five ten or eleven, maybe 170 pounds. Wore dark clothes, a watch cap over his head, and gloves. I almost had the punk by the stairwell. He threw something at me." His gaze went to Meghan's, held. "I recognized it as your flashlight. He took off down the stairs, and I went back for you." And he'd found her. Hurt. Bleeding. There was a single vicious twist in his gut at the memory. He never should have left her in the darkness alone. He hadn't been there when she'd needed him. It would be a long time before he forgave himself that.

"So we just happened to be in the wrong place at the wrong time?" Meghan looked from one detective to the other. "Maybe this guy was a thief hoping to ransack some of the compartments, came upon us and panicked."

"Maybe." Because he couldn't resist that hopeful tone in her voice, he tempered his own. "Or maybe he wanted to see what we were up to." He despised himself then when he saw the flash of fear in her eyes, but she wouldn't thank him for trying to sugarcoat the truth. That much, at least, he knew about her. "The lighting went out just before things started to break."

Cal nodded. "The fuse box for each floor is located in the stairwell, right behind the door. Looks like our guy went up the stairs, checking each floor on his way. The first two levels had the lights out, too."

"So he hit the third floor and heard us talking," Gabe surmised. "He cut the lights and made his move."

Meghan folded her arms across her chest, each hand tightly clutching the opposite arm. "So you think he meant to attack us all along."

In an uncustomary urge to soothe, Gabe consciously softened his voice. "Maybe not. He might have thought we'd leave when the lights were cut. And if I hadn't heard him moving, maybe we would have."

Shaking her head, she said, "But why? Why did he want us out of there?"

"Maybe he was after the same thing the two of you were looking for," Cal suggested. He met Gabe's gaze meaningfully. "Whatever that might have been."

"But there wasn't anything!" Meghan's words were exasperated. "Which is exactly what I tried to tell Gabe yesterday."

Ignoring her words, Gabe looked at Cal. "You searched the compartment?"

The man nodded. "Didn't look like it had been bothered much. One box was open." He sent a questioning look at his partner and Gabe nodded.

"We'd just started on the fourth one."

"Can't really tell if anything was missing, but the boxes didn't look disturbed. If he'd been through them he wouldn't have been careful."

"Did you happen to find any pictures on the floor? Polaroids, like the one Meghan gave us of her sister?"

"Nope."

Gabe drilled Meghan with a look. "How many did you say were there?"

She stared from one man to the other. "Nine, but why..."

"What did you do with them after I left you?"

"I...I laid them down just before you left," she said slowly. Her face was set, still, as if she were keeping dangerous emotion suppressed. "I was holding the flashlight. It seemed like you were gone a long time. I kept hearing sounds...I saw a shape, thought you had come back."

Gabe's mouth flattened to a thin hard line. "He wasn't in the compartment long enough to do any searching. If the pictures are all that's missing, then we have to figure that maybe they were what he was looking for."

"No." Agitated, Meghan rose to pace. "Those pictures wouldn't mean anything to anyone else."

"They might have meant something to this guy because he was the cameraman. Or knows who was."

"Was there something incriminating pictured in them?"

Wearily, Meghan shook her head. "They were the only current pictures I could find of either Sandra or Danny. They weren't even of particular good quality. I had already brought the best ones here. You have one of them."

"Then I think it's time we took a closer look at the others," Gabe said quietly.

Things were moving too fast. Meghan stared at him, only dimly aware of the noises Danny was making as he staged a major naval war in his bath. She'd wanted Sandra's death investigated, hadn't she? Then why was she filled with this mind-numbing fear as it appeared more and more likely that they just might discover something that would provide her with some of the answers she craved?

Releasing a shuddering breath, she stood silently and led them to her studio. She opened a drawer beneath a counter, drew out the two remaining photos. Thrusting them at Gabe, she muttered, "I have to check on Danny."

He watched her leave the room, and fought the urge to follow her. Any comfort he could offer wouldn't be welcome, and he was damn poor at offering comfort, at any rate. The best thing he could do for her was to find D'Brusco, and maybe clear up a little of the mystery surrounding her sister's final days. He gave the photos in his hands a cursory glance. There was nothing in either of them to suggest their importance. Maybe the technician downtown could find something.

Cal gave a short whistle, and Gabe looked up. "What?" In the next instant he wasn't certain he wanted to know. The smirk on his partner's face didn't bode well.

"Better wipe off your chin, man, you're drooling."

Gabe glared at him. "What are you talking about?"

Chuckling, his partner answered, "I mean you've got it bad. The tension between the two of you is thick enough to cut with a knife."

Turning on his heel, Gabe stalked from the studio, leaving his partner to trail after him. "You're imagining things," he said shortly. "The thing is, I kinda promised to look into her sister's death for her, in return for her allowing us to use the kid for an ID of D'Brusco's friend. Then with Barton's connection with D'Brusco..." He gave a shrug. "That keeps her involved."

"Involved." Cal stroked his chin consideringly. "Yeah, that's what it looks like to me, too. Like the two of you are involved."

Gabe's beeper went off then, followed a moment later by Cal's. "Who's gonna call in?" Gabe asked, half-relieved by the interruption. When Cal got something in his head, it was difficult to shake it. The two men silently engaged in rock-paper-scissors, and Gabe lost. It was almost worth it. He went to Meghan's phone and punched in the number to headquarters.

Danny entered the room at a run, with Meghan following more sedately. "Slow down, you're not late."

He skidded to a stop near the front door and yanked the closet door open. "I like to get to Alex's early so we can watch cartoons before we hafta leave."

"Alex is coming here this morning, remember? It's my turn to take you guys to school."

Gabe disassociated himself from the scene and focused on the voice on the phone. After a few terse questions he hung up and caught his partner's eye. "We better get moving."

"Why? What's going on?"

Keenly aware of Meghan and Danny in the room, Gabe chose his words carefully. "D'Brusco has surfaced."

"Great." Cal started for the door. "Where's he being held?"

"West Harrison." He saw the comprehension in his partner's glance. They wouldn't be getting any answers out of Lenny D'Brusco. Nobody would. Because right now he was occupying a slab in the police morgue.

"Cause of death, knife wound to the throat. I'll need to conduct the autopsy before I can give you a full description of the wounds, but I'm betting he was dead before he hit the water." Doug Trump spoke cheerfully to the detectives from across the bloated corpse. "The fish had quite a time with the body before it was discovered."

Cal winced. "Spare us the gory details, Doug. Are you going to be able to estimate the date of death with any accuracy?"

"Depends." The medical examiner pulled the sheet back over the body. "From the looks of it, I'd guess he was in the water two or three days. Have to wait and see what shows up inside. Water isn't much of a preservative."

"We'd appreciate it if you could put a rush on the autopsy."

"Of course you would. Everyone is appreciative." The medical examiner rolled his eyes. "And everyone's in a rush. We're knee-deep in bodies here. With these damn budget cuts there's a hiring freeze on the vacant position in my department, but there's no freeze on the work, y'know?''

Gabe and Cal exchanged a glance. "They won't give you the help you need? That's rotten, Doug."

"Yeah, you guys are the backbone of the outfit. How do they expect us to solve any cases if you don't get the help you need?" Gabe chimed in.

The medical examiner eyed them suspiciously. "The original Frick and Frack aren't you? Did you really think that patronizing crap was going to work?"

Shrugging, Gabe said, "We thought it was worth a try."

Doug snorted. "Well next time try a case of prime scotch. Otherwise your guy waits his turn."

The detectives were ushered out of the morgue, and both took a deep breath of the relatively fresh air in the hallway. "Think it's worth a case of scotch?" inquired Cal as they headed back upstairs.

"Let's wait and see. Somehow I don't think we're going to find out a whole lot about D'Brusco's murderer from the autopsy. Not after he was in the water that long."

As soon as they entered the squad room back at headquarters, Gabe was immediately aware of the covert glances sent their way. By the time he'd reached his desk his suspicions had heightened noticeably. "All right, what's going on." Dead silence met his question. He looked at the most likely suspect. "Fiskes? What'd you do, start a fire in my desk drawer again?" As if to make sure, he reached down and pulled the drawer out a ways.

"The lieutenant's got company," the detective answered. All eyes traveled to the direction of the lieutenant's office, which had the blinds closed. A bad sign.

"It must be your lucky day, boys." Fiskes grinned wickedly as he went back to the report he was typing. "Because I heard your names being mentioned."

As if on cue, the door to the office opened and Lieutenant Burney appeared. "Connally. Madison. Could you come in here, please?"

The partners exchanged a glance before obeying. "What's up, Lieutenant?" Gabe asked in a low voice as he passed by him into the cramped office. The door was closed behind the detectives, and Gabe saw the answer for himself. Two men were seated inside already and turned at their approach. Gabe pegged them in an instant as suits. Feds, definitely. Then his gaze fell on the file open on the lieutenant's desk. He glanced at Cal and knew the other man recognized it, too. It was a copy of the D'Brusco file.

"Gentlemen, Detectives Connally and Madison." Lieutenant Burney rounded his desk and sat down. "Agents Gallo and Torley. Justice."

Justice. The two detectives pulled out chairs and sat.

"Detectives." The tall thin one, Torley, nodded in their direction. He was pushing fifty, Gabe figured, and looked every day of it. "We understand from your lieutenant that you've been investigating some questionable monetary activity."

Hooking one foot over the opposite knee, Gabe returned the man's regard steadily. "That's right."

"Guess this is your lucky day, then. We're about to lighten your caseload for you."

"That's kind of you. Isn't that kind of them, Cal?"

Recognizing the sarcasm in his tone, the lieutenant threw Gabe a warning look.

"Actually it has come to our attention that your case dovetails neatly with an ongoing investigation we've been conducting." Agent Gallo was speaking now, with a slight Boston accent. He was a couple of decades younger than his partner, but didn't seem any less uptight.

"Dovetails neatly," Gabe muttered in an aside to Cal. "Geez. Where do they get these guys?" He was about to say more, but, catching the lieutenant's eye, wisely refrained.

"I've received a request from these agents' superior asking for a complete copy of your investigation to date."

"Sorry we couldn't arrange to have that delivered on a silver platter for you," Gabe said with mock politeness.

Torley leaned forward, locked gazes with him. "Do you have something you want to say, Connally?"

Burney cleared his throat. "I don't think…"

"Yeah, Lieutenant, I do." Addressing Torley, Gabe said, "Justice was sniffing around this case from the beginning. But you backed off until now. Why? Did you need someone to do the groundwork for you first?"

"We weren't sure then about the connection to the case we're building," the agent retorted. "Now we are. You should be thanking us, Detectives. We're making your life easier."

As the lieutenant showed the men out of his office, Cal looked at his partner. "They didn't think we were grateful. Imagine that."

Burney returned to his desk, leaned against it and folded his arms across his chest. "You must have a lot of friends, Connally. What with your winning manner."

"C'mon, Lieutenant." Gabe made no effort to curb the frustration in his voice. "This case is ours in about eight different ways. It's just like Justice to waltz in here after we've done the work…."

"This department wouldn't have completed a laundering investigation and you know it, Detective. It's routine for another agency to take it over at some point. And it's not like you're off the case completely." He waited until Gabe met his gaze before continuing, "You've still got a dead body on your hands, don't you? Looks like you two still have a homicide investigation to conduct." Pushing off from the desk, he went to the door, held it open.

Gabe and Cal exchanged glances as they exited the office.

D'Brusco's murder was intertwined with his activities that may have led to it. The lieutenant was right.

They still had a case to work. And Gabe figured their best lead would be to identify the last-known guy to have seen D'Brusco alive.

"It's out of the question." Meghan turned from Gabe's level stare and scrubbed at an imaginary stain on the counter.

"Why is it out of the question?"

"Because he's a five-year-old boy, that's why!" She whirled on him, fire in her eyes, fear in her heart. "Can you even imagine the trauma he's been through in recent months? Do you even care? I'm not going to allow you to put him through more."

Something settled in his eyes—a cold chill. "Working with a sketch artist isn't going to send your nephew over the edge. You agreed to cooperate when we first entered into our bargain, remember? I've upheld my end. You got your second look into your sister's accident."

"What I got were even more questions."

"That's right. And those questions point to a connection between your sister and the corpse we've got downtown." She winced at his description, but he didn't seem to notice. "By helping us solve the D'Brusco case you just might get a few more answers to those questions."

She firmed lips that were beginning to tremble. "You can't guarantee that."

"No." His low voice curled around her like a lover's embrace, and reminded her, just for a moment, of the way it had sounded the night she'd been in his arms.

Open your eyes. Look at me, Meghan.

The memory alone was seductive enough to send a shiver over her skin. It wasn't what she ought to be concentrating on, however. It was the choice she'd made that night. And all the reasons for it.

"I'll have to consult his therapist," she hedged. "To see if he can handle it. And if the timing is right."

His eyes were shrewd. "Why does he have a therapist? He seems all right to me."

Her gaze slid from his and she went to the sink, took her time arranging the damp dishcloth over the faucet to dry. "He had some trouble adjusting...problems at school. She's helped him a lot. Helped us both." The words were a masterful understatement. She would never have made it this far with Danny without Raina's help.

"Okay, so we'll ask the therapist."

"No!" She knew the vehemence in her voice would only give rise to more questions, but she couldn't control it. Gabe couldn't meet Raina. The thought had her blood turning glacial. She didn't doubt the woman's discretion, but neither did she doubt the detective's persistence. He wouldn't be satisfied until he'd learned all there was to know about Danny's therapist. And from there it would only be a step until the next secret was revealed. The one she was determined he'd never discover.

She wet her lips, strove for composure. "I'll talk to her. Then I'll let you know what she says."

He was watching her with that sardonic, knowing expression that he wore far too frequently. "If she happens to say no, I'll be wanting to talk to her myself."

She turned her back on him then, her fingers clenching the edge of the counter in frustration. Her mind was whirling, but she didn't see a way out of this. She should never have made that ridiculous agreement; should never have believed she could get away with using the man, as she'd originally intended. There would be no denying Gabe Connally. At least, she hadn't figured a way yet.

She sensed his presence behind her and closed her eyes. Two hard fists propped on the counter on either side of her hands. She could feel his heat at her back, a bare fraction of space between them. When he spoke, she imagined she could feel his lips brushing against her hair. "He's already involved in this, Meghan. *You're* already involved."

She shook her head in silent denial, all the while knowing he spoke the truth. She was trapped, in much the same way she was caged between the counter and the equally unyielding man at her back. A breath shuddered out of her when his cheek brushed her hair. He was right, and the acknowledgment brought only desperation. She was involved. Involuntarily, intricately.

And she could see no way out.

Chapter 9

"I understand your reluctance." Raina's hand touched Meghan's, as gentle as her voice. "But you have a choice here, no? And if Danny can help, you may also learn more about Sandra. Both of you have questions about her death."

Her gazed streaked to Raina's. "Danny has questions? What has he said?"

"He was living with his mother when she was involved in all this," Raina reminded her. "He's too young to be able to verbalize all of what he feels, but he is able to sense quite a bit. And he felt the danger his mother was in. It made him very afraid."

Agitated, Meghan rose to pace. "All the more reason then to keep him out of this investigation. There's no telling who he may come into contact with at a police station. Can you imagine the kind of things he might sense if there happens to be a criminal in custody?"

"So it is his reactions you fear."

Honesty compelled Meghan to admit, "Not totally. Going to the police station we run the risk that someone might start asking questions, putting two and two together.''

''You do not trust this Detective Connally to keep him safe?''

The older woman's question hung in the air, and Meghan considered it honestly. The key word was *trust*. She shouldn't trust any cop, after what the department had done to her family. She held Wadrell responsible for her sister's name being made public. The thought of the same thing happening to Danny; the thought of him following a path blazed by his mother, seeking the public eye, only to eventually die from it, turned her heart to ice. There was nothing she wouldn't do to prevent that.

But she wasn't dealing with Wadrell here, she was dealing with Gabe. And thoughts of the man muddied the waters. She knew he was trustworthy up to a point. She could expect him to be up-front with her and not try to hide his motives. But things could happen that were outside of his control. She wouldn't trust him with Danny's ability; it wasn't her secret to share, at any rate.

Aware that Raina was awaiting her answer, she finally said, ''I know he would do what he could. But that may not be enough and I can't take that chance, can I?''

''It sounds as though you have made up your mind.''

''I have.'' Meghan stared at the corner where her nephew was busily drawing. ''I'll tell Gabe we've decided not to let Danny cooperate.''

An hour later Meghan opened the door to the apartment and Danny ran by her. ''Time for...Pokémon!'' Grasping the remote, Danny scrambled up on the couch and turned on his favorite show.

''How about time to hang up your coat?'' she inquired, amused. On Callie's advice, she limited her nephew's TV watching to an hour a day, and he tended to take advantage of every minute of it.

Without removing his gaze from the TV screen, Danny dropped his school bag and shrugged out of his coat. He looked at the TV and then the closet, clearly torn.

Taking pity on him, Meghan said, ''I'll hang it for you this time.''

''Thanks, Aunt Meggie.''

By the time she'd turned back to her nephew he was staring raptly at the television set again. Meghan followed his gaze with her own, wondering, not for the first time, what magic the show had that transfixed a five-year-old boy. Its power was lost on her. ''Did you bring home a note from your teacher today?''

Her only answer was a head shake.

Half-amused she asked, ''How about papers? Did you bring home any of your work to show me?'' Her question warranted a distracted nod. ''Shall I get them out of your bag for you?'' Another nod. It appeared that nothing short of a natural disaster could divert the boy's attention.

Crossing to the couch, she sat down beside him, reached for his bag and unzipped it. They'd worked out something of a routine in the short time they'd lived together. Ordinarily Danny insisted on emptying his bag himself, presenting each of his papers with the gravity of a master exhibiting a finished piece of art.

Meghan drew the papers out of the bag and looked at them one by one. She paused at Danny's rendering of a dinosaur. For the last week he'd chosen to paint dinosaurs at school as a not-so-subtle hint about his birthday present. Although Meghan continued to play noncommittal, she'd already bought and wrapped the two dinosaurs the boy had his heart set on. They were safely tucked away in her bedroom closet.

She tipped the bag upside down to be certain she'd taken out everything. A boy's treasures, she'd found, weren't limited to papers from school. Hearing a rattle she uprighted the bag, peered inside. When she found that pocket empty she unzipped the others until she discovered what had caused the sound.

"What's this key go to?"

Danny's head whipped around and he stared at the key in her hand, eyes wide. His lips began to quiver, but he squared his chin with an effort and didn't say a word.

More than a little concerned about his reaction, Meghan asked, "Did you find it? Someone may be looking for it." There was adhesive tape wrapped around the top, with the number 498 written on it. "Although I'm not sure what it could go to," she mused. "It's too big for a suitcase, not the right shape for a car..." Her words broke off when she saw the huge tears welling in the boy's eyes.

"Hey, there's nothing to worry about." There was a tinge of panic in her voice. Her nephew's tears were increasingly infrequent, and never failed to make her feel inadequate. "If you found it at school we can just turn it in to the lost and found there."

"It's the secret."

The thin thread of desperation that ran through her nephew's voice had Meghan reaching over for the remote and clicking off the TV. It was a measure of Danny's upset that he didn't seem to notice. With an effort at calm she said, "Tell me about the secret."

The boy cast his gaze downward. If possible his voice got even lower. "I was supposed to give it to you, but I didn't. Mom told me the secret and then she got dead." When his gaze raised to hers again it was filled with such heart-wrenching despair that it squeezed her heart. "I don't want you to get dead, too, Aunt Meggie."

A sense of foreboding settled in her chest. She was about to reassure the boy, but the words went unuttered. Danny deserved more than empty assurances. She asked the next question, more than a little certain that she wouldn't like the answer. "When did your mom give you this?"

He shrugged miserably. His concept of time, she knew,

centered on school days and cartoon days. "Was it after I came to your apartment? When we met for the first time?" A slow solemn nod was her answer. "How long..." She drew in a breath and forced the words out. "How many cartoon days did you have it before you came to live with me?"

"We went shopping on cartoon day and I got a new bag."

Meghan handed the now-empty bag to the boy, and he hugged it fiercely to his chest. "Mom put the key in it at night, before I went to bed. She said to give it to you if I saw you again. She said it was a secret. I hate secrets! I hate them!" The boy's voice rose a little wildly. "Put the key back, Aunt Meggie!"

His obvious agitation melted her reserve the way nothing else could have. She moved over and put her arms around the boy, feeling the trembling that was shaking his rigid body. "Shh," she whispered. Unconsciously her body began to sway in a rocking motion. From the boy's description she guessed that Sandra had given him the key about a week after she'd last seen her sister. "That key can't hurt anyone. And once we all know the secret we'll know what your mom was thinking when she gave it to you, won't we?"

"We could throw it away." The words were muffled against her chest.

"I think you realize we can't do that. But I can promise you that I'll take care of it. And whatever the secret is, I won't let anything hurt you." The words were uttered to soothe. She surprised herself by the conviction in them. She had a bond of responsibility with this boy. And she had the same sort of bond with Sandra. She owed it to both of them to lay all the secrets to rest. No matter what they were.

Danny heard the tone in his aunt's voice but didn't respond. He couldn't. The bad feeling had started as soon as his mom had dropped the key in his bag. It came back every time he thought about it being in there. Thought about how

he hadn't told Aunt Meggie the secret like his mom had
said to. Fiercely he willed himself to believe his aunt's
words. He wanted to. He wondered if the bad feeling would
leave once she found out the secret. But somehow he didn't
think so.

"Can you blow it up any more?"

Stan Vandevanter, the police technician, shrugged at
Gabe's question. "I can, but with every enlargement the
picture will get grainier. This was the biggest I could make
it without losing clarity. See what happens here?" The man
tapped a command into the computer, and the picture enlarged again. As the man had warned, it became noticeably
less detailed.

Gabe took another moment to study the reproduction of
the first of the pictures he'd taken from Meghan before
glancing at Cal. At his quizzical look, his partner shook his
head. "Nothing's jumping out at me."

"Let's see the next one."

Obligingly Stan tacked up the enlargement of the second
photo. Gabe squinted at it. Where the first had been taken
of Sandra and Danny on a crowded street, this one had been
taken in a park. Sandra was seated on a park bench, looking
at a newspaper. It would be difficult to say whether she or
Danny had been the focus of the picture. The boy was standing next to the bench, blowing bubbles. A smile pulled at
the corner of Gabe's mouth. Danny's face was a study in
concentration. It reminded him of the night the boy had
asked him for a bedtime story and he'd told him about
trains. For several minutes he'd fought sleep with just that
same fierce concentration, as if to hear every word Gabe
had uttered. It had been a novel experience to be the focus
of that intense regard.

Stan brought the last of the pictures to the screen, and
without waiting to be asked, began to enlarge it. "Wait!"
Interest suddenly heightened, Gabe leaned forward. "Can

you zoom in right here and enlarge this part?'' He tapped a finger against the foreground.

"No problem." The technician moved the mouse to the area the detective had indicated and clicked several times until Gabe halted him. "Okay, right there." He tilted his head. "Tell me what you see, Cal."

His partner peered more closely at the picture. "I can't be sure. I'd have to compare it to the other one."

"Bring the first picture back," Gabe ordered. A buzz of adrenaline was humming through his veins, the feeling he got when pieces of a case were dropping into place. They leaned in to study the picture that filled the screen again.

"Yeah, maybe," Cal muttered. "Let's see a closer shot."

"Zoom in here." Gabe indicated a spot in the crowd behind Sandra and Danny.

"Want a comparison shot?" Without waiting for the detectives' assent Stan brought a boxed-in likeness of the enlarged sections of both photos and arranged them side by side on the computer screen.

"I'll be damned," breathed Gabe. Through computer enhancement they were able to clearly see parts of the foregrounds that had lacked clarity before. And in two of the pictures, the same man could be seen standing a distance away from Sandra.

"What are the chances that the same guy would just happen to be hanging around while pictures are being shot of Barton and her kid?"

"Somewhere between slim and none," Cal replied. "It doesn't look like Barton was aware these pictures were being taken. But something tells me this guy knew." He pointed at the screen.

"Yeah. Now all we have to do is figure out why." Gabe's voice was grim. There was no longer any doubt that the intruder at the storage compartment had had more than a passing interest in the rest of these pictures. Someone knew he'd shown up in these photos and had been desperate to recover them.

"Can you get us a hard copy of that close-up?" he asked Stan. The man nodded and tapped a command into the computer. A moment later the printer was spitting out a color photo. Gabe snatched it. "Thanks, Stan. C'mon, Cal. Let's see if we've got a pinup of this guy."

The tedium of the next two hours paid off when Gabe whistled softly. "Hello. I've got a match."

Cal abruptly shut the book of mug shots he was looking at and rounded the desk to peer over Gabe's shoulder. "Looks like him. Shadrach Collins. Let's see what we can find out about our friend in the database."

Gabe deferred to his partner's superior ability on the computer. "Oh, he's been busy, hasn't he?" he murmured, leaning over Cal's shoulder to read the man's rap sheet.

"Well, well. What's this?"

"He's been flagged," Gabe murmured. "Not surprising that some other CEO has taken an interest, with this guy's record."

Cal scrolled down to the bottom of the screen, and a name jumped out at Gabe. "Wadrell. What'd he want this guy for?"

"I don't know. But there are getting to be way too many connections from his last case to ours, don't you think?"

The clerk interrupted before Gabe could answer. "Detective Connally, call on line two."

Reluctantly Gabe turned from the computer to cross to his desk. His mind still on their findings, his voice was brusque when he answered. "Detective Connally."

The female on the other end of the line had his attention within the first few words. His expression growing grimmer, he listened for a moment more then said, "You did the right thing to call me. I'll take care of it."

He returned the receiver to the hook and turned back to his partner.

"Trouble?" Cal inquired.

"Maybe." He reached over to grab his jacket. "I think Meghan might be closing in on another piece of the puzzle regarding her sister. And I'm going to make damn sure I'm there when she finds it."

The key didn't fit. Meghan let out the breath she'd been holding and stepped away from the locker in the train station. The pounding of her heart quieted. It occurred to her, not for the first time, that she may well have sent herself on a wild-goose chase. But she was no amateur sleuth. A transit locker had seemed the most obvious solution. The key didn't look as if it would fit a suitcase, car or door. And whatever it did unlock would have to be something she'd have access to. Something Sandra knew she could find with little effort.

It was significant that her first inclination after she'd quieted Danny's fears was to call Gabe. She dismissed the thought just as quickly. There was no way of knowing what, if anything, she'd find. But if she did discover something she wanted to view it free of a cop's eyes, a cop's reaction.

And she couldn't take the chance that whatever she found might allude to Danny's gift. She had to protect his secret at all costs. Even from Gabe. *Especially* from Gabe.

Turning away from the row of lockers, she headed back toward the double front doors and the parking lot beyond. It was too early to contemplate failure. Similar lockers could be found at the bus depot, as well as in some subway stations. Her head down as she contemplated the possibilities, she almost ran into the man who stepped in front of her.

"Planning a trip?"

Dismay sank like a brick in her stomach. "What are you doing here?"

Gabe gave her a humorless smile. "I asked you first." With a nudge he got her moving again. "I got a call from your friend, Callie. Said she was having a difficult time

getting your nephew calmed down. That you'd told her
you'd gone out to buy him a birthday present, but he keeps
talking about a bad secret that was going to hurt you. Something you were trying to find of his mother's.'' He lifted
his head and scanned the crowd before ushering her out
through the doors and outside.

Her throat went dry and she forced a shrug. ''Kids can
be dramatic.''

''I wouldn't know.'' Although his manner was easy
enough, there was a tightness to his mouth that warned of
a simmering temper. ''Your nephew kept telling Callie that
you took the key to the trains. For future reference you
might consider that if you can't even deceive a little kid,
you probably ought to give it up. You're not too good at
it.''

She was, she thought miserably, much better than he
could have guessed. And she was fiercely glad that he'd
concluded Danny's accurate guess of her location came
from her poor acting skills. Her palms dampened as she
realized that the boy had managed to focus on her across
the city and come up with hints of her whereabouts.

The familiar tightness was in her chest, the same feeling
she'd always had when Sandra had carelessly plucked one
of her carefully guarded thoughts and exposed it for the
perusal of those around her. The accompanying feelings of
violation, vulnerability.

But how, she wondered, as Gabe fairly dragged her in
his wake, did she come to terms with those feelings regarding a five-year-old boy? He tried so hard to live the lessons
Raina taught him, and the effort almost broke her heart.
Somehow she knew it had been fear that had motivated him
this time, just as it had been preoccupation that had lowered
her customary guard, allowing it.

She looked up when they stopped, and frowned. ''My car
is across the lot.''

''Tough. You're riding with me.''

His high-handed manner had her narrowing her eyes at him. "No, I'm not."

His gaze met hers, hard and unyielding. "Where's the key, Meghan? Good idea to check transit lockers first. That's what I would have recommended myself."

She ignored the little flare of pride his words inspired. Under the circumstances, it was ridiculous. She'd be better off spending her time planning how she could shake Gabe, if and when they found what Sandra had left. Something told her that would require more than a little ingenuity.

They got in his car, and Gabe glanced at her across the front seat. Rarely had he seen Meghan this anxious. Although she was striving not to show it, nerves were hovering just below her mask of calmness. Her fingers twisted in her lap. And clutched in those fingers was the key.

"Maybe we're on the wrong track altogether." He heard the thread of hope in her voice.

"We'll check the bus depot next." Uncustomarily, Gabe kept his gaze firmly on the road as he spoke. There was something about the worry stamped on her pale face that evoked a deeply protective response. He couldn't afford to be sidetracked by it. There was too much at stake to compromise his objectivity. And the admission that his objectivity was an issue was an uncomfortable realization better dealt with another time.

With effort he forced his mind back to their conversation. "Some of the subway stations may have lockers, too. I'd have to contact the Transit Department to figure out which ones. But I think we're on the right path. The key doesn't go to anything you found in her apartment, does it?" He felt, rather than saw, the shake of her head. "And it doesn't look like any safety deposit key I've ever seen."

He pulled into the parking lot for the bus depot and found a spot to park. Even after he'd switched off the ignition of the car, Meghan sat, taut with apprehension. He waited with uncustomary patience.

"I'm starting to think that we'd be better off not knowing what Sandra left behind," she burst out. The key was clutched so tightly in her hand that her palm would surely be branded with its imprint. "When we were growing up, my sister's 'surprises' were most often unpleasant." Her gaze flew to his, guilt and remorse mingled in it. "I know that sounded incredibly self-centered."

Because he felt an unusual urge to soothe, he covered her hands with one of his, stilling their movement. "Times like these, I guess you're entitled."

She squeezed his fingers, just for an instant, then released them. He could see her draw herself up, as if reaching deep down inside an inner well of strength belied by her fragile exterior. Not for the first time, she earned his admiration. And something else. Something much more complex.

"Well let's get on with it, shall we?" Although her smile was strained, her voice sounded steady enough. He rounded the car and placed his hand at the base of her back as they walked toward the depot. As support it wasn't much. He didn't know if she took any comfort from that light touch, but he knew that he did. And he'd worry about the meaning of that later.

After the agony of indecision all afternoon, the discovery of Sandra's secret was almost anticlimatic. "A videotape." Meghan reached into the locker the key had opened and withdrew its lone content. She drew a deep breath. "I'm guessing it's not a home movie."

"No." He took the tape from her hand. "But it may shed some light on her relationship with D'Brusco. And it just might answer some of those questions you've had about your sister's death, Meghan."

She lifted her gaze to meet his whiskey-colored eyes and knew he was right. But that didn't stop one thought from echoing in her mind.

Maybe some questions were better left unanswered.

"Let me clear some of this out of the way."

Meghan looked around Gabe's living room curiously. She was unsure whether she was more surprised at his slight embarrassment over the clutter, or at being in his home in the first place. He swept up some newspapers, a plate and an empty beer bottle in his hands and strode out of the room. She moved a bit so she could track him with her gaze. The kitchen adjoining this room lacked the same homey untidiness. Somehow she thought this room got a lot more use than the kitchen.

Not for the first time she considered grabbing the video-tape and fleeing. No amount of protesting had swayed Gabe from his determination to view the tape with her. Her argument about privacy and property had gone head-to-head with his insistence that the tape might well shed some light on his ongoing investigation. Her presence in his home was testament to the winner in that battle of wills.

Roaming over to a built-in bookcase, she studied its contents. A surprisingly large number of books were arranged neatly by size. Gabe's taste ran to police mysteries and thrillers. In front of the books were several framed photographs, and it was these that held Meghan's attention the longest. There were several pictures of him with an older couple, and another one of him and the man in the pictures. Gabe was holding a huge fish and wearing a carefree expression that she'd never observed. With a jolt she wondered if she ever would.

There was a picture of a younger Gabe in uniform and another of him receiving a medal in some sort of ceremony. She continued scanning the pictures, intrigued by these snippets of his life. She recognized Detective Madison in two of the pictures, taken at what was obviously his wedding. She stared, longer than necessary, at the image of Gabe in a tux.

She heard him enter the room behind her. "Your partner looks happy in these photos. Are they recent?" She felt no compunction at her prying. It was occurring to her that he knew a great deal more about her life than she did about his.

"Cal was out of his mind that day. Quite rightly, too. Unbelievable that a gal like Becky settled for him, and as his best man it was my duty to tell him so."

She felt a flicker of amusement. "I'm sure you fulfilled that duty admirably."

"Remind him every chance I get. He's a home-and-hearth kind of guy. Domestic life suits him."

But not Gabe. He may not have said the words but they were there, nonetheless. She tried to imagine him in the place of the groom, wearing that exuberant expression. She failed to summon the picture. He seemed to limit that kind of enthusiasm to his fishing exploits.

She turned to find him standing too close, and for a moment she stilled. His large form had a way of projecting a comfort that owed nothing to size and everything to presence. It would be a temptation to some women, she imagined. Women who made it a habit to lean on the strongest shoulder available. Because the opportunity had never presented itself, she'd grown up quite different. Wary. Reserved. Strong.

But there was a fleeting moment when she wished she could close the distance between them and rest her head against that broad chest; to feel the worries she'd carried for months slip away. And because the strength of that urge frightened her, she veered around him and crossed to the couch facing the television. He was, after all, a source of a great deal of those concerns.

"Well." Her voice was brittle but steady. "Show time."

He picked up the tape and slid it into the VCR. Meghan settled back on the couch, hoping the tension she felt didn't show, afraid that it did. But not knowing would have to be worse than the actual viewing. She owed Danny and Sandra at least this much. If there was anything on the tape that hinted of Danny's ability, she'd embark on damage control. It helped, she thought wryly, that Gabe didn't seem to put a great deal of stock in such things.

The screen was blank for a few moments, then Sandra's image filled it. Suddenly Meghan was hit with a certainty that she hadn't been ready for this moment at all. That she could never have been prepared enough.

"Well, Meghan, here we are. Ready for another of our sisterly chats?" Sandra smiled, a smile devoid of amusement, reached for a bottle on the table before her, and filled her glass. "Our last one really didn't last long enough, did it?" She brought the wine to her lips and drained the glass. It didn't look as though it had been her first, although the bottle was almost full. Meghan recognized the brightness in her sister's eyes, the edge to her voice. She didn't doubt that there was an empty bottle out of sight in the kitchen.

"We've never been the type for heart-to-hearts, have we? So I'll make this short and sweet, and hope like hell that you never have the opportunity to watch this." Gabe and Meghan watched intently as Sandra explained how she'd met a couple of guys in a bar one night and gotten a nasty picture of what they were involved in; how she went to the police with the information and agreed to help Wadrell with it.

"The detective was quite impressed with my talents. One by one he was able to haul in these guys' friends, and a major drug-trafficking ring was broken up. If Wadrell had been as good as he thought he was, though, I wouldn't be making this damn tape." The bitterness was apparent in Sandra's voice as she leaned forward and filled her glass once more. "I practically gave him the two ringleaders on a silver platter. He had their names, for godsakes. But they'd gone underground, he claimed, and he couldn't seem to find them. Unfortunately, that didn't stop them from finding me."

The words leaped from the TV and clawed viciously at

Meghan's heart like slashing little blades. They'd found her sister. And she didn't need to watch the rest of the video to imagine most of what happened next.

Sandra leaned back and wrapped a finger in one of her long strands of hair. The gesture was so jarringly familiar it stole Meghan's breath.

"I started getting photographs in the mail. Pictures of me on the street, in a store or a park. In some of them I was alone, others had Danny in them." At the mention of her son, the first hint of real emotion crept into the woman's voice. "I never thought any of this would affect Danny. I never would have…"

She stopped, pressed her lips together. "I was on my way to a club one night and there they were. Seems they weren't as far underground as Wadrell had thought. They forced me into a car, and during the course of that pleasure ride they managed to convince me that I was going to work for them this time. They threatened the kid if I didn't. They'd gotten close enough to snap those pictures. It didn't take much to guess they could get close enough to hurt Danny.

"At first all they wanted was for me to start feeding inaccurate information to Wadrell, throw him off their trail. I'm not completely stupid, though, my academic record notwithstanding." Sandra crossed one jean-clad leg over the other. "I told Wadrell about the whole thing. He convinced me to play along with them."

"Son of a bitch." The venom in Gabe's voice didn't register. Meghan's world had narrowed to a twenty-four-inch television screen.

"So they laid out the deal and I pretended to agree to it. After a while though, there was more. They wanted me to meet some guy and tell them if he was skimming profits." Her foot jittered nervously. "I did it. Met with D'Brusco twice, as a matter of fact. Wadrell was hot to grab them the next time we met, only they've never arranged another meeting. They call from different cell phones every time, and I'm starting to get a real bad feeling about the whole thing.''

The trepidation in Sandra's voice was reflected in her face. ''What's to stop them from carrying out their threats now that they've got what they wanted? I'm not figuring on sticking around to find out. I'm taking the kid, and we're going to disappear for a while. But if someone arranges to have me disappear completely, I wanted you to know what was going on.''

She lifted her shoulder in a gesture of derision. ''Somehow I don't think I could count on Wadrell to supply all the details. And Danny should know. If something happens, I mean. He should know that I did what I could to protect him.'' Her lips quivered for an instant before she brought the glass to her mouth and drew the only kind of courage she could from it.

Then she lowered the glass and leaned into the camera, and it seemed to Meghan as though she was staring right into her eyes. ''You were always the good girl, weren't you, Meghan? I'm hoping that hasn't changed. You'll do what has to be done, and you'll see that Danny is taken care of.'' A sly look crossed her sister's face. ''Kind of ironic, isn't it? The thought of you taking care of Danny? Be like when we were kids. Meggie and the freak, together again.''

She got up from the chair then and leaned into the camera. An instant later the screen went blank. Meghan sat, staring at the wall of nothingness. Guilt warred with old regrets, until they nearly rose and choked her. So many wounds. And the opportunity for healing them had long passed.

Kind of ironic, isn't it? Sandra had asked. And irony seemed far too tame for the cruel joke life had played. It was ironic that Meghan would end up guardian to a boy who possessed the same ability that had made their childhood a nightmare.

But the most cruel irony of all was that her sister's worst fears had come true. The same ability she'd alternately ignored or exploited all her life, had, in fact, ended up killing her.

Chapter 10

Gabe's face was hard when he took the tape from the machine, his movements tightly controlled. "Seems like Wadrell has a lot to answer for." And he was going to make damn sure the detective was held accountable for his actions. Using a psychic in a police investigation wasn't unheard of. But encouraging Sandra to continue when she'd been endangered, without providing her with adequate protection, was inexcusable. Oh, there would be questions, Gabe promised himself savagely. And Wadrell would provide explanations, if Gabe had to choke them out of the man himself.

Meghan rose, crossed her arms and hugged her shoulders. "So I was right all along. Her death was caused by her involvement in that case." She'd known, in some distant part of herself. But instead of feeling a sense of closure she felt strangely empty. She thought of Sandra making that video, more than half-convinced that it would never be seen. And tried not to wonder about her sister's last thoughts when she'd gone over that cliff.

Watching her closely, Gabe said, "We can't assume that." She rounded on him, and he held up one hand, stemming her argument. "I admit it seems likely, in light of what she told us. But we're really no closer to proving it."

She took a deep breath and then another. He was right, of course. Once emotion was brushed away, she had to admit that the tape hadn't verified whether Sandra had been forced off that cliff. But it had certainly pointed to a motive for someone to do so—a motive Meghan had suspected from the beginning.

"The tape did establish a connection between the case your sister was involved in and my own. D'Brusco is the common element," he murmured. She could almost see him shifting puzzle pieces in his mind, snapping some in place. "All we have to do is figure out his part in both these cases."

His gaze met hers and he immediately switched gears. "You're exhausted. We need to get some food into you, and then you can crash."

Just the thought of food had nausea rising in her stomach. "I don't have an appetite. Just take me back to my car, and I'll head home."

He leaned against the sofa, folded his arms. "I'm not going to do that."

His obstinance, combined with the events of the day, gave root to the beginnings of a headache. "You should have let me drive my own car. I told you that before."

"I remember." He didn't remind her of the reasons they'd ended up here to watch it in the first place. He had no doubt that she would have much preferred to watch that tape in private. He couldn't even begin to imagine the emotional upheaval it had put her through. And he was fiercely glad she hadn't gone through it alone.

Aware that her glare was turning dangerous, he continued imperturbably, "It doesn't make sense for either of us to venture out this time of night. Danny calmed down as soon as you called him, didn't he? And Callie agreed to keep him for the night?''

Looking away, she nodded.

''So there's no need for you to go home at this hour. And a lot of reasons not to.'' He waited for her reaction and he wasn't disappointed. As comprehension dawned, her chin angled, and shock widened her eyes. Shock and something else. Something that refused to be identified.

''I'm not staying here.''

''You won't have to sleep on the couch. I've got a spare bedroom.''

''It's out of the question.''

Shock had faded, to be replaced by a thread of panic. Recognizing it, his voice went persuasive. ''The last thing you need tonight is to go back to your empty apartment and replay this tape over and over in your mind. I can't stop you from the memories,'' he added, catching the look in her eyes, ''but I can make sure you don't face them alone. Now I'm going to find you something to eat.''

He pushed away from the couch and strode to the kitchen, leaving her feeling as though she'd just encountered a bulldozer and come out on the losing end. There was no way she would stay here. Tension seeped into her limbs, drove her to move. She crossed to the window and contemplated the glow of the streetlights. Gabe's plan seemed to tempt fate. Although he'd gone to great pains to convince her otherwise at first, she'd found out for herself that the attraction was real, and it certainly wasn't all one-sided.

She was surprised at the little kick to her pulse at the recollection. There was no question that this was a bad idea. And totally unnecessary. Regardless of what Gabe thought, she'd be all right alone. Certainly that was how she'd spent most of her life, emotionally if not physically.

But there was no denying that his protectiveness warmed her. He'd displayed it before, after she'd been hurt and he'd stayed to watch over both her and Danny. There was a kindness to Gabe Connally, one she doubted he let many people see. And it had the power to disarm her completely.

"I've got some soup heating in the microwave."

She turned to find him regarding her soberly from the doorway of the kitchen.

"Even if you don't feel like eating, maybe you should get something in your stomach. You don't look like you can afford to miss too many meals."

She cocked her head, wondering if she should be insulted. "And you don't look like you have much experience making them."

One corner of his mouth pulled up. "Got me. But you have to admit that the pizza box was a giveaway."

If the banter was meant to calm jittering nerves, it was having the desired effect. "Am I taking my life in my hands with you acting as chef?"

"You would be if it was more than soup." The buzzer sounded, and he cocked an eyebrow at her. "How adventurous do you feel?"

He might, she decided, be more agreeable about taking her home if she indulged him a little. It was that thought that had her moving past him to the kitchen, sitting down to a bowl of soup she didn't want.

But once she saw the meal of soup, cheese and crackers he'd prepared, her appetite improved. She began eating and he opened the refrigerator, taking out a beer and a carton of milk. He took the precaution of checking the date on the milk, which raised some doubts. But she accepted the glass he poured for her silently, and he sat down opposite her with the beer in hand.

If a stranger observed the scene, it would appear cozy, she supposed. A man and a woman sharing the evening after a long day. A stranger wouldn't be privy to the churning in her stomach. A stranger wouldn't note the self-consciousness that tinged her actions as the intimacy of the scene worked on her. She could only hope Gabe didn't observe it, either.

"What did your sister mean there at the end when she said it was ironic?"

His tone was easy, his question wasn't. She took inordinate care to swallow around the sudden knot in her throat. Damage control, she recalled. Somehow she'd always known she would need it.

Her mind scrambled for an answer, and she settled for a slice of honesty. "We weren't particularly close, Sandra and me. Not as children, and when we grew up it just seemed…too late, somehow." Too much had transpired between them for Meghan to mend it. She'd hoped there would be time for that later. But Sandra's death had shattered that wish.

She felt his gaze on her and strove to keep her voice even. "My mother handled Sandra badly." In truth she had handled them both badly, but she knew far more damage had been done to her sister. "One time when Sandra was a teenager she and my mother had a terrible fight. I think she'd been kicked out of her third or fourth boarding school. Sandra was yelling and Mother was speaking in that tight, clipped voice she uses when she's angry. Mother wouldn't listen when Sandra tried to explain why she'd been sent home; just went on about how she'd disappointed the family again. And then she said she didn't know why nature had cursed her with a freak for a daughter." Memory transported Megan back to less pleasant times. The air in the room had thickened, holding everyone in the tableau frozen. "Mother apologized later, of course, but we both knew. That's what she thought of her. And after that time it was how Sandra referred to herself."

She caught the look in his eye and knew she had to tread carefully. "Sandra could be indiscriminate about the way she used her ability."

"She used it on you."

It was a statement rather than a question, and had the power to jolt her. She forgot sometimes just how observant he was. "It caused problems." The words, simply uttered, were anything but simple. But there was no need to rake up old wounds again. And certainly they paled against the reality they were faced with. "We were never close, and now I'm raising her son. She's right. It's ironic."

"Yeah." He was silent for a moment, contemplating the label on the bottle in his hand. Then he tipped it to his lips and drank. "Life has a way of working out that way sometimes."

She made a point to avoid his gaze. There would be no way for him to guess that the irony Sandra referred to was Meghan raising a boy with the same ability that had made her childhood a war zone. No reason, she thought, bringing the spoon to her lips, to contemplate such an explanation for Sandra's words. There were few battles Meghan had won when faced with the strength of his will. But she'd managed, so far, to protect Danny's secret. She hoped it would be enough.

"He's lucky, you know." When her startled gaze met his, he continued. "He's had it rough, but he landed okay with you. You're good with the kid. You'll do right by him."

The quiet assurance in his voice was a comfort, and she wished she could believe his words. There were far too many nights when she lay awake, feeling as though she'd stepped through the looking glass. Far too much self-doubt, and downright ignorance, about taking care of the young boy.

She pushed aside the troubling thoughts and concentrated on the man before her. "Well, you've fed me, thereby satisfying yourself that I won't collapse. Now why don't we discuss my going home again?"

"You can discuss it." He got up from the table, clearing his dishes and carrying them to the counter.

"A discussion usually involves at least two people," she pointed out.

He turned, pinned her with a steady look. "I don't think the full weight of the day has hit you yet. When it does, you shouldn't be alone."

With effort she ignored the generosity in his thought and focused on her mission. "I could call a cab."

"And I could cancel it." He must have recognized the exasperation crossing her features, for his voice softened. "This is hard for you, isn't it? Accepting help from someone else."

"And it's easy for you?" she shot back.

His mouth quirked, surprising her. "I don't think my foster parents ever used the term *gracious* to describe me once I came to live with them, but I did get used to the idea. Eventually."

She saw old ghosts in his eyes. "Did you lose your parents, or weren't they able to take care of you?"

"My mother's alive." He brushed by her to reach for her dishes, piled them with the others, and left her to grapple with his words. His answer raised more questions, but she recognized the No Trespassing signs in his expression.

Resigning herself to the inevitable, she said, "I'll have to be home quite early. I want to be there to get Danny ready for school."

"You will be." If he was surprised at her capitulation, he didn't show it. There was likely no shock in learning that he'd gotten his way. She imagined he was quite used to it. She watched him for a moment as he shoved the dishes in the dishwasher, raising her eyebrows a bit at his technique. Luckily the dishes were shatterproof. He turned, caught her eyes on him. Silence stretched, long enough to be awkward.

"If you want to show me to my room, I think I'll turn in." She thought she saw relief on his face as he nodded and started out of the room. Certainly she didn't share that

emotion. She wouldn't be relieved until she was safely en-
sconced in her own apartment again. Away from the questions that still badgered her. And away from an enigmatic
man whose unexpected bits of kindness meant far more to
her than they should.

Late at night, lying awake in bed, Meghan could understand Danny's fear of the dark. Night was a dangerous time,
and fortunately the child's fears could be banished with a
light. Her own demons were less easily dealt with. Somewhere between sleep and wakefulness the memories slith-
ered beneath the doors she kept them caged behind and
played across her mind.

She remembered Sandra's twelfth birthday party. Her sister had insisted that each boy and girl deliver their present
to her individually, and had then delighted in announcing
its contents before she'd opened it. Meghan supposed that
the children had been surprised at the accuracy of her
guesses, which had been nothing of the kind. But one by
one Sandra had alienated her guests, and when the cake and
ice cream had been served, she'd been sitting by herself,
her friends huddled in their own group.

Meghan could still recall the look on her sister's face that
day. One of utter desolation. Although she hadn't been able
to identify the emotion then, she could recognize its effect.
And she wondered if Sandra had carried that same feeling
into adulthood: that feeling of isolation, no matter the
crowd. She thought she had. And she ached for the woman
who no one could ever get close to. Not even Meghan.

Silently she rose and slipped back into her clothes. Making her way into the darkened living room, she switched
the TV on, turning the volume low. And that was where
Gabe found her minutes, or hours, later, staring blindly at
her sister's face on the screen.

"You need to sleep." His low voice glazed her chilled
skin with a coat of warmth. He moved in front of her and

stopped the VCR, letting the all-night TV programming take over. Standing before her in the glow of the screen, he looked rumpled. The jeans he'd dragged on were unbuttoned, and he was barefoot. But his eyes were alert, his face quietly observant.

"She was like a mouse in a maze." She didn't speak her sister's name, knowing he'd understand. "She'd use her ability in ways that frightened and angered people. And then she would seek the very contact she'd alienated by ignoring her ability for periods of time. She never found a way to have both. And that breaks my heart."

He sank down beside her on the couch, not saying anything. She was grateful for that. Most people would be driven to platitudes and comforting phrases. It wasn't comfort she sought now. It was understanding.

"I failed her. I couldn't do anything back then. I was just a child. But I could have made more of an effort as an adult. She carried turmoil with her like a cloud carries rain. It was simpler to stand away from the storm."

"It wouldn't have changed anything, Meghan. The result would be the same."

"But then maybe I could forgive myself."

Her voice was a mere whisper of sound threading through the darkness. It shouldn't have had the power to curl inside his chest and squeeze his heart. A lifetime ago he'd been that mouse in a maze, and the memory still throbbed. He understood how guilt and regret could work a person until they felt they had nothing to lose. He'd been lucky to learn differently.

Without a thought he leaned forward, brushed his lips against her forehead. "Let it go." He heard the weary little sigh she released. His advice would be difficult to follow. But he was certain of the truth in his words. "You can't change the past, and you sure as hell can't change another person. Trying to do either will just make you crazy."

Her face turned up to his, and it would have been the

most natural thing in the world for him to touch his lips to hers. He pulled away a little and made the mistake of looking in her eyes. What he saw there tempted him beyond all bearing. Because there was awareness there, and memory. Not the one she'd just spoken of but the memory of the last time he'd laid his hands on her. And the last time she'd touched him back.

His fingers dug into his palms. She couldn't realize the danger of turning that look on a man; letting him know without words that she was aware of him as a male. It could have unintended results. Far-reaching ramifications. It could, quite simply, make a man forget about promises uttered in more honorable moments; unleash a passion that had been kept tightly harnessed.

Her eyes drifted shut, and this time it was she who closed the distance between them; her lips pressing against his; her hand tracing his jaw. The actions shouldn't have had the power to scrape his skin with edgy needles of torment. She couldn't know that her slightest touch, spontaneous and freely given, packed a greater punch than the most experienced seduction. He endured the light pressure of her lips for endless moments, every nerve in his body drawing tighter, before she moved a fraction away.

His fingers wrapped around her wrist. "The last thing either of us needs is more regrets." He saw the comprehension in her eyes. He also noted that it failed to dim the desire there. His blood leaped with lust and something else, something he couldn't name.

"Then let's not regret this."

Her words fired his veins, and he felt a flash of frustration. He wouldn't be the one regretting this decision in the morning. It would never be him wishing to reset the clock to alter events. But he feared, quite desperately, that she might.

It shouldn't matter. But he knew, in a place he wasn't

willing to acknowledge, that it had begun to matter all too much.

She caught his bottom lip in her teeth and scored it with her teeth. He managed, barely, to resist crushing her lips in return. If the pace she was setting was guaranteed to give her time to pull back, then he'd give her the time. But even as he thought it his body called him a liar. His mouth was already moving on hers, calling for a response, receiving one. The pace abruptly quickened. And when she lowered her head to trace his collarbone with her tongue, any thought of halting had fled.

He gathered her to him and rose, striding to his bedroom. Following her down on the bed, he tried to quiet the voice inside him that whispered of choices and regrets and to-morrows. She'd have no regrets. Not if he could help it.

His mouth went to her neck. Her pulse scrambled beneath his lips and the evidence of her excitement was satisfying. Her flavor was intoxicating and went right to his head. And when he felt her hands on his chest, stroking and kneading, his senses swam and reason receded.

Meghan flexed her fingers, traced the curve of his ribs. She felt muscles quiver under her touch and thrilled to his response. She'd never before considered the heady power of evoking this kind of reaction. Never allowed herself to react in turn. But there was no thought of controlling the need careening inside her. Since it couldn't be tamed, it would have to be set free.

He drew her blouse over her head and scored her shoulder with his teeth. The rasp of his beard aroused, the stroke of his tongue soothed. His hands were quick and knowing, a glide of fingers across the top of her breasts made her long, quite fiercely, for a more intimate touch. When he released her bra and filled his hands with her, she couldn't resist a gasp.

She'd thought she'd known need before, so it was hard to recognize it in this whipping of her pulse, this thrumming in her blood. Impossible to identify the fierce pleasure at the press of naked breast against rock-hard chest. Fires, when stoked, burned brighter. Hotter. She was caught in the heat of one now, a longing flaming in her blood. And as if he recognized that craving, returned it, he pressed her back on the bed and feasted on her.

A whimper escaped her. His quick, knowing fingers cupped one breast, his mouth teased the other. The dual assault was explosive. Her back arched, urging him to take more. He was drawing her up, sensations sprinting and colliding inside her. And when she thought there was no more he took her higher.

Gabe found a savage satisfaction in the taste of flesh, an emotion that should have warned him. Need this fast, this brilliant, held an edge all its own. Brutal demands pounded through his system, honed his desire. Every need, once satisfied, failed to soothe. Every temptation, once tasted, urged him to the next sensation.

He battled for the zipper of her jeans, dragged them over her hips. With swift efficient movements he had her naked, and his blood began to hammer. There were secrets to discover in every long soft inch of her. Secrets that would take a lifetime to possess. And as the moments spun out between them, each spiraling into the next, it was easy to believe that they had at least that long.

Her hands went to the waistband of his jeans, and he helped her remove them. Then there was nothing between them but exquisitely sensitive skin against skin.

They rolled on his bed, a tangle of limbs on dark sheets. Pleasures given and returned. Pleas uttered and answered. He felt her lift one leg to slide it along his, and his vision hazed. He stroked her smooth skin, felt the whisper of muscle quivering beneath, and then moved higher and found her where she was damp and inviting. Slipping his fingers inside her, he swallowed her moan.

She could no longer pinpoint the focus of her pleasure.

Hot lashing kisses warred with a wicked touch that teased, promised, then retreated. Sensation battered her system, until abruptly it overloaded and she was flung from desperation to release with a suddenness that sent shock waves of sensation crashing inside her.

Her reaction fired an immediate visceral response in him. The more Gabe took, the more he wanted. It was a hunger that couldn't be assuaged. He didn't think of eliminating doubts from her mind now. He didn't think at all. Need, primal and urgent, clawed through him. He'd never had a woman in his blood, the wanting a hot and savage beat. He explored every inch of her with his hands, and then his mouth. Her taste mingled with the fever in his veins and sent it raging.

There was primitive pleasure to be had in the bite of her nails on his shoulders, of damp flesh moving on damp flesh. Her pulses rocketed beneath his touch. His own echoed them. There was a fire ignited inside him, and he was being consumed. His control began fragmenting, and his touch grew more desperate.

He moved and braced himself over her. There was just enough light to see the emotions flickering over her face, and the sight torched his desire. He slipped inside her, and his world abruptly tilted. The delicate pulsations of her adjustment gripped him, seated him more closely. He drew her legs up around his hips and pressed deeper. He waited for her hips to move helplessly, seeking, and only then did he rock against her, his breath strangling in his lungs. Her arms wrapped around his shoulders, and each movement of his hips drew a cry from her lips.

"Gabe."

Her voice was a plea, and it shattered his restraint. His hips pounded against hers, a desperate quest for fulfillment that could never be completely assuaged. He felt the shimmers of release that eddied through her body and felt the desperate clutch of her fingers as she arched and bucked beneath him. And when she moaned his name, he swallowed the sound from her lips and followed her into pleasure.

Chapter 11

The night spun hours to gold. Time shimmered, almost still, as they reached for each other, again and again. When greed was appeased, hunger remained. Satisfaction was fleeting before the wanting would build again.

Meghan watched the predawn sky lighten outside Gabe's bedroom window and felt a pang of disappointment. Last night it had been too easy to believe that this moment could be suspended indefinitely while they floated above reality. But dawn's approach heralded a clearer head, albeit on a pleasantly boneless body.

He'd spoken of regrets, but she didn't have any. At least, not the kind he meant. She could feel no remorse for allowing that glorious heat to burst to conflagration, to rage out of control. But she was experiencing an all-too-familiar trace of guilt. It was one thing to give in to the temptation of wanting this man. It was another to do so while engaged in deception.

She stirred, the thought weighing uneasily, and his arm tightened around her waist. Reluctant to awaken him, she stilled. He put a high price on honesty. Would he make allowances for good intentions? For difficult decisions made for the most honorable reasons? Trepidation tightened in her chest. Somehow she didn't think so. Although she knew he was a trustworthy man, he didn't strike her as a particularly forgiving one.

It occurred to her then that she'd been caught in her own deception. It had seemed so easy at the beginning, when she'd figured to use Gabe the way the department had used her sister. She'd get the information she wanted and give nothing in return. There had been no contemplation of a deeper relationship with the man. In theory the plan could have worked. Reality had proved much more complex.

She still didn't dare tell him about Danny. It wasn't a matter of trust; it was a matter of control. Gabe had reports to file, superiors to answer to. Once he shared Danny's ability with even one other person, the chances of it leaking even further doubled. She had no faith that the department would keep the information private. Not after the debacle with Sandra.

But there was also no denying that anyone who was in her life on a long-term basis would eventually have to be told. Danny was trying hard, but setting boundaries around his ability would take time. And time couldn't be summoned at will.

She was left with a sick certainty that for her and Gabe, it was quickly running out.

Gabe leaned against the wall waiting silently for Cal to finish viewing the tape. He couldn't watch it again without remembering Meghan's face when she'd seen it. Her reaction after. And then the memories shifted, refocused. There had been something in her eyes this morning. Not the regret that he had half feared seeing, but something shadowed. To dispel that sadness he'd tried to distract her, and he thought he'd succeeded. Although she would never again believe his line of saving time by showering together, he thought the time had been well spent. When he'd put her in her car and given her a deep, hard kiss, the only look in her eyes had been desire. The recollection of that look would return again and again to torment him.

He couldn't find it in him to care, and that did have caution rearing. Women were infinitely pleasurable, but no woman distracted him. Not ever. But there was something different about Meghan, something that he didn't want to examine too closely. It was enough for now that their relationship had changed, expanded. That she trusted him.

And she did trust him, on some level. He knew her well enough to be certain that she didn't let people into her life easily. He'd wedged his way in, and now he was going to make a place for himself there. He realized he'd have to convince her of the wisdom of that. And he found himself looking forward to doing just that.

"Jesus." Gabe's attention shifted back to his partner. "Meghan saw this?"

"Yeah." Telling Cal about the search he and Meghan had undertaken took only a few minutes. He was carefully select with the rest of the evening's details. He didn't want to expose what he'd shared with Meghan last night with anyone, even his partner.

"After you left last night I did a little more digging, myself," Cal said. "Ran a search on our pinup boy and then looked into his known associates. Ran them through the database, and damned if another one didn't show up flagged. A Chafe Robinson."

Gabe stared at him, his mind racing. "Latest arrest records?"

"Nothing for the last couple years on either of them. But I contacted Wadrell, asked about the flag. Seems like both these guys were involved in the drug case he was using Barton on. Wadrell was real cagey. Didn't want to give me much. He was more interested in what our angle was."

Gabe looked at him sharply, and Cal shrugged. "I was purposefully vague. Just mentioned we were following a lead and left it at that."

Talk of the other detective was enough to set Gabe's temper simmering again, but he pushed the feeling aside for the moment. Taking care of Wadrell himself, however satisfying, would have short-lived consequences. Before this whole thing was through, the other detective was going to have a whole lot of heat directed at him. Turning the tape over to Lieutenant Burney would light the match. Gabe was looking forward to watching the other man go down in flames.

He shifted his attention back to the matter at hand. "Wadrell told me he'd rounded up most of the members of the drug ring." He spoke slowly, fitting pieces together as he went. "Only the ringleaders were still at large, he said."

"I didn't tell you the most interesting part. I pulled out those surveillance shots we had of the people coming and going from the video place, and I matched Collins to three of them and Robinson to a full half dozen."

"So these mopes are trafficking drugs. Lenny somehow gets placed managing a bunch of video stores where he handles money all day. We trace him to a half-dozen different banks and find him using that many aliases."

Gabe rose, paced a bit. He always thought better on the move. "The video stores were sinks, all right. Drug money was brought in daily to be mixed with the store's deposits, ending up freshly laundered. The cash that goes through those places daily, Lenny could easily have been smurfing several hundred dollars a day at each branch. Let's be conservative and figure a couple grand, all told."

"They're open every day of the year," Cal observed. "Even holidays. So where are we at now?" He cocked his head, mentally calculated. "I figure they could launder well over a million a year that way."

"Might not have taken care of all of that drug money but

it would have been a healthy start. So what did they do with the rest of it?'' They looked at each other and spoke simultaneously. "Ran it through other holdings.''

"Son of a gun,'' Gabe said. "Robinson and Collins must have been the ones Barton talked about, the drug lords Wadrell couldn't catch up with. They tried to get her to start giving phony information to Wadrell, and then used her to tip off their boss that D'Brusco was skimming.''

"That would mean either Robinson or Collins was probably behind Meghan's attack. Must have realized they left some loose strings with those threatening pictures. And there was another development last night after you left. Apparently there's been a major shakeup in the organization lately. Robinson's body was discovered yesterday. It was found under a railroad bridge, minus a hand.''

"First D'Brusco ends up dead and now Robinson,'' Gabe mused. "Are you thinking what I'm thinking?''

Cal was already on his feet. "Let's get to this Collins before he ends up in a body bag, too.''

They kicked over a lot of rocks that day before finding Fast Eddie. They finally spotted him coming out of one of the five-dollar peep shows wedged like garish old hags on a seedy side street a few blocks from his home. They crossed the street, dodging traffic, and fell into step with the man, flanking him.

Eddie looked up, dismay quickly replacing recognition on his face. "Hey, don't be hassling me, now. I'm done with the two of you, right? I gave you what I had, and I'm done with you.''

"You'd think so, wouldn't you? But as it happens we have a few more questions for you, Eddie.''

The man was already shaking his head. "I don't got no more answers. Our deal's done. And you ain't doing me no good, coming up to me like this on the street. People might get the wrong idea, you know?''

"Well we wouldn't want to ruin your good name," Gabe said. He looked at his partner. "Do we want to ruin his sterling reputation, Cal?"

His partner didn't miss a beat. "Wouldn't think of it. And that's why we're going to get out of the public eye." The detectives veered as one, steering the man into a nearby tavern. With a few well-orchestrated moves, they had him seated in a booth in the back, with Gabe penning him in and Cal surveying him across the table.

"What can you tell us about a scumbag goes by the name of Shadrach Collins?" Gabe let Cal begin with the exchange they'd perfected while searching for the weasel. He waved away the waitress who had shambled in their direction and then he lounged with an ease that gave lie to the adrenaline pumping inside him.

"I can't tell you nuthin', man, 'cuz I ain't never heard of him. Don't know him, can't help you. So I'll be headin' home." Eddie half rose, and Gabe grabbed his jacket, jerked him back to the seat.

"Maybe this will jog your memory." He pulled out the photo of the man they'd enlarged from one of the pictures Meghan had given them. He watched Eddie, saw the flicker of recognition in his eyes, and closed in. "Ever seen him?"

"Nope."

"Well, see that's kind of funny. 'Cuz we caught him on film a few times heading into the video store. You claimed you hung out there for a while with Lenny, and you say you've never seen this guy. I'm not sure I buy that." His gaze shifted to meet his partner's. "Do you buy it, Cal?"

Eddie fidgeted in his seat. "Listen, I don't owe you nuthin'. They dropped that charge when I gave you that information. And it was real good info, too." His gaze flicked from one man to another. "My guy said that info was gold, man. You moved on it, din't ya?"

Ignoring the question, Gabe leaned forward. "You got the last pandering charge dropped for the trade, but you're back at it again, now, Eddie, and somehow I don't think the scales of justice are on your side this time. Caught you on the police blotter this morning, you bonehead. Came to bail out one of your girls last night, didn't you?"

Eddie's head was shaking so furiously it was in danger of flying off. "Just helpin' out a friend, man, there ain't no harm in that. You can't prove nuthin' by it."

"You're probably right." Gabe sat back, waited for the relief to cross the man's face. "You're not worth our time. We'd hand you over to vice, right Cal?"

His partner shrugged, looking bored with the whole thing. "I'm not gonna spend time looking into that sleazy stable you call a living, but vice probably will. Yeah, if we express an interest, they'll be crawling over you every time you step in the street."

"Hey, cut me some slack, huh?" Eddie swiped his nose with his coat sleeve. His gaze darted around the bar furtively. "You two are bad luck, you know? I give you info on Lenny, and a few days later he's a floater."

"We appreciate your concern for Collins," Cal said dryly.

"I don't care about that homie, I'm talking about me. It in't healthy being around you."

"So the sooner you tell us what we want to hear, the sooner you can regain your health." Gabe's voice was mild, his gaze wasn't.

"Oh, man." Eddie slumped in the booth. "I need a drink."

Gabe held up a finger, and the waitress ambled in their direction. He let Eddie order a beer, and when the waitress left he said, "Why don't you tell us what you know about Collins, Eddie. Is he connected?"

"Don't know about that, but he's got someone behind him. Someone big." Reaching out with shaking hands to take the glass the waitress set in front of him, Eddie downed half of it. "He and some Robinson dude were pulling in a pretty big territory until things got hot a few months ago. I hear they're rebuilding, but they have to stay low. Got warrants out on both of them.''

Gabe and Cal exchanged a glance. Apparently the man hadn't heard that Robinson was no longer in the picture.

"Go on."

"I don't know nuthin' about their business, just what it is, you know? And I know they got muscle behind them because folks just don't mess with either of them. It just ain't smart.''

Gabe's mood went grim. If the dealers were tough enough to warrant that kind of respect on the street, they would have been bad news indeed when they'd found Sandra. And one of them had had his hands on Meghan, as well. His fingers curled into fists. For that fact alone, he wanted to find the one still alive and spend five minutes alone with him.

"Where do we find Collins?" he said in a hard voice.

"I don't know for sure." Recognizing the danger in Gabe's eyes, he hastened to add, "But I got a few places you could look. He's been moving around, you know? Staying one step ahead of the cops.''

"Give us locations, Eddie. And then maybe you can stay one step ahead, too.''

They found Collins at the last place Eddie had named, a hole-in-the-wall high-rise on Tenth and Maple. Trouble was, someone else had found him first.

The aroma of dried blood and death permeated the air. "He really pissed someone off," Cal observed. He and Gabe perused the body, careful not to contaminate the scene. Collins's throat had been cut, nearly severing his head.

"This ties the whole mess up in a neat little bundle, doesn't it?" Gabe's voice was rife with frustration. "Wadrell enlists Barton...Robinson and Collins force her to ap proach D'Brusco...and Barton ends up dead. A few months later Lenny is dead, and now the bodies are starting to pile up. All the players in that little scene are eliminated. What does that leave us with?''

''A whole lot of nothing?'' Cal suggested.

''Maybe. Maybe not.'' Gabe was surprised at the reluctance he felt about the idea swirling in his mind. ''We've still got an eyewitness to the guy seen with D'Brusco.''

Cal looked at him a little strangely, and Gabe turned away to call the scene in. He didn't want to take the chance that his partner would recognize something on his face. Something that felt very much like dread.

''So how's this for service?'' Gabe strolled into the door Meghan opened for him carrying a large pizza. She looked good. His palms itched with the need to touch her. Her hair, which only hours ago had been a riot of curls spread across his chest, was piled on top of her head in a knot that looked as if it would give with the least bit of help. He was tempted to provide it. Her slim legs were showcased in formfitting jeans, and her pink shirt was short enough to show flashes of her flat stomach. All in all she looked tastier than the meal he carried.

''I usually tip the other delivery guy,'' she noted.

He moved swiftly then and caught her mouth with his own. The taste was all too brief. ''I'll settle for this.''

Laughter lurked in her wide, blue eyes. ''That's what the other delivery guy always says, too.'' She moved away before he could reach for her again, and headed toward the kitchen. He followed, hormones already kicking to life. Then another door in the apartment burst open and Danny sped into the living room, with another boy in fast pursuit.

''I smelled it first.''

''No, I did!''

Gabe cocked a brow at Meghan. ''I hope they're talking about the pizza.'' He set the carton on the counter. When she moved by him to search for the plates, he remained motionless, so her body had to brush his.

"Deviant," she murmured.

He grinned, unrepentant. "Hey, with you, I'll take what I can get." He waited while she served the boys, who seemed to have more interest in adding to noise pollution than in eating. His smile faded as he considered his purpose for coming here, other than the far more personal one. It was that distinction, the professional warring with the personal that had uneasiness churning in his stomach.

"I need to talk to you." His voice low, he met Meghan's quick glance. If he hadn't been looking so intently he might have missed that flash of wariness that appeared on her face, only to vanish the next moment.

"You guys try to keep most of the pizza in your mouths, okay?" After pouring each of them some juice, she left the kitchen. Gabe trailed behind her. She led him a distance away and turned to face him. He wanted nothing more than to reach for her, possess her mouth once more. Because he couldn't trust himself not to do just that, he shoved his hands in his pockets. He wouldn't take that kind of advantage. He wouldn't kiss her until her body melted against his and her eyes got drowsy and languorous. Not when he suspected what her reaction would be to what he had to say.

As if aware of his warring emotions, she retreated a step. "What is it?"

"We identified the men who threatened Sandra," he told her bluntly. "Both of them are dead. One a couple days ago and the other today. And with those two homicides we've lost every lead we've got in this case." He watched her carefully. "Except for one."

It didn't take long for comprehension to streak across her face. He expected the sliver of panic that showed, but he hadn't expected the resignation that followed. She turned her back to him, went to the windows that were showcasing a spectacular sunset. "You have the tape."

He heard the hope in her voice and damned himself for shattering it. "With these guys dead the tape is no good to us. Other than to be used to make things very uncomfortable for Wadrell." The fierce satisfaction the thought gave him crept into his voice. "But with them gone, it's more important than ever that we get an ID on the guy Danny saw with D'Brusco."

She looked too solitary standing there, and he was damned if he'd let her feel alone. Striding to her, he cupped her shoulders with his hands, drew her back against his chest. It was a measure of her distress that she sagged against him for just a moment. The tiny sign of weakness, one that was just as quickly masked, elicited a protective, answering emotion. Personal feelings waged war with professional obligations. It was a hell of an uncomfortable battle. But he'd spoken no more than the truth. They needed this lead more than ever before. "It'll be painless, I promise. I'll line a sketch artist to work with Danny. That will save him from having to look at pictures for hours."

Silence stretched between them. He wondered what she was thinking, was afraid he already knew. So he was surprised at the steadiness of her voice when she spoke, and even more surprised by her words. "How about if we compromise?"

"I don't see how we can..."

"How about if I be the sketch artist?" She spun in his grasp and met his gaze. "Portraits aren't my strength, but I just finished the one for Danny's birthday of his mother. And it doesn't have to be a work of art, does it? Just a reasonable depiction for you to go on?"

He hesitated, unwilling to destroy even that one small concession and reach for the total capitulation he needed. "Sketch artists are specially trained, Meghan. I don't know if you can expect to get the same results."

"At least let me try." There was a fierceness in her voice

that caught him. "If it doesn't work—" her hesitation was infinitesimal "—then we can discuss it again."

He looked into her face and knew he was lost. He couldn't deny her this, not when it would cost them so little. Not even when he was certain they were only delaying the inevitable.

With an effort he looked away from her, and damned himself for losing his famed objectivity. "It has to be tonight. We can't afford to waste any more time."

"Then tonight it is."

"What kind of game is this, Aunt Meggie?" Danny wanted to know. He and Alex were seated on stools in the studio, and the specialness of the occasion wasn't lost on him. He was supposed to stay out of the studio because things here spilled easily. Or broke. Or tore.

"It's called…Funny Faces," she improvised, avoiding Gabe's gaze. He had refused the seat she'd offered and was roaming her studio in a fashion that made her decidedly nervous. "I've got an easel with paper for each of you."

"Are we going to paint?" asked Alex.

"No, you're going to describe a funny face for me to draw. Danny can start with one and I'll make a picture of it. Then Alex can describe one. When I finish with them, you can change anything you want on them. If you want the noses to be different, you just tell me. If you want a scary scar—" she raised her eyebrows at the boys' delighted expressions "—I can add one. Let's see who ends up with the funniest face."

She sensed the exact moment when Gabe's interest sharpened. Although she didn't raise her gaze from the easels in front of her, she felt his close attention. She took the boys through the process, and had them in fits of laughter over the pictures they described.

"Change my guy's nose, now," demanded Alex. "Make it long with a big bump on the end."

"I want my guy's eyes to be different. Make them squinty like this." Danny demonstrated by screwing up his face comically. She acceded to that change, and all the others the two came up with. If she hadn't finally called an end to the projects, she thought the boys would have been entertained for hours.

Ripping the sheets off the pads, she handed each boy's picture to him.

"That was fun, Aunt Meggie. Let's do another one."

"We're going to do one again, but this time we'll do it a little differently. I want you to describe someone you've seen. Do you remember what the men looked like that you saw running outside of the toy store that day?"

Instantly Danny's eyes clouded, and his gaze slid to Gabe. "Yeah. Sort of."

Meghan squatted down until she was eye level with her nephew. "We're going to let you do a little detective work."

"You are?" The dubious tone in Danny's voice said better than words that he wasn't totally comfortable with the idea.

"I am. And we're going to do it here, the way we did these drawings."

If she could help Gabe with the case in this way, it might relieve her conscience a bit. May make her feel less deceitful. But she wouldn't compromise her nephew's well-being for the investigation. And Gabe...well, he'd just have to accept that.

Danny considered her words. "Which man?"

Giving a sigh of relief, she looked at Gabe questioningly.

"The second one," he said. "The one you said was tall and thin."

"He had a skull face."

Meghan rose, went to the pad. "Tell me what you mean. What was his face shaped like?" Slowly, a little at a time, she drew details from the boy, drew, erased, revised. Gabe

came over to stand behind her. The questions he directed
at Danny helped elicit more specifics. Finally Danny said,
"That's how I remember him looking. Can we go watch
our movie now?"

Meghan looked at Gabe, and he nodded, not taking his
eyes away from the picture. "I'll be damned," he murmured. "I can see what the kid meant." The figure in the
sketch had deep-set eyes, broad cheekbones and a long narrow chin. The close-cropped dark hair she'd added only
accentuated the skeletal features.

It was easier to concentrate on putting away her supplies
than on the menacing face she'd drawn. If anything, she
was more certain than ever that she'd done the right thing
by protecting Danny. If the news of his ability leaked the
way Sandra's had, he could be endangered by the man in
the drawing, or someone like him. She shuddered at the
thought.

"You did great, Meghan." Gabe's words of praise spread
a honeyed warmth through her veins. The warmth notched
up a few degrees when he drew her into his arms. "You're
very talented."

She tilted her head to look up at him. Being in his embrace was too new, too stimulating, to take one moment of
it for granted. But the thrill was marred by a feeling of
dishonesty she couldn't seem to shake. She wanted, desperately, to believe that the sketch somehow made up for
the other secrets she was keeping from him.

But she couldn't quite manage to make herself believe it.
"I think that statement could be a considered compliment
if you didn't sound so surprised."

"Oh, it's a compliment," he assured her. "I think I'm
becoming a real fan of your talents. Both in the studio—"
he dipped his head, nuzzled her neck "—and out of it."

A breathless laugh escaped her, and she twined her arms
around his neck. "I have lots of talents. Would you care to
be more specific?"

There was a promising gleam in his eyes that sent rivers of delight cascading through her veins. "I'd like to do just that. What's on your schedule tonight?"

"Alex is here for an overnight."

"Lucky Alex."

"Bedtime is nine o'clock, because the boys don't have school tomorrow." The look of disappointment on his face filled her with a soft, womanly satisfaction. "I have it on good authority that you're a very early riser."

His brows rose. "With the birds."

"Then maybe we can work out an overnight for you, too."

His lips took hers in a quick hard kiss that wanted to linger. "I'm a very considerate houseguest."

She linked her arms around his neck and smiled up at him. "I'm counting on it."

"Sit down, Paul."

The man in the chair observed his employee over steepled fingers. "You dispatched our last bit of business with your usual aplomb."

Paulie shrugged gaunt shoulders. "Collins was no problem."

"No," the man murmured. "He won't be anymore. I've always found his type to be eminently dispensable." He reached into his Italian-tailored suit jacket and withdrew a leather wallet, setting it on the desk. With one well-manicured index finger he nudged the wallet across the desk.

It was a mark of wariness that Paul didn't count the money before slipping it inside his coat. There wasn't a man on earth he feared, but this one at least commanded a certain respect. It helped, of course, that he was well paid for work he enjoyed.

"Was Shadrach able to be of some use to us before you finished him?"

Paulie remained motionless with that eerie stillness that was so much a part of him. Perhaps the hours spent waiting for prey had trained him. It was difficult to be sure. But he got results. And if he approached his work with a rather distasteful amount of enthusiasm, that really was of little consequence.

"It was pretty much like you thought. Apparently he and his friend got Barton to help them by sending pictures they took of her and her kid. Collins could be identified in most of them."

"Incompetent fool." The diamond in the man's pinkie ring glinted as he drummed his fingers on the desktop of polished cherry. Nothing was more an affront than stupidity. He breathed deeply, attempting to shove back the remembered fury. Stress of this type wasn't healthy. "Well, at least they gave us D'Brusco. It hardly made up for the mess they made of things, but it was something."

"Do you have anything else for me?"

"Perhaps." The man pursed his lips, calmer now. "I'll have to discern how much damage has been done. I know how to contact you if I need you."

The dismissal in his tone was obvious, and Paulie silently rose to leave. He'd be summoned again. His services were in great demand. Especially among men like this one.

Chapter 12

"Connally, this came for you earlier, special messenger."

Gabe took the large manila envelope the desk clerk held out to him. "Is it ticking?"

"If it was I'd have put it in your desk."

"You're heartless, Mona. After all I've done for you." The wounded expression he affected didn't soften the woman's expression appreciably.

"Let's see. Would that be the time you put the rubber rat in my desk drawer or the time you sent a singing telegram to my birthday party."

"I'm told he had an excellent voice."

"He was nearly naked," the woman retorted. "I thought my mother was going to have a heart attack. She's almost ninety, you know."

Gabe grinned all the way back to his desk. Although he couldn't claim all the credit for that particular masterpiece, it had been his brainchild and he felt a resulting pride.

His partner wasn't in yet. Gabe was early again, having left Meghan's before the boys could awaken. He sensed she felt awkward about his presence there with Danny in the apartment, and he was willing to do what it took to allay her concerns. But he couldn't deny an underlying visceral satisfaction. Her obvious discomfort with having a man spend the night probably meant he was the first to do so in a while. And though he'd never been possessive about a woman in his life, there was no doubt that he was interested in keeping this an exclusive relationship.

The recognition of that fact should have scared the hell out of him. The distance he maintained with other women didn't seem to apply to her. He wasn't quite ready to examine the reasons for that.

Dropping the envelope on his desk, he strolled over to pour himself a cup of what passed for coffee in the place. Only then did he settle in at his desk and tear open the envelope to examine the contents.

When Cal arrived later, the cup of coffee sat forgotten on Gabe's desk. "You beat me here again? What gives, Connally? Is one of your favorite greasy spoons running a sunrise special on cholesterol-packed breakfasts? No, even then they'd have to be free," he said, immediately correcting himself. "There's not much else that would get you up early."

It took a moment for the words to register. It took another for Gabe's concentration to shift. "It's not free breakfasts—but someone is giving away information. C'mere and take a look at this."

Cal rounded the desks and peered over Gabe's shoulder. After several minutes of scanning the papers his partner showed him, he said, "That looks like…"

"It is. Someone's gone to an awful lot of trouble to compile all this." He riffled the stack of pages. "It tracks various holdings of Golden Enterprises. According to this, Ultimate Video is only one of its many businesses. And talk about coincidences…" He stabbed his index finger at a line on one sheet. "The Sunrise Lounge is owned by the same group."

Cal reached around him and flipped through some more pages.

"Trying to keep track of who's actually at the helm of Golden Enterprises is like shooting in the dark. There's more blind trusts and offshore companies listed here than I can even keep track of. And that raises some interesting questions."

"Like why go to all this trouble of hiding something that's legit."

Gabe nodded. "Exactly."

"Why would this information be sent to us? We're not even handling the laundering aspect anymore."

Piling the papers back into some semblance of order, Gabe said, "That's just the question I'm going to ask."

"Did I miss something here? Are you saying you know who this package is from?"

Gabe rose and stuffed the contents back into the envelope. "I think I have a pretty good idea."

Gabe and Cal were on their third cup of coffee when Dare McKay slipped into the diner booth. "Detectives. Always a pleasure to receive an invitation from some of Chicago's overworked public servants." He gave an easy smile at a waitress passing by and said, "Anne, would you mind bringing me a cup?"

The woman smiled warmly at him. "Sure thing, sugar."

"Come here often, McKay?" Gabe inquired blandly.

Dare took the cup the waitress brought, in half the time it had taken her to wait on him and Cal, Gabe noted, and reached for the pot on the table. "You don't mind, do you?" Without waiting for an answer he filled his mug. "I get here once or twice a week. They serve a hell of a pancake breakfast."

Although Cal rolled his eyes, Gabe felt a spark of interest.

"Yeah?" Catching his partner's look, he shifted back to business. Picking up the envelope and emptying its contents on the table, he asked, "Recognize these?"

Bringing the cup to his lips, Dare raised his eyebrows over the rim. He took a drink, returned the cup to the table. "Should I?"

"I figure so. They were sent anonymously this morning by someone who seems to have an interest in our case."

Dare gave the sheets a cursory glance. "Guess that's a lucky break for you, huh? Might help you make a big break in the investigation."

"Only problem is," Cal put in, "we're not working the money angle anymore. Justice is. Seems odd that this information would be sent to us rather than the agents assigned to it."

"Maybe Justice already has this information," Dare suggested. He waited for the detectives to digest his remark. "I'm no expert in financial matters but it looks kind of complicated to me. Corporations, offshore accounts..." He shook his head. "Hard to tell what might be lurking behind all those blinds, isn't it?"

"Hard to tell how someone came by this information," Cal said.

"I couldn't say." Having emptied his cup, Dare refilled it. "But life is surely full of mysteries." The man smiled broadly. "Keeps things interesting, doesn't it?"

"Like we said, we're just working the murder of Lenny D'Brusco."

Dare tapped an index finger on the envelope and said, "My dad always told me that money was the root of all evil. I'd guess someone's telling you that you might turn up the murderer if you follow the money."

"Thank you so much," Gabe said with mock politeness. "Without that piece of wisdom we could never do the jobs we're trained for."

"Tough to follow the maze of corporate ownerships isn't

it?'' Dare drained his cup and rose. ''Suppose it might be interesting to see who the corporation acquired some of those properties from.'' He winked. ''Thanks for the coffee, guys. And, hey, if you ever want to try out their breakfasts here, you should arrive around seven. You'll beat the rush.'' He sauntered away from the booth and out of the diner.

''You think he sent the information?''

''He sent it,'' Gabe said surely.

Cal looked at his watch and then reached for his cup. ''If Justice already has this information, why the hell didn't they tell us about it?''

Leaning back in the booth, Gabe said, ''You know how the suits are. They think the information highway is a one-way street. Let's get back to Area One. I've got a sketch of the guy with D'Brusco the day we went to question him, and I want to run it by the lieutenant. Then we can start digging through this pile—'' he lifted the envelope ''—and find whatever the hell it is that McKay wants found.''

Cal's attention had been snared by an earlier sentence. ''You've got a sketch? How the hell did you manage that?''

''Meghan did it.'' He didn't like the look that came over his partner's face at his words.

''Oh, *Meghan* did it. She do police sketches a lot, does she?''

Gabe shifted uncomfortably in the booth. ''Don't be stupid. I asked about having the kid come in, but she wasn't keen on the idea. She suggested trying her hand first. Did a decent job of it, too. We both got what we wanted.''

''Did you, now?'' The gleam in Cal's eyes was more than matched by his suggestive tone, and both added to Gabe's discomfort.

''C'mon, knock it off.''

''What? I'm just thinking that Meghan Patterson is a really nice lady.''

''Yeah.'' Gabe stood, dug for some bills and threw them on the table.

"Not your usual type, though." Cal stood, as well, enjoying himself hugely. It was a rare treat to see Gabe this uncomfortable talking about a woman. "And by that I mean she seems to have an IQ higher than her body temperature."

Walking quickly to the door, Gabe said, "Sounds like you've been looking. Wait until Becky finds out." The sound of his partner's chuckle scraped across his nerves.

"Becky knows she's got nothing to worry about. You, though...you I'm not so sure about."

That his partner's words should so closely parrot his earlier thoughts didn't fill Gabe with any particular sense of calm. "Yeah, well don't worry about me. I know what I'm doing."

Tongue in cheek, Cal replied, "I think that's what Samson said before Delilah showed him the true meaning of the phrase 'bad hair day.'"

"Well, Detective, I had no idea." Meghan walked around his basement bemusedly. "So this is how you spend your free time, huh?" Large platforms were set up in his basement, and each was covered with miniature track. The plywood had been cleverly designed so that it appeared as though the trains were running through countryside, over hills and bridges. One of the scenes was unfinished, and she went to examine it. A city was taking shape, she observed. Miniature skyscrapers crowded streets, with a partially finished lake nearby.

"Wow, this is cool, Gabe!" Danny went excitedly from one platform to the other. "Did you get all of these from your foster dad? They're neat."

Meghan and Gabe both looked sharply at the boy, who didn't seem to notice. "How'd you know about that?" Gabe asked him.

"You said." Danny was eyeing a old fashioned steam engine with fascination. "That night you stayed."

Although Meghan still wore a puzzled look, Gabe quickly

recalled the night in question. It was the one when he'd remained to make sure Meghan was okay. The night when they'd been in each other's arms for the first time. The night, he remembered wryly, that he'd ended up frustrated and aching on her couch.

He'd been unable to come up with a bedtime story for the boy, so he'd told him about trains instead. He'd surprised himself then by how much he'd talked, but an even greater shock was that he'd mentioned his foster father. Family, with its tangles and dysfunctions, wasn't something he often spoke of. He must have been more distracted that night than he'd remembered.

"Make 'em go," the boy demanded. Gabe went over and flipped the switch on one platform, and the miniature train began its ascent over a hill.

"Cool!" It was clear that Danny was impressed. It was equally clear, Meghan thought amusedly, that the man enjoyed explaining the different functions of various pieces of track and equipment. Who would have thought that the big, tough detective spent his time in such a fashion? The many facets of Gabe Connally were a tempting invitation for exploration. She only hoped that she'd have the chance to do so.

She watched the two males silently, their heads bent close together as Gabe explained the intricacies of some mechanism. The bond she'd noted before seemed even stronger, and she wondered at it. She'd never known Danny to take to someone as readily as he did Gabe, not even her. A pang accompanied the thought. With Raina's help she was trying to put to rest those old fears about his ability. For Danny's sake, for both their sakes, she was going to have to find a way to do so.

A phone rang somewhere nearby. Gabe was engrossed in demonstrating the lift bridge to the boy. "Would you mind getting that?"

"No problem." She crossed to the desk that held the

telephone and picked up the receiver. After a moment she handed it to Gabe. "It's for you," she said quietly. "She sounds upset."

He frowned, took the phone from her. He listened for a moment, then said, "Ma, calm down."

Meghan listened, making no attempt to disguise her interest. There was apparently no end to the details she was learning about Gabe tonight. The longer he spoke on the phone, the grimmer he looked. He resembled, she thought, the distrustful cop who'd shown up at her door that first time. And she wondered what his mother could possibly be saying that would put that look on his face.

"Where'd he get the cash?" After listening for a moment, his expression grew sterner. "Yeah, I'll be there. No, don't do anything. I'll take care of it." He cut the connection abruptly and swiped a hand over his jaw.

Meghan's voice was tentative. "Bad news?"

"There's something I need to take care of. I don't know how long it will take."

She watched him carefully, wondering at the rigid control he was exerting. But his eyes told a different story. And she was very glad she wasn't on the receiving end of the kind of fury she saw brewing there. "We can just take a cab."

Her question seemed to distract him. "You don't have to do that. I'll take you." There was a minute of hesitation before he added, "After I take care of this."

Gabe had been less than communicative in the car, so Danny had done most of the talking. Meghan hadn't been sure what to expect, but she was surprised when Gabe pulled into the general hospital's parking lot.

"Shall we wait for you here?" she asked tentatively.

He looked impatient. "I don't know how long I'll be. You better come in."

As an invitation it lacked civility, but his meaning was clear enough. She and Danny trailed in his wake into the emergency waiting room. Meghan held back as an older woman launched herself at Gabe.

"Gabriel! Oh, thank God you're here. They were talking about putting him in detox, and that would just kill Butch. You know it would."

He stood stiffly in her embrace for an instant, before disentangling her arms from his neck. "Why don't you let me get the information so we know what we're dealing with here?"

"Oh, my, yes." Joyce Reddington clasped her hands together to keep them from trembling. "You talk to them. I just can't seem to make sense of what they're saying." Without another word Gabe strode away. Joyce turned to Meghan and smiled uncertainly.

"Are you with Gabriel?"

Gabriel, the archangel. The whimsical thought flitted across Meghan's mind. Somehow she didn't think Gabe would appreciate the comparison.

"Yes."

Joyce spotted Danny then, and her smile faltered. Her gaze went back to Meghan. "Are you Gabriel's wife?"

"No." Realizing the woman was on the edge of collapse, Meghan gently steered her toward one of the chairs lining the walls. "You'd certainly know if Gabe was married."

"Yes." Joyce's voice was strangely uncertain. "He would probably tell me." But as if she remained unconvinced, her gaze kept darting to Danny, who'd discovered a magazine graced with what else—a dinosaur—and was already engrossed.

Gabe reappeared, and if possible his jaw was even tighter. Joyce bounced out of her chair. "Did you get Butch released? I can take care of him if they'd just send him home. Are they going to send him home?"

"No, they're keeping him in detox where he belongs. And after that there'll be a psych eval."

"No!" Joyce clutched Gabe's arm tightly. "Maybe they

could just keep him overnight. Just until he calms down. He's been clean a long time. One little mistake isn't reason for him to start all over again.''

"Was it just one mistake, Ma?" Gabe peered into her eyes dispassionately, then took one of her arms in his hand and rolled up the sleeve of her sweater.

"Gabriel." She managed to sound indignant and sad at the same time. "The last time was 'it' for me. I quit for good. Didn't I promise you that?"

"You made a lot of promises."

His voice was flat, expressionless, but his words vibrated like a plucked harp string. Joyce's shoulders sagged. "I know I did. But this is one I'm keeping."

Gabe's jaw clenched. "If you really want to stay clean, the last person you should be living with is another addict."

"Butch isn't an addict anymore. He's not," Joyce said insistently when Gabe muttered a curse. "He stumbled this time, but he'll pick himself up again. And he'll be stronger for it, you'll see."

"Yeah." It was clear from the set of Gabe's shoulders that he was done arguing with the woman. But the emotion hadn't been dismissed. It seethed in his eyes. With abrupt motions he jerked out his wallet. "How are you fixed for cash? Do you have a way home?"

"I got my purse. I'll take a bus home tomorrow. I want to stay the night here, make sure Butch is okay."

He nodded, took some bills out of his wallet and handed them to her. "The cafeteria is open until midnight, the desk nurse said. She can show you where it is, and tell you where you can wait."

Joyce took the bills, but her gaze was on her son's face. "All right."

"I'll call you here tomorrow. I'm going to want to talk to his doctor myself."

She folded the bills nervously over and over in her hands. "Thank you, Gabriel. You're so good to me."

Gabe had started to turn away, but at those words he froze for a moment, every vertebra going rigid. Then he strode to where Meghan was collecting Danny. With his hand resting at the base of her spine, he ushered them away and out to his car.

"He was asleep before his head hit the pillow." Meghan's voice was soft as she joined Gabe in the living room.

"Asleep without his nightly bowl of ice cream? That must be a record." Conversation was a welcome distraction from the scene that played and replayed in his mind. Endless repeats. Variations on a theme. It took only the puzzled look on her face for comprehension to register. "He doesn't have a bowl of double-fudge ripple before going to bed at night?"

Her reaction spoke more loudly than her words. "Good heavens, no. That sounds like an open invitation to nightmares if I ever heard one."

"Damn." He felt a flicker of amusement. "I thought the little creep was scamming me that night, but I wasn't sure. Guess I don't know much about kids."

She studied him for a moment as he prowled the area, then went to the kitchen where he could hear the sound of cupboards opening. Minutes later she came back carrying a tumbler. Offering it to him, she said simply, "Whiskey. I'm told it's an excellent quality."

He reached for it, took a swallow. "At this point quality is wasted on me." The liquor seared a path down his throat and pooled warmly in his stomach. He sipped again, willing the warmth it produced to spread to his veins, melting the ice that had formed the minute he'd heard his mother's voice on the phone.

Meghan watched him for a moment, then sat on the couch. "Who was it that your mother was so worried about?"

"Butch VanGowen. Her boyfriend."

"Did the doctors say he was going to be all right?"

His mouth twisted. "His kind have a way of surviving. He'll live to spread misery another day." The last words were uttered with such loathing that he surprised even himself. But if he despised the weakness that kept his mother clinging to the man, he despised the man more. "As you might have picked up from the conversation, he has fallen off that pinnacle of abstinence he teetered on." He brought the glass to his lips and watched her over its rim. "He's a drug addict. Just like my mother."

He waited for the shock on her face, and he waited for the pity. When he saw neither, the vise in his gut eased just a fraction.

"She seemed sincere. When she said she'd quit for good."

"She's good at sincerity. Almost as good as she is at quitting. She's done it dozens of times over the years. Hopefully this time it took." He gave a dismissive shrug that hinted at none of the emotions crashing and churning inside him. "Maybe it has."

Driven to move, he roamed her large living room. Her pricey apartment and high-rent neighborhood were about as far away from the squalor of his childhood as it was possible to imagine.

And yet, it wasn't difficult to recall those times. The memories lurked in the dark corners of his mind, striking when least expected. When consciousness faded. When defenses were weakened. Then the echoes from the past would pounce, packing enough realism to leave him sweating and shaking.

"What I remember most about my childhood was the smell." Poverty had an aroma all its own. Rotting garbage. Stale beer. Human waste. "Sometimes when I have a call on the west side I'll walk into a tenement and I'll catch that scent…" He shook his head, as if to dislodge the images that clung despite his efforts to carve them out of his mind. And then he sipped from the cut-crystal tumbler in his hand, enjoyed the bite of fine whiskey and tried to remember how far away he was from those years.

"For me it's Chanel Number Five."

His attention jerked to Meghan and she gave a half smile. "Both my mother and grandmother used it. When one or both of them would call me on the carpet, which was fairly often, I'd stand there waiting for the lecture to be over and smell that perfume. To this day whenever I encounter that fragrance I'm filled with an overwhelming urge to flee."

"I can't imagine that you were too troublesome as a kid."

"Well, it didn't take much to disappoint the Tremaynes." Her voice was casual as if the thoughts no longer mattered. "It occurred much more frequently than you think. But you were troublesome, weren't you? You told me once that you were a delinquent."

"Where I lived it was a way of life. I joined a gang when I was twelve." He managed, finally, to shock her. He saw it in her widened gaze, her fixed expression. "My mother spent whatever money she earned on drugs and stayed pretty strung-out most of the time. By the time I was thirteen we were homeless and lived under a bridge for the summer." He lifted a shoulder. "By that time I was living in the streets anyway."

There'd been promises back then, so many promises. That she'd get a real job. That she'd stop using. That they'd get a real house. Promises as empty as the air they were uttered in.

"How did you end up in the system?" When he merely looked at her she elaborated. "You mentioned foster parents. I assume Social Services stepped in at some time."

"I took four bullets to the chest the fall I turned fourteen." Pumped out of a .35 caliber midnight special blasting out of a window of a stolen hatchback. A rival gang had been looking for notches and they'd found one. He'd nearly bled to death in a filthy gutter filled with crack vials and broken bottles. It was a long time before he'd been glad he survived.

"It woke my mother up." He gave a humorless smile. "At least to what the life was doing to me. The cop assigned to my case told her I'd be in jail before I was eighteen. She begged him to take me home instead." The fact that Joseph Maine had, in fact, done just that, still had the power to amaze him. He'd stayed at first because the small house in the suburbs had been preferable to juvie. But at the end he'd stayed because he'd wanted to. Joseph and Dora had slowly won his trust and then his respect and finally a fierce devotion that remained strong to this day. He didn't understand people like them, who had the patience and desire to take in a half-wild street punk. But he knew where he'd be today without them.

"It sounds like your mother made the right decision."

"It was the best thing she ever did for me." He went over to the wall and examined the bright splash of colors on the canvas adorning it. "She spent the next four years trying to undo it."

Her visits at first, he remembered, had been full of familiar promises and empty vows. Maybe she'd sensed when his reluctance to stay with the Maines had dissipated, to be replaced by an appreciation for the modest comforts his new life provided. Hell, maybe she'd been jealous. But for whatever reason, before the first year was up, the focus of the visits had undergone a drastic change.

"She began to argue with the Maines, threaten them if they didn't let me go back with her. They had the system on their side by then, of course. There was no way I would have been allowed to return as long as she continued her lifestyle. But somehow she twisted all of it, made it seem like it was Joseph who had stolen me from her. And she certainly held him and Dora responsible for my reluctance to leave.''

''How long did that go on?''

''On and off for years.'' Slowly his ambivalence about life had changed to a new appreciation for it. But whenever he would start to get comfortable, she'd show up again, spouting threats and worthless promises. ''The last time was when I was seventeen. She'd sworn to me that she was off drugs for good, and I was starting to believe her.'' He hadn't particularly wanted to think about leaving his foster family by that time, but he'd have done it, out of loyalty if not love.

''She disappeared for a few months. Said she was getting a new life together for us. When she turned up again she was stoned out of her mind and about seven months pregnant.''

The sick feeling of betrayal was easily recalled. ''That meeting ended badly,'' he said in gross understatement. ''I didn't see her again for ten years.''

''And she's been straight ever since.''

He gave a humorless laugh. ''With an addict it's never as easy as that.'' Every time he saw Joyce he couldn't suppress the suspicion that surged, couldn't prevent himself from silently searching for signs of drug use. As long as she remained clean, he took care of her. Found her a place to live and made sure she had clothes to wear, food to eat. He was careful with the money. Butch had a way of selling whatever he could get his hands on. A more worthless human being Gabe had rarely seen, but Joyce stuck by him with pathetic devotion. She'd exchanged, he supposed, one addiction for another.

''What happened to the baby?''

''I don't know. She was vague with the details. I assume it went in the system, wherever she happened to be when she gave birth.'' He knew too well the outlook for babies born with addictions. Had dealt with the offspring of addicted mothers for most of his career. Suddenly he was weary, clear down to his bones. Tired of thinking of it, and damned tired of talking about it. He slid a gaze to Meghan. It wasn't like him to let all this spill in the light of day. Cal knew bits and pieces of it. No one else. He didn't know what it was, about this woman, that had elicited his candor. Maybe because he knew something of what she'd gone through, too. Crash victims experienced similar camaraderie.

But even as he had the thought, he knew it was a lie. He didn't feel the inclination to spill his guts to anyone else. It wasn't the experiences they shared, it was *her*. And he was past the point of questioning why.

She rose and approached him. Slipping her arms around his waist, she tipped her face up to his and said, "You became a good man in spite of it all, Gabe. Decent. Honorable. And probably more empathetic than you're entirely comfortable with."

He wasn't at ease with the accolades, but her proximity accomplished what no amount of whiskey ever would. The tension began to seep from his body, one small bit at a time. Sliding a hand into her hair, he lowered his mouth to hers for a kiss that held a curious tenderness. When it was over he leaned his forehead against hers and released a breath. It felt like ridding his lungs of poison.

"You know you forgot to list some of my most winning qualities, don't you?"

Recognizing the lightening of his mood, she responded in kind. She cocked her head, pretended to think. "Hmm...I can't think of any."

"You forgot charming." When she rolled her eyes, his brows raised. "Handsome."

"Conceited," she offered, and was rewarded with a pinch.

"I was going to say, 'dangerously susceptible to blue-eyed blondes with long, curly hair and tight, curvy little bodies.'''

"Lucky for me your taste is so specific."

He set his tumbler down on a nearby table and toyed with the top button of her blouse. "Honey, my taste grew more specific the moment I met you." The kiss she rewarded him with started out with a laugh and quickly turned into more. His mouth angled against hers and feasted, drawing in her flavor like a starving man devoured a meal.

It was a kind of healing. The sweetness of her mouth, the catch of her breath. And then the evidence of her rising passion, as her mouth twisted under his and her arms tightened. The taste of her was a balm to old wounds and just that easily she stripped his mind clean. He took the kiss deeper and thought of nothing but her.

Meghan felt herself go boneless. The dizzying speed of it arced through her senses. Nothing in her experience had prepared her for the way one touch from him could rocket her system. He tasted of warm whiskey and primal male hunger. It was an irresistible combination.

His hand moved between them, and moments later cool air kissed her bare skin. Her teeth closed over his lip, and as his hand covered her breast she gave a satisfied sigh. He pushed her blouse down her arms, released the catch of her bra. Bending his head, he took the tip of one breast between his lips. The fleeting satisfaction shattered, transformed into a sudden, vicious ache.

The scent of her lingered in provocative traces between her breasts, in the delicate hollow at the base of her throat. He filled his senses with her and used teeth, tongue and lips to feast on her satiny flesh. He could feel her heartbeat stumble as she arched closer to him, and he responded to the demand by taking her deeper.

She fumbled with his shirt, pulled it from his jeans and unfastened it. He raised his head and pressed against her, a kiss of sensitized flesh that fired nerve endings to flash point.

A whisper of sanity had Meghan twisting her mouth from his. "Not here." The words were panted, barely audible, but her meaning was clear. He picked her up and carried her to her darkened bedroom, setting her down just inside the doorway. Then he was swinging the door closed and crowding her against the wall. He shrugged out of his shirt with barely restrained violence and sucked in his stomach when her hands went to the button of his jeans.

Raw, wicked need thrummed in his veins. Hands tangled as each battled to be the first to strip the other. Divested of clothing, they had no barriers between them. Free to touch and be touched, they filled themselves with the pleasures of the senses. Their breathing grew quick and labored. Her hand slid down his stomach and lower, then she found him, wrapping her fingers around his shaft.

His senses careened. He swept his hands up her silky leg, followed the crease of her thigh until he found her damp heat. He entered her with his fingers and took her to the peak that first time by touch alone.

Meghan had to fight to get air into her lungs. Her senses were filled with him. Her world had narrowed until he was the focal point. She reached for him blindly; striving to bring him to that same barbed edge. A hunger that couldn't be satiated, that wouldn't be denied.

Long lingering strokes, quick bursts of pleasure. He tolerated her teasing until his mind reeled. Then he moved between her legs, cupped her bottom in his hands and entered her with a single savage thrust. He paused, every pulse in his body throbbing like a wound. Her arms clung to his shoulders, her teeth grazed his lips. The tiny pain enflamed him, and his hips began moving against hers, slowly at first, then with increasing urgency. His eyes were open but he couldn't see. Could only feel the quick bursts of breath escaping her, hear her moans as he hammered himself into her. Her legs were wrapped around his waist, and her hips arched beneath his, urging him on.

Gabe could feel her body tense, in a taut quest for fulfillment. He moved against her faster, deeper, climbing the jagged brink to his own release. Then she crested, twisting in his arms. He allowed free rein to the savage need pounding through him and followed her over the edge, swallowing her cry of pleasure. And free-falling into sensation, nothing existed but the two of them.

Chapter 13

He left her sleeping, soft and depleted from their love-making. Slipping into his clothes he made the mistake of looking back at her and nearly reversed his decision. The fall of her hair barely revealed the curve of her cheek. He didn't have to touch it again to remember its exquisite smoothness.

After another moment he stiffened his resolve. If he gave in to the temptation riding him, he wouldn't be getting back out of her bed at all. Opening the door he strode to the kitchen for some juice before he made his way home. The thought had never been so uninviting. He didn't want to slip from her bed at the first hint of dawn, and he damn well didn't want her slipping from his. Discretion was going to grow burdensome quickly.

He opened a cupboard and removed a glass. Taking the juice from the refrigerator, he poured his glass full, then drained it. He refilled it and replaced the container in the refrigerator. Even as he chafed at the restraints she placed on their time together, he had a grudging understanding for her reasons. That's what parenthood called for, he supposed, leaning against the counter. A constant balancing act of adult needs against the child's. And if the parent was committed, the child's took precedence. Danny was lucky to have landed with Meghan. Her sense of responsibility and compassion ran deep. And there was no question of her feelings for the boy.

There was a small sound, then Danny appeared, clad only in his underwear and T-shirt. He rubbed his eyes and yawned. Gabe stilled, guilt stealing through him. This was exactly the kind of scene that Meghan had hoped to avoid having her nephew witness.

But the boy just shuffled to the table and pulled out a chair. Climbing up on it, he said, "I want some juice."

Gabe watched him for a moment, but thirst seemed to be the only thing on the boy's mind. "You got it." He took out another glass, filled it and handed it to Danny. "You're up early."

The boy took a long drink. "Is it time for school yet?"

"You don't have school today, remember? It's Sunday."

"Can we go back to your house today? We didn't get to see the trains very long."

"We'll see." The idea had merit. They could spend the afternoon together. Maybe grill outside, if the weather warmed up. He thought he had a couple fillets in his freezer. He wondered if Meghan liked steak. Then she appeared in the doorway, as if summoned by his thoughts, looking drowsy, soft and mussed.

"She likes hers with steak sauce," Danny said. Another huge yawn overtook him. "But I'd rather have hamburgers. Do you have any hamburgers in your freezer?"

Gabe's glass halted halfway to his lips. Then slowly, a fraction of an inch at a time, he lowered it. His voice hoarse, he asked, "What did you say?"

"Danny, what do you want for breakfast?" Meghan

forced herself to keep her voice steady, to move. Anything to shatter the frozen vista before her.

Around another yawn the boy said, "Fruity O's and chocolate milk." He was sleepy enough not to realize the impact of his words to Gabe. Not to feel the intense regard of the man standing near him. But she felt it. And it made her bones quake.

She busied herself preparing the boy's meal. "How about Cheerios and regular milk?"

He uttered a complaint, but was too hungry to protest for long. She set the dishes down in front of him and finally allowed herself to meet Gabe's gaze. What she saw there tore at her heart.

Pushing away from the table, he stalked out of the room, his body rigid. She forced herself to follow him and then to meet the condemnation in his eyes.

"You lied to me."

The flat, harsh words were barbed and stabbed deep. Guilt reared. "I was trying to protect him...."

"You've been lying all along. Through this whole case." He paced the room in short vicious strides, then whirled to face her again. "It was like he walked right into my head and read what I was thinking."

She looked away, battling back the old fears. She could well imagine his shock. She had, after all, lived all her life with her sister's ability to do the same.

He didn't give her time to respond. "He's done it before. I just didn't realize it. I never mentioned my foster father to him. He saw it somehow. Hell, I don't know. Why don't you explain it to me, Meghan." His tone was barely a whisper, but savage despite its softness. "What the hell do you call that...that thing he does?"

"He's telepathic," she said wearily. "His therapist thinks he has some clairvoyant tendencies, too, but it's not nearly so well developed."

His eyes seared into hers. "Like his mother."

She flinched visibly. "Yes. Pretty much."

He looked as if he was on the verge of violence. But she was strangely unafraid. If she'd learned one thing about Gabe it was that she had nothing to fear from him physically. But emotionally... She swallowed hard.

"I should have figured out the way you were dragging your feet about having him cooperate that there was something you were trying to hide. And there is, isn't there, Meghan?" She didn't respond, and he reached her in two quick steps, taking her chin in his hand and forcing it up so she met his gaze. "He knows something, doesn't he? Something you didn't give us."

"He picked up a little from the men," she began, then flinched when he abruptly dropped his hand and turned. Sensing his intention she grabbed his arm. "You'll just upset him. I can tell you what he saw. It doesn't make much sense."

He stopped and looked pointedly at the hand she'd placed on his arm until she released him. His tone was biting. "I wouldn't believe anything you said right now if you came down the mountain carrying stone tablets. I'll talk to the boy."

She followed him to the kitchen, dreading the scene to come, expecting the worst. She would intercede on Danny's behalf if Gabe upset him. Her responsibility was to the boy.

But that didn't mean she felt no obligation to the man. The man who'd provided some of the answers about Sandra's death. The man who'd held her in his arms and taken her to heights she'd never dreamed existed. The man, she thought achingly, who valued honesty above all else.

Gabe casually picked up his glass and sat in the chair next to Danny. "How're the Cheerios?"

Mouth full, Danny said, "Fruity O's are better."

"No kidding. I like the sugared flakes myself. Ever had them?"

Danny nodded and swallowed. "I had those at Alex's

once. Aunt Meggie won't buy good cereal very often. She says my teeth will rot if I eat too much junk."

"She's probably right." His face serious, Gabe then said, "I need your help, buddy." He waited for the boy's gaze to meet his before going on. "Your aunt says maybe you know something else about those two guys you saw outside the toy store that day."

"I told you the first one was scared." Uneasily Danny looked at Meghan, seeking her support.

Gabe nodded. "You did. And you helped a lot already by describing the tall guy. But I really need anything else you can tell me. Anything at all."

The uncertainty on the boy's face tore at Meghan's heart. Swiftly she crossed to his chair and sank to her knees beside it. "It's okay, Danny. You can tell Gabe everything."

"Everything?"

She tried a smile for reassurance and nodded her head.

His gaze slid to the detective's. "You know the first guy? The short one? He was scared of Pollynife, the skull guy. He got in the car with him, but he didn't want to. He wanted to run away instead." He stopped, looked at his aunt.

"Go on," she urged softly. "Tell him the rest."

"Pollynife had a nursery rhyme song in his head. The one about the weasel. We sing it at my school, too." Gabe's arrested expression seemed to stop him then, and he glanced at Meghan uncertainly.

"That's good, Danny." She made her voice reassuring. "That's just the way you told it to me, isn't it?"

He nodded. "Can I go play now?"

"A bath first." His expected groan of dismay would have made her smile on any other occasion. "We got home too late last night for you to have one."

He slipped from the chair, his shoulders drooping, and trudged toward the bathroom. Watching his theatrics reminded her achingly of how short-lived this disappointment would be for him. In a few minutes he'd have his toys engaged in a full-blown sea battle. The apprehension pooling in her stomach, however, would not be nearly as easily dissipated.

Forcing herself to turn and meet Gabe's gaze, she nearly flinched from the condemnation in it. "Are you sure that's everything he knows?"

"Telepathics don't always 'see' words. People's thoughts are rarely that clear. It's usually more perceptions, fragments they can sense when people don't have a natural guard raised. Or at least," she added, "that's what his therapist tells me. I told you before, what he got from them doesn't make much sense." Silence stretched endlessly. "You have to understand..." Her voice faltered under his scathing look. "I couldn't let him be endangered like his mother had been. She made her own choices. Someone had to watch out for the boy."

"And you didn't trust me to do that. You're wrong. I understand perfectly."

His words hit their mark. But that didn't mean the quiet sound of the door closing didn't feel like a shot to her heart. It didn't mean the sorrow and disappointment weren't welling up inside her in a tidal pool of grief.

Something told her she'd have to live with the feelings for quite some time.

Monday morning Gabe was at his desk again when Cal arrived. He had a stack of copies of the sketch Meghan had made on his desk. He didn't look up when his partner clasped his chest dramatically and said, "I don't think my heart can take any more of these shocks. If giving up nicotine has turned you into an early riser, maybe you should have gone cold turkey a long time ago." When Gabe made no response, concern chased the humor from Cal's tone. Peering closely at his partner he said, "You look like hell, pal."

"Thanks." He could have told him that he felt worse.

Much worse. The little sleep he'd gotten last night hadn't been particularly restful. The images of Meghan that he'd managed to keep at bay during the daylight hours hadn't waited for an invitation to pounce. He'd woken from dreams of her, of them together, and reality had seemed even bleaker.

Aware that his partner was going to demand an explanation, Gabe said, "There was a deal with my mother this weekend." He didn't elaborate and could tell from Cal's expression that he didn't need to. He'd spent most of yesterday dealing with her at the hospital. He'd finally convinced her to let him drive her home when it became apparent that Butch was going to be kept a few more days. Not that Gabe held out much hope that the psychiatric evaluation would go anywhere. The man would probably walk out of the hospital in a few days with only his word that he would show up for the treatment program the hospital arranged for him. As if his word meant anything.

"Well you may be beating me into the office these days, but I've been getting a little work done once you leave." Cal went to his desk and opened a drawer, pulling out the file McKay had sent them. "Lookie what I found when I did a little digging last night." He handed the folder to Gabe.

Without much enthusiasm Gabe reached for it, flipped it open. And then his interest sharpened as he scanned down a list Cal had tucked inside. "Some coincidence."

"A full dozen of Golden Enterprises's businesses were sold to the corporation by Victor Mannen." Cal sat on the edge of his desk, supremely pleased with himself. "And all of the sales took place within eight months of each other about three years ago. Hell of a coincidence, I'd say. Now why don't you tell me what you've got?" He nodded toward the scribblings on the tablet in front of Gabe. "You working on something?"

"I'm not sure. I got more from the boy yesterday morning. Maybe a name, I don't know."

His brow furrowed, Cal said, "A name? How would he come up with that? He wasn't close enough to hear D'Brusco and the other guy..." Gabe just looked at him until comprehension and incredulity warred on his face. "No way. He's just a kid. He couldn't..."

"He does." Gabe's voice was short.

Cal was still grappling with the information. "How long have you known?"

"Since yesterday."

"Ah."

There was a wealth of meaning in the sound. Gabe chose to ignore it. He handed the tablet to his partner. Cal read what was written there and asked, "Pollynife? What kind of name is that? A person? A place?"

"From what the boy said, a person. Namely the person with D'Brusco."

"Skull face?" Unknowingly Cal mimicked Danny's words. He shook his head. "I don't know, Gabe. This isn't much. What are we supposed to do with it?"

"You can't think of anyone out there who goes by the nickname of Polly?" At his partner's negative answer he admitted, "Me, either. And I've tried every angle I can think of to match that sketch with our database. No luck. But the answer's on that tablet. I can feel it."

Slowly Cal said, "You know, Gabe, this hocus-pocus stuff...well, it's weird, okay? And not exactly the kind of thing you'd normally go for."

"It's real." Gabe knew that for a fact. He'd had a thought plucked cleanly out of his mind as if he'd voiced it. But he hadn't. And although he still was half disbelieving about the whole thing, he couldn't refute what he'd witnessed for himself.

He looked past his partner to a man wending his way toward their desks. "Hey, Doug. You lost?"

The medical examiner stopped in front of their desks. "I thought you'd want to see this right away. And since there's a case of scotch in it for me…" He let his words trail away and held a sheaf of papers in the air.

"You got something for us?" Gabe made a grab for the papers, but the man held them out of reach. "Yeah, all right, the case is yours. Gimme."

The man dropped the papers on Gabe's desk, and Cal came to peer over Gabe's shoulder. "You said you were looking for a connection between the D'Brusco and Collins homicides. I've got it for you, fellas, tied up here in a neat little bow. I even brought you another surprise."

Scanning the information on the papers, Cal and Gabe saw what they were looking for at the same time. "Same knife?"

Doug pulled a chair up and sat. "Yes, indeedy. They were both killed with a wicked blade of the same approximate width and length. If it's not the same one it's identical. It's probably the same killer did both, and the boy knows his stuff. It's tougher than people think to achieve an almost instant kill by slitting someone's throat. Most who try have to effect a sawing motion—" he pantomimed with his index finger at his throat "—to sever the cartoid artery. It takes a specialized weapon. The victims killed by this method usually bleed to death."

"But not these two?" questioned Cal.

Shaking his head, Doug leaned forward in his chair. "Their deaths occurred in moments. This guy has the right tool for his trade. There were kidney wounds on both vics indicating a rear attack. Then their heads would have been pulled back, like so." He tipped his head back, baring his throat. "The blade is thrust in here, pressed forward and severs the front of the throat and neck."

"So you're saying this guy's a pro," Gabe said slowly.

"Absolutely. And the surprise I mentioned earlier? Autopsied another vic a few days ago killed exactly the same way.''

He had both men's rapt attention now, and enjoyed it to the fullest. ''A Chafe Robinson. Only difference was the corpse was missing a hand.'' He lifted a shoulder as if to say the significance of that detail escaped him.

''I'll be damned to hell.''

Doug agreed with Gabe's pronouncement cheerfully. ''Very probably.'' He rose to his feet. ''Don't forget that scotch, fellas. And don't think that's the end of it. You're gonna owe me for this one a lo-o-ong time.''

Gabe looked at Cal, his mind racing. ''So there's a pro out there.''

''Lots of them. We can feed the MO into the computer and see what it spits out.''

''Maybe.'' Something nagged at the edge of Gabe's mind, but sleep deprivation had his concentration fuzzy. ''If he's never been arrested we're not going to get a match.'' In frustration he pressed his fist to his eyes. *Pollynife.* ''What if the part of the name the kid picked up was knife?'' He was thinking out loud, trying to make sense of it. ''Some pro who specializes with a knife.'' Even as he spoke it, the answer blazed across his mind. ''Paulie the Knife.'' He slapped his hand on the desk. ''It fits, Cal. It has to.''

''Paulie the Knife.'' Cal's brows were raised to his receding hairline. ''You know there's never been a picture of him. No one's ever been able to identify him.'' Witnesses, of course, had a way of disappearing. ''You're talking connections, there, Gabe. And money. Hired assassins don't come cheap.''

''And whose name keeps popping up who would have both?''

They voiced the words simultaneously. ''Victor Mannen.''

"This is thin," Cal said halfheartedly. He was already rising and reaching for his coat. "Really thin."

Gabe grabbed his jacket and headed toward the door. "Thin's my middle name."

"Detectives." Victor Mannen didn't rise from his desk when they entered, just waved a hand for them to take a seat, the action oddly regal. Setting his pen down precisely beside the papers on his desk, he folded his hands and surveyed them. "To what do I owe this...pleasure?"

"You could tell us about your dealings with Golden Enterprises," Gabe suggested.

Mannen raised his brows politely. "I'm afraid I don't follow you."

"That's the name of the corporation you sold several of your holdings to, among which were Ultimate Video and Sunrise Lounge. Both places have figured in an investigation we're running. You used to own them."

"The key phrase, I believe, is used to."

"Who'd you deal with when you sold them to Golden Enterprises?" Gabe roamed the opulent office, taking in the teak furniture and the artwork that even he could tell was museum quality.

"I can't even say for sure if it was Golden Enterprises that I sold to." He lifted one immaculately clad shoulder. "The transactions occurred some time ago."

"Maybe we can help your memory. That *was* the corporation you sold to." Cal's voice was easy. "Courthouses keep records of stuff like that."

Mannen inclined his head. "As you say. Well, if that's what the records show, then it must be so. But I fail to see why it would generate such interest."

"Why'd you get rid of them?" At Mannen's silence Gabe looked over at him, met his gaze blandly. "Were they losing money for you?"

"I believe at the time I was seeking to diversify." His

voice was cool as he watched the detective pick up a Ming vase, examine it, then set it down audibly. His lips tightened. "Please make whatever point you've come for, Detectives. My time is quite valuable."

Gabe approached his desk, dropped a copy of the sketch on it. "Have you ever seen this man before?"

Mannen studied the sheet for a minute before raising his gaze again. "I can't say that I have, fortunately. He doesn't look like the type I'd normally run into in my circle."

"We've got copies of this sketch circulating throughout the city. We think he's responsible for three deaths related to the case we're working," Cal interjected. "He's known as Paulie the Knife."

"Colorful." A faint smile crossed Mannen's lips, then vanished. "But what does this have to do with me?"

"That's what we're wondering." Gabe stared at the man steadily. "Somehow you're the common thread running through this whole mess."

"Because I used to own a few businesses you've mentioned?" Mannen's tone was amused. "Since when is it suspicious for a man to divest himself of some investments that ceased to be profitable?"

"So the video place and the Sunrise were losers, huh? And the rest of them?" Gabe strolled over to a glass case showcasing antique firearms. "Where'd you place the money you got from them?" He looked back at Victor. "Stocks, bonds, that kind of thing?"

Mannen clasped his hands on his desk. "I hardly think my portfolio is pertinent to your investigation. And it isn't up for discussion, at any rate. Now if you've finished your business..." He rose and pressed a button on his intercom. A burly man wearing an ill-fitting suit stepped into the room. "Peter, the detectives are done here. Could you show them out?"

"You know, I'm thinking your portfolio might be more

pertinent than you believe.'' Gabe smiled easily. ''We'll let you know when we do some more checking.''

Mannen pressed his lips in a thin, hard line and waited for the door to close behind the detectives. He could trust Peter to show them to the street. Crossing the room, he opened an adjoining door and said, ''They're gone.''

The man known as Paulie the Knife reentered the room he'd recently vacated. At birth he had been given the name Paul Delgado. It had been so long since he thought of himself that way that the name had little meaning for him. The conversation he'd just heard did.

''I gotta leave town. I need the rest of the money you owe me.''

The demand in the man's tone rankled, but Victor remained outwardly unruffled. ''I'm not sure you're due any more money. Obviously, you bungled one of the jobs.''

''Those hits were clean.''

''You left a witness.'' The truth hung in the air, irrefutable. ''Therefore, the job isn't finished.''

The words landed squarely on Paulie's pride. It was the first time ever that he'd been identified. He looked at the sketch lying on Mannen's desk and cursed. It wasn't perfect, but it was close enough for him to be recognized. Pride struggled with survival, and the battle was short-lived. ''Forget it. I'm out of here.''

Mannen allowed him to get as far as the door before saying, ''I think you're forgetting one very expedient point. A sketch is worth nothing if there isn't an eyewitness to back it up.'' It was tedious, he thought, having to explain every detail to his employees, but then, it wasn't their brainpower most of them had been hired for.

Paulie turned, warily looked at him.

Steepling his fingers, Mannen reached for patience. ''Collins and Robinson, as it turns out, have been useful in one small way. They linked Barton's sister with this police detective, so it takes very little intelligence to guess the identity of the eyewitness, doesn't it?'' He watched comprehension flood the other man's face before indicating a seat. "Sit down.'' He waited for the man to do as he bade. "Now listen carefully. I want my wishes carried out to the letter.''

"What'd you think?''

"He's got the money to afford a pro,'' Gabe said. "And he's sure got the ego. What are you gonna do next?''

Cal didn't take his eyes off the road. "Be kind of interesting to find out what Mannen's into now, wouldn't it? We'll have to have more to go on before approaching Burney with this. You know how tough he can be to…'' His words tapered off. "What do you mean, me? What are you going to do?''

"I'm going to talk to the lieutenant about taking some personal time this afternoon.'' There was a feeling in his gut, too edgy and raw to be ignored. "I want to make sure Meghan and Danny aren't in any danger now that we've spread around those sketches of Paulie.'' He shrugged, unable to explain the uneasy feeling he had. It wasn't a meeting he was looking forward to. Some of the anger from this morning had subsided, but there was lingering emotion that still stung. He'd have preferred to have all those feelings under control before he saw her again. Reacted to her again.

Uncharacteristically Cal chanced taking his eyes off the road to glance at his partner. "They shouldn't be in any danger. The kid told us the first day that neither man saw him.''

Rolling his shoulders, Gabe said, "So, great. But it still wouldn't hurt to let her know what went down. She deserves to know, since it affects her nephew, doesn't she?''

With raised brows Cal turned his attention back to the road. He knew better than to press Connally when he was in a mood, and as moods went, this one was downright surly. Only a woman could get a man so worked up that he couldn't think quite clearly. Suppressing a smile, he continued his sedate journey back to Area One. The guess he'd made days earlier had been right on. Connally was definitely smitten.

The man loomed out of nowhere. Meghan had just begun to get out of the car when he appeared before her, suddenly enough to give her heart a jolt. And then in the next instant recognition set in, followed by terror. The sketch she'd done of the man from Danny's description had been eerily accurate. She dove back inside the car, frantically trying to shut and lock the door behind her. But her split second hesitation had given the man the opening he'd needed. He yanked the door open, and crowded in behind her, forcing her across the seat. She threw herself at the opposite door then abruptly halted when she felt the kiss of cold steel at her neck.

"Bad move. Now sit up. That's right." The knife traveled lower, out of sight of anyone passing by. She could feel its edge pricking the skin at the top of her thigh through the denim jeans.

The man snatched her purse, found the keys on top. "Your femoral artery is right there, know that?" He started the car and pulled into the traffic. "If I slice you open there it'd take less than ten minutes for you to bleed out." She sent an anguished look around, but amazingly everything looked normal. No one seemed to have noticed anything amiss.

"It'd be a messy way to die. Painful, too, I guess. And if you move a muscle that'll be the way to go. Serve you right, too. Where were you? I was extremely careful. You weren't in the alley, no one was."

She stared at him, realization arriving in a flood. He thought she was the witness, the one who'd ID'd him. "The window," she murmured. If she could take comfort from one thing it was knowing that by her lie, Danny would be safe. "I was looking out the toy store window."

His face tightened. The pressure on her leg increased and she flinched. "Is this how you killed D'Brusco?"

"As I said, it's messy. Strictly for amateurs, unless an emergency arises. I'm a professional. An artist, you could say." His thin lips stretched into a chilling smile. "Kinda like you."

She stared at the scenery speeding by, trying to shove aside panic to think. It helped to focus on something besides her fright, so she kept track of the directions they traveled in. She watched for landmarks, memorized them. And she tried not to consider the fact that she'd probably have very little use for either.

She thought then of Danny, and the knot in her throat threatened to choke her. He'd been frantic when she'd returned from the hospital the night she'd been attacked. Raina had told her that he'd probably picked up on some of her fear and pain. Strong emotions, the woman had said, send out powerful signals. It was an incredibly helpless feeling, knowing that the boy could well be experiencing her fear at this very moment.

Lost in anguish at the consideration, another moment passed before the significance of the thought struck her. A tiny bud of hope unfurled inside her, and she grew even more intent on her surroundings. That same psychic ability that had been used to torment her for years, might be her only salvation.

Sandra had been right. It was very ironic.

"Open it."

The super of Meghan's apartment building balked. "I can't do that, Detective. If Miss Patterson's in there and doesn't want to see you, that's her business. And if she's not in there, there's no point. I overstepped my bounds by even letting you in the building. She had plenty to say to me just the other day about allowing you access."

Gabe leaned on the doorbell. "You're sure you never saw her go out?"

The other man sighed. "I told you a half a dozen times…"

"Yeah, yeah. You were fixing the plumbing in 218." A thought struck him, and Gabe walked down the hallway a few doors and rang Callie's bell. His edginess was due to a combination of exhaustion and adrenaline, he told himself. But that didn't explain the sick sensation in his gut when Meghan hadn't answered her bell or her telephone.

Callie opened the door, and her eyes widened in recognition. "Detective, thank heavens. Do you know where Meghan is? Is she with you?"

The sick sensation rose, fueled by the first stirrings of fear. "No. I can't get an answer—" He stopped, aware for the first time of the voices in her apartment. "What's going on?"

Neither saw the super throw his hands in the air and walk away, muttering about crazy tenants and their guests.

She stepped aside, an invitation to enter. "It's Danny. He's been like this ever since I picked him up. It was Meghan's day to get him, but when she didn't show up the school called me."

"She never showed up?" Dread circled, spreading through his veins.

"Gabe!" Danny sped across the room and threw his arms around Gabe's legs. "Aunt Meggie's in a bad place. A really bad place. You gotta find her."

He squatted, holding the boy at arm's length. "Wait a minute, champ. Slow down."

Tears formed in the boy's eyes and slid down his cheeks. Manfully he tried to keep his lips from wobbling. "She's scared, Gabe. Real scared of the man."

"What man?"

"Pollynife. Pollynife's making her afraid."

Chapter 14

Ice pierced Gabe's heart, sent glacial splinters to his veins. "How can you be sure of that?"

"I can tell. Just like I could tell when I knew she went to see the big trains."

He looked hard at the boy. He'd assumed when he'd caught up with Meghan that day that she'd told Danny where she was going, but he realized now that the boy's knowledge had come from a far different place. One less easily explained.

He pushed aside a thread of panic. "Do you think you can do that again, Danny?" He was only peripherally aware of Callie watching them with an expression of confusion and fear. "Can you try and make it happen or does it just…" He didn't have the words to phrase it.

"I didn't know about the big trains on purpose. It was a accident. I'm not supposed to do it on purpose. Raina and Aunt Meggie said."

"Raina." His gaze flicked to Callie. "Do you have a key

to Meghan's apartment?'' She didn't speak, just nodded. Gabe rose, took Danny by the hand. ''Get it.''

In the shadowy interior of the abandoned building, Meghan's captor reached out, caught her hair. Yanking her head back, he pressed the tip of his knife to her throat with enough pressure to break the skin. The air clogged in her lungs. She thought she would see murder in his eyes or an insane lust. But the only emotion she read there was the vicious satisfaction of a man engaged in an act he enjoyed. There would be no appealing to such a creature. Certain she was about to die, her mind whirled with a dizzying array of images. Sandra. Danny. Gabe. Of promises made and love left unspoken.

''You're not gonna go quick. Not like your sister.'' He watched the horrified comprehension flood her face and gave an ugly laugh. Running the flat end of the blade along her cheek, he said, ''I wonder if you'll scream like she did when I ran her off that cliff.''

''You killed Sandra.'' She forced the words through numb lips, but didn't need the savage smile on his face to know he spoke the truth.

''Not my style. Babe like her deserves some attention before she buys it.'' His breath bouncing off her face was rank, the hand he ran over her revolting. ''I got the time to spend with you, though. You decide how you want the end to be. It can be fast or slow, depending on how nice you are to me first. Either way, you'll be with your sister soon. Tell her Paulie Delgado sends his regards.''

Emotion bombarded Meghan, revulsion, terror and— most welcome—a simmering rage. Whatever her faults, Sandra hadn't deserved to have her life snatched away so suddenly. Hadn't deserved to be sent to her death at this monster's whim. Life—nature—had been unfair to her. Death had been even more so.

Panic wrestled with fury in a greasy tangle in her stomach. "Were you singing to yourself when you killed her?" Meghan barely noted the stillness that crept over his features. The words tumbled out of her, fueled by anger. "Or was that little mental serenade only for D'Brusco?"

"What?" Wariness threaded through the word.

"'Round and round the mulberry bush...'" Repeating the lyrics Danny had picked up from his brief encounter with the killer left a bitter taste on her tongue. His reaction, however, was fiercely satisfying. Her head thudded painfully against the floor as he shoved her away from him.

"Shut up."

"'...the monkey chased the weasel...'"

"Shut up!" Steel glinted, and the blade was presented against her throat again, but this time there was a slight tremor in the hand that held it. "How'd you know about that, huh?"

The momentary satisfaction she'd felt abruptly vanished. How had she known about that? Oh, God, she couldn't let him guess about Danny! She couldn't...

"You're a spook. Just like your sister."

The conclusion he reached was so at odds with the lance of fear piercing her that it took a moment for her to comprehend. In the next instant he balled his fist and slugged her. Lights wheeled behind her eyelids as pain exploded in her jaw. He grabbed her shoulders his hands and shook her. "Aren't you? You're just like her?"

The metallic taste of blood pooled in her mouth, and she fought desperately against the haze that threatened to drag her to unconsciousness. Dimly she was aware that he'd just handed her a possible lifeline.

Feeling as though she were clawing her way through a thick mental fog she forced her eyes open, tried to stop her head from spinning. "That's right. I am."

He rose suddenly, as if loath to remain near her. As if

Meghan, with her imagined abilities, was somehow more freakish than his own lack of conscience. She welcomed the respite, her mind working overtime. "Do you want to know what D'Brusco was thinking when the two of you ran by the window?"

His lips stretched in a chilling smile. "Change of plans, bitch. You're gonna die quick, after all."

She shocked herself with the steadiness of her tone. "I think you're overlooking just how useful my ability can be." When she saw him hesitate in his approach toward her she knew she had his attention. "I can pick up all kinds of things that go through a person's head. Where they keep their money. Combinations to their safes. How to shut off their alarm systems."

"You're lying."

"Am I? There's a list in my purse of possible targets. Go ahead and look." She held her breath for the space of the minute he stared at her. Then he found her purse on the floor and dumped it out, fishing for the folded-up sheet listing donors to the fund-raiser. He brought the paper close, scanned it. Then his expressionless gaze landed on Meghan again. "So what. It's a bunch of names."

"Names that include a bank president. A respected gemologist. A federal appeals judge." She knew she didn't imagine the cold calculation that crossed his face. "Check them out for yourself. And while you do, imagine how much you stand to gain by letting me live."

Desperation was all that kept her words steady. Desperation and a certain fragile hope that she could buy herself some time. Enough time for Danny to help Gabe find her.

The soothing sounds of ocean tides filled the dimly lit room. "Concentrate on the waves, Danny. Hear them rushing in and then out again. Listen to that rhythm."

Raina's gentle voice was as lyrical as the sound of the

recording. Neither had a calming effect on Gabe's razor-edged nerves. His fists clenched tightly, he chafed at the forced inactivity. But unless Danny could give them something, some tiny clue about Meghan's whereabouts, any attempt at rescue would be doomed.

C'mon, kid, he coached Danny silently. You did it to me easily enough. Give me something to work with. He was only half aware of the hand Cal placed on his shoulder. His attention was focused intently on the boy. If it hadn't been, he would have missed the way Danny's small fingers squeezed the older woman's.

"Aunt Meggie's scared." Tears were in his voice.

"Tell us more, Danny."

"Her car's outside." The detectives looked at each other. Meghan's car wasn't in the apartment garage. Gabe suspected she'd been on her way to Danny's school when Paulie had found her. Which meant he'd been watching her. Waiting for an opportunity. And Gabe had been too late to prevent it.

"Is it?" Raina spoke quietly in her slightly accented voice. "Where is Meghan?"

"It's empty and dark. She's inside with the bad man." His lips quivered. "There's water, only not like on the tape. And big lions on the wall. There's one outside with his mouth open."

"There used to be a restaurant called the Red Lion on the east pier," Cal murmured to Gabe. "Had a big lion out in front that almost looked real. I took Becky there on our first date."

Gabe met his partner's gaze. "Got your cell phone?" Cal nodded. "Then let's go."

When Meghan heard the squeak of a door hinge, and a heavy tread approaching, her stomach plummeted. She had no way of knowing how long Delgado had been gone, only

that it hadn't been for long enough. She blinked away the
tears of frustration that wanted to gather and forced that
thin shaft of despair away.

It had been futile to think she could project her whereabouts to Danny; futile to believe that a five-year-old child
could do more with that bombardment of emotion than be
terrified by it. Who, after all, had she thought could help
the boy? From Gabe's icy fury that morning, it had been
all too obvious that the fragile relationship they'd been
building had shattered.

Delgado walked over to where she sat on the floor, bound
to the radiator. "Your lucky—you get to live. For a while
at least." He'd checked out the names on the list, she
thought dully. Greed had managed to circumvent his blood-
lust. At least for the moment.

"Your boyfriend, though…he's not going to be so
lucky." He watched for the comprehension to flicker in her
eyes. "I might be able to fake your death, but I still got a
job to do on him." His hand went to her hair, and snakes
of revulsion twisted in her stomach. "I think I'll let you
watch me gut him. We'll take him at his house after dark,
how 'bout that? But there's plenty of daylight left. And I
know just how we can spend it."

Her protest was muffled by her gag, but Meghan struggled violently as he reached for her, kicking out and catching him in the thigh.

He loomed over her, menacing. "Bitch. You'll learn how
to…"

The blow she was steeled for never came. The door
crashed in, and a figure came hurtling inside in a dive, dropping to the floor and rolling to his feet again. Gabe. She
had an instant to recognize him before she saw the glint of
Delgado's blade flashing. Descending. She kicked out
again, her scream sounding only in her mind. Tearing pain,
followed by numbness.

The scene was rushing by in blurred fast-speed frames. She recognized Cal, heard the struggle Gabe was involved in and then the room began to shift in and out of focus. Senses dulled, grew distant. The last thing she remembered before the black rush of unconsciousness overswept her was the sound of Gabe calling her name.

"A hell of a story." Dare McKay scribbled madly in his notebook.

"Yeah." Gabe leaned back in the hospital chair, bone tired with worry and exhaustion. Meghan was sleeping, heavily sedated. He'd had the doctor's assurance, repeatedly, that she was out of danger. But he couldn't bring himself to stray farther than outside her door.

"Thanks for the exclusive."

"Well that informant we mysteriously acquired had a hand in all this."

Dare shrugged modestly. "Glad to hear it."

Gabe narrowed a look at the other man. "How'd you happen to know so much about Mannen, anyway? What's your angle in all this?"

"I often find myself wondering about his *angles* myself."

The blond woman approaching them wore a tailored navy suit and a professional manner. But there was no mistaking the slight edge to her words. "McKay makes it a habit of turning up in all sorts of odd places."

The reporter, Gabe noted interestedly, seemed to lose a little of his famed affability when he saw the woman, but his voice was even enough when he answered. "Turning up in odd places is my business, Addie, you know that."

With an air of dismissal the woman turned her back on McKay and extended her hand. "Addison Jacobs, assistant state attorney for Cook County. I'll be determining charges in the case."

Shaking her hand, he responded, "Detective Gabe Connally. My partner and I made the arrest. He took the perp to lockup, and I came here with the victim.''

"I talked to Detective Madison already and thought I'd get your report before talking to the victim. Is she…'' The attorney broke off as her cellular phone rang. With an apologetic smile, she reached for it. "Would you excuse me?''

As she moved away to answer her call, Gabe looked between her and Dare consideringly. "Now I'm the one sensing a story.''

The other man pretended to misunderstand him. "About me and Mannen? Maybe I'll tell you about it over a beer sometime.''

"And the one about you and Jacobs?''

McKay's gaze strayed to the pretty blonde. "That story will take a six-pack.'' Tearing his gaze away from the woman, he tucked his pen in his shirt pocket. "You know, there's one thing you didn't explain about the events today.'' He paused a beat. "You never said how you knew right where to find the victim.''

A mist of ice formed and settled in Gabe's chest. "We acted on an anonymous tip.''

"Funny thing about tips. You never know where they're going to lead. For instance, did you know Meghan Patterson and her nephew are regular visitors of Raina Nausman?'' He watched the detective's eyes go opaque. "The woman's famous in some circles. Noted for her expertise in parapsychology.''

Gabe didn't ask how the hell the reporter had gotten that information and he didn't waste time on denials. Damage control was his first concern. "Leave the boy out of it, McKay.''

Dare's gaze never wavered. "Are you asking or telling me?''

Emotions were a complicated business, Gabe was discovering. They rippled out, touched others. And because he felt a responsibility to all involved, he said, "I'm asking."

The other man nodded, tapped his pen against his tablet. "You got it." He rose and gathered his jacket. "I hope Miss Patterson recovers soon." Then he turned and strolled away.

And Gabe was left with the discovery of how instinctive it was to seek to protect a child. And a new appreciation for the lengths people would go to, to do so.

"Are you sure you're up to this?" Callie asked worriedly. She fussed with the cake Meghan had ordered, while she repeated the question for the fifth time.

"I'd better be. The first of the little demons is already on his way upstairs." As if to punctuate her words, the bell rang, and Danny threw the door open, greeting his friend and ushering him inside.

"I still think you should have postponed this until you're feeling better."

Meghan stifled a sigh. "Callie, I feel fine. And this is the first birthday party Danny's ever had. He's been counting the days until his birthday for weeks. I couldn't disappoint him." Or more important, she refused to. There had been so much turmoil in the boy's young life, that this slice of normalcy was the very least he deserved. And the very least she owed him.

It also provided her with a much-needed distraction from the recent events in her life. And the man who was noticeably absent from it.

The buzzer sounded and again Danny answered the door. "Well, I'm going to stick around to make sure you don't overdo it," Callie said firmly. There was a whoop and what sounded like a pack of elephants running through the living room. "I'll also provide the whip and the chair."

Meghan forced a smile. "They might come in handy. I'm not sure how I'm going to keep the kids occupied all afternoon."

Callie waved her worry away. "Don't be concerned about that. They'll entertain themselves. That's the part that will make you most miserable. Oh, there's the buzzer again. How many of the little maniacs did you let him invite, anyway?" She left the kitchen to go to the door.

"Do you want to show him into Danny's room, Callie?" Meghan called from the other room. "Oh, make him take off his shoes first. And show him where the bathroom is. I've found that that's a pretty urgent thing for—" She looked up from the pitcher of drink she was stirring and her words stumbled.

"Actually, I've been housebroken for a few years now," Gabe said, propping one shoulder against the wall.

Her voice was strangled. "I...thought...you were..."

"Five. I got that." His gaze swept her form once, then again. She looked okay, he thought with something approaching relief. Better than okay, actually. There was some color in her cheeks, a welcome change from the way she'd looked lying in that hospital bed. Just the memory made his gut churn.

"So this doesn't look like following doctor's orders."

She shrugged, then winced when the action pulled at the wound in her shoulder. "I'm taking it easy. And Callie's helping."

He raised his arm to show her the box he was carrying. "I brought the kid something." His gaze skimmed the room because it was easier than watching that polite, blank expression on her face.

"A train set. He'll like that."

"Yeah. I guess every kid needs a train."

"I can go get him if you like."

"It can wait." This wasn't going exactly the way he'd

figured. His stomach was jittery with what felt suspiciously like nerves. Hell. He frowned. He'd rather face a storm of bullets than see Meghan look at him with that polite dispassionate mask.

"So. I thought you'd want to know…Delgado was denied bail. They've got charges of kidnapping and attempted murder pending against him."

She winced a little. "He was planning to kill you, too."

"Yeah, so you said, but so far we haven't had any luck trying to get him to talk about who hired him." Gabe had his suspicions, though. Meghan must have been snatched not too long after he and Cal had left Mannen. He was a long way from proving the man's involvement, but it was a connection he was determined to make. "If we catch some luck, the knife Delgado had on him might match the wounds on the corpses that have been piling up in this case. We'll have enough charges against him to keep him in prison the rest of his life." And maybe, he thought grimly, that would be incentive for him to flip on whoever had hired him. That would be their best chance of tying him to Mannen.

"And you should probably know about Wadrell." Her gaze jerked to his. "He's on suspension, pending a full investigation into his conduct in your sister's case."

Meghan waited for satisfaction to fill her, or at least a sense of vindication. But there was nothing. What happened to Wadrell now, however deserved, wouldn't bring Sandra back. "It's not enough." She was unaware she'd spoken the words aloud until she heard his response.

"No, it's not. But sometimes we have to take what we can get."

As if they'd both run out of words, the silence stretched then, long enough to be considered awkward. Gabe cleared his throat. "Well, you look good. Last time I saw you, you were kind of out of it. I think they'd just given you a painkiller again.''

She went still. "You saw me…in the hospital?"

"Yeah, both nights."

"I don't remember." She recalled little past the time he'd burst in that door, struggled with Delgado. Gabe had ridden in the ambulance with her, and she'd annoyed the medic by insisting on telling him everything she'd learned while Delgado had been holding her. But once she'd gotten to the hospital…she had no memory of seeing him while she'd been there, and she'd drawn her own conclusions from his absence.

She couldn't allow herself the indulgence of believing that finding out differently changed things. She tucked that dismal little tendril of hope away and faced him. "I owe you an apology." She was going to step out from behind her carefully constructed defenses and offer him, finally, honesty. It might be too late, but it was no more than his due. "For not telling you about Danny."

His voice was deliberately expressionless when he answered. "You were trying to protect him."

"That's true. But telling you wouldn't have been easy for me, in any case." Determined not to spare herself, she met his gaze head-on. "I don't have much experience trusting people. I didn't get much practice at it when I was a kid, and now…well, I guess I'm too much of a coward."

His eyes narrowed. "That's the last thing I'd accuse you of."

A corner of her mouth lifted wryly. "Oh, yes I am, emotionally at least. *Trust* means lowering my guard and opening up to someone, and that terrifies me." *He* terrified her, because he'd managed to smash through her defenses with so little effort. Had found a place in her heart without her permission and lodged there. There had been loneliness within those inner walls, but there had been safety, too. Right now she felt stripped bare. Vulnerable and exposed. So the words she had to force through her lips sounded rushed. "I guess what I'm saying is that I'm not a good risk. I don't have a lot of experience with long-term relationships, and there's absolutely no reason to believe I'll get better at them. But I want to." The ache in her heart sounded in her voice. "Because I love you."

For one long moment he stared at her, and then finally, slowly, his mouth curved. "I know."

She stared blankly. "You know?"

"Remind me not to tell you any state secrets. You're inclined to babble when you're on low dosages of medication."

Her gaze abruptly narrowed. "Babble what?"

"That first night in the hospital you told me you loved me." He hadn't quite believed it; hadn't allowed himself to. She'd also mentioned something about climbing the Sears Tower in grip boots, and he hadn't intended to hold her to that, had he? But she'd repeated the words now, and damned if he wasn't going to hold her to it.

"I did?" Emotional bravery, she was beginning to believe, was vastly overrated. Her chest was in a vise, squeezing the oxygen from her lungs. "Well, what did you say?"

"I think I said something along the lines of...ditto."

Her lungs eased a little, but there was no denying a sense of disappointment. "Ditto? Ditto? You're lucky you didn't send me into insulin shock with your sugary sentimentality."

His smile settled into his eyes. Her fire was back. He preferred it to the ice. Closing the distance between them, he cupped her face in his hands. "I couldn't do much better at the time. Do you know what it did to me, hearing Danny describe how afraid you were...knowing Delgado had you?" The ugly images crawled across his mind, still trailing ice. "Every minute it took to find you was an agony."

He shoved away the memories before they could settle and concentrated on the present. And the future. "I love

you.'' He lifted one of her hands, pressed a kiss to the palm.
And when he saw the shimmer of tears in her eyes, a little
slice of peace settled in his heart. After a lifetime of dodging
ties, he found himself craving ones that would bind her
close to him. ''I want us to be a family. You, me and
Danny.'' He thought of his mother then, and mentally included her, as well. Meghan wasn't the only one who had
to learn to trust. ''I'm talking forever.''

Joy was tap dancing in her chest, but there was trepidation, too. ''Forever? With our backgrounds do you think we
can pull that off?''

He ran his hand down her spine, pleased by the way she
instinctively arched against him. ''I know we can. I'm crazy
about you. Cal says I'm smitten.''

She smiled, slow and secretive and feminine. ''Smitten.
I like the sounds of that.''

He brushed her mouth with his. ''I thought you would.
When do these monsters go home? I intend to show you
just how smitten I really am.''

''Well, there are the presents to open.'' She leaned forward, to punctuate each phrase with a kiss. ''Cake and ice
cream to eat.'' Another brush to his mouth. ''Games to
play.'' Her lips touched his, moved away too quickly. ''I'd
guess...four more hours.''

''Four hours?''

Her eyes laughed at the dismay in his tone. ''Yes. And
then Alex has an overnight.''

He lowered his face to hers. ''What are the chances of
me wrangling an overnight, too?''

Meghan linked her arms around his neck and smiled bril-
liantly. ''I'd say your chances are growing better by the
minute.''

* * * * *

*And there are more extraordinary stories by
Kylie Brant available in the next three months.*

*In November, Intimate Moments's exciting continuity
series features BORN IN SECRET by Kylie Brant.*

*Then she returns to
CHARMED AND DANGEROUS
in December with Dare McKay in
HARD TO RESIST.*

*And again in January with
HARD TO TAME.*

Don't miss any of these wonderful titles!

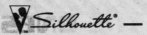

CALL THE ONES YOU LOVE OVER THE HOLIDAYS!

Save $25 off future book purchases when you buy any four Harlequin® or Silhouette® books in October, November and December 2001,

PLUS

receive a phone card good for 15 minutes of long-distance calls to anyone you want in North America!

WHAT AN INCREDIBLE DEAL!

Just fill out this form and attach 4 proofs of purchase (cash register receipts) from October, November and December 2001 books, and Harlequin Books will send you a coupon booklet worth a total savings of $25 off future purchases of Harlequin® and Silhouette® books, AND a 15-minute phone card to call the ones you love, anywhere in North America.

Please send this form, along with your cash register receipts as proofs of purchase, to:
In the USA: Harlequin Books, P.O. Box 9057, Buffalo, NY 14269-9057
In Canada: Harlequin Books, P.O. Box 622, Fort Erie, Ontario L2A 5X3
Cash register receipts must be dated no later than December 31, 2001.
Limit of 1 coupon booklet and phone card per household.
Please allow 4-6 weeks for delivery.

I accept your offer! Please send me my coupon booklet and a 15-minute phone card:

Name: _____

Address: _____ City: _____

State/Prov.: _____ Zip/Postal Code: _____

Account Number (if available): _____

---

097 KJB DAGL
PHQ4012

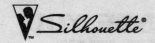

COMING NEXT MONTH

INTIMATE MOMENTS

#1111 BY HONOR BOUND—Ruth Langan
The Lassiter Law

Pru Street had no idea that her sexy new neighbor had been secretly hired by her father to protect her. But Micah Lassiter's hero status in the security business made him determined to keep the feisty graduate student safe from her stalker—and to welcome her into his passionate embrace!

#1112 BORN IN SECRET—Kylie Brant
Firstborn Sons

International spy Walker James was not happy when he learned that his partner in his latest assignment was former flame Jasmine LeBarr. Could the headstrong duo stop the threat of biological terrorism and rekindle the fire of their turbulent past?

#1113 JACK'S CHRISTMAS MISSION—Beverly Barton
The Protectors

Successful TV personality Peggy Jo Riley's life was in danger and she was forced to go under the guard of macho man Jack Parker. Now Peggy Jo's daughter was convinced that Jack would not only keep them both safe but that he would stay at their house for Christmas—and forever!

#1114 THE RENEGADE AND THE HEIRESS—Judith Duncan
Wide Open Spaces

Mallory O'Brien was running for her life when Finn Donovan found her in the snowy mountains. He vowed to keep her safe but soon discovered that protecting her from kidnappers was one thing, while protecting her heart was another altogether.

#1115 ONCE FORBIDDEN...—Carla Cassidy
The Delaney Heirs

Their love had once been forbidden—the rich girl and the boy from the wrong side of the tracks. Now Jerrod McKay was back in Johnna Delaney's life, asking for her help. Yet, how could she give him her assistance without exposing her most closely guarded secret?

#1116 THAT KIND OF GIRL—Kim McKade

Colt Bonner had returned home for the first time in twelve years, and virginal Becca Danvers hoped to draw his attention. But Colt had always considered her to be just the girl next door. Could Becca convince him that he was the one man in her life she'd been waiting for?

SIMCNM1001